Judaism's Gifts to the World

EDITOR
Rabbi Mordechai Dinerman

AUTHORS
Rabbi Baruch Shalom Davidson
Rabbi Lazer Gurkow
Rabbi Shmuel Super

Printed in the United States of America

by **THE ROHR JEWISH LEARNING INSTITUTE**
822 Eastern Parkway, Brooklyn, NY 11213

Cover Art: *The Feast of the Rejoicing of the Law at the Synagogue in Leghorn, Italy* (detail), Solomon Hart, oil on canvas, 1850. (The Jewish Museum, New York)

(888) YOUR-JLI/718-221-6900
WWW.MYJLI.COM

ב"ה

Judaism's Gifts to the World

HOW MAJOR JEWISH IDEAS EVOLVED INTO UNIVERSAL VALUES

STUDENT TEXTBOOK

ADVISORY BOARD OF GOVERNORS

YAAKOV AND KAREN COHEN
Potomac, MD

YITZCHOK AND JULIE GNIWISCH
Montreal, QC

BARBARA HINES
Aspen, CO

DANIEL AND ROSIE MATTIO
Seattle, WA

DAVID MINTZ
Tenafly, NJ

DR. STEPHEN F. SERBIN
Columbia, SC

LEONARD A. WIEN, JR.
Miami Beach, FL

PARTNERING FOUNDATIONS

AVI CHAI FOUNDATION

COMMUNITY CEMETERY EDUCATION PROJECT BY JEWISH REACH

CRAIN-MALING FOUNDATION

ESTATE OF ELLIOT JAMES BELKIN

GOLDSTEIN FAMILY FOUNDATION

KOHELET FOUNDATION

KOSINS FAMILY FOUNDATION

MAYBERG FOUNDATION

MEROMIM FOUNDATION

MYRA REINHARD FAMILY FOUNDATION

OLAMI—WOLFSON FOUNDATION

RUDERMAN FAMILY FOUNDATION

WILLIAM DAVIDSON FOUNDATION

WORLD ZIONIST ORGANIZATION

YEHUDA AND ANNE NEUBERGER PHILANTHROPIC FUND

PRINCIPAL BENEFACTOR

GEORGE ROHR
New York, NY

PILLARS OF JEWISH LITERACY

KEVIN BERMEISTER
Sydney, Australia

SHAYA BOYMELGREEN
Miami Beach, FL

PABLO AND SARA BRIMAN
Mexico City, Mexico

GORDON DIAMOND
Vancouver, BC

ZALMAN AND MIMI FELLIG
Miami Beach, FL

YOSEF GOROWITZ
Redondo Beach, CA

DR. VERA KOCH GROSZMANN
S. Paulo, Brazil

HERSCHEL LAZAROFF
Monsey, NY

JENNY LJUNGBERG
New York, NY

DAVID MAGERMAN
Gladwyne, PA

DR. MICHAEL MALING
Deerfield, IL

YITZCHAK MIRILASHVILI
Herzliya, Israel

BEN NASH
New Jersey

THE ROBBINS FAMILY
Vaughan, ON

LEE AND PATTI SCHEAR
Dayton, OH

ISADORE SCHOEN
Fairfax, VA

YAIR SHAMIR
Savyon, Israel

LARRY SIFEN
Virginia Beach, VA

SPONSORS

MARK AND REBECCA BOLINSKY
Long Beach, NY

DANIEL AND ETA COTLAR
Houston, TX

AMIR AND DAFNA ELYASHAR
Ramat Aviv, Israel

BRIAN AND DANA GAVIN
Houston, TX

SHMUEL AND SHARONE GOODMAN
Chicago, IL

CAROLYN HESSEL
New York, NY

JOE AND SHIRA LIPSEY
Aspen, CO

ELLEN MARKS
S. Diego, CA

RACHELLE NEDOW
El Paso, T'X

PETER AND HAZEL PFLAUM
Newport Beach, CA

FRANK AND FRUMETH POLASKY OB"M
Saginaw, MI

MOSHE AND YAFFA POPACK
Fisher Island, FL

HERCHEL AND JULIE PORTMAN
Denver, CO

EYAL AND AVIVA POSTELNIK
Marietta, GA

DR. ZE'EV RAV-NOY
Los Angeles, CA

CLIVE AND ZOE ROCK
Irvine, CA

ZVI RYZMAN
Los Angeles, CA

ALAN ZEKELMAN
Bloomfield Hills, MI

MYRNA ZISMAN
Cedarhurst, NY

JANICE AND IVAN ZUCKERMAN
Coral Gables, FL

The Rohr Jewish Learning Institute
gratefully acknowledges the pioneering
and ongoing support of

George and Pamela Rohr

Since its inception, the Rohr JLI has been a beneficiary of the vision, generosity, care, and concern of the Rohr family.

In the merit of the tens of thousands of hours of Torah study by JLI students worldwide, may they be blessed with health, *Yiddishe nachas* from all their loved ones, and extraordinary success in all their endeavors.

LOCAL COURSE SPONSORSHIPS

Mr. and Mrs. David Beesemer
AMSTERDAM, NL

In memory of Lawrence and Mildred Weiss
BLOOMFIELD HILLS, MI

Mr. and Mrs. Jim and Renee Hon
BOISE, ID

Dr. Yura Stoly
BROOKLYN, NY

Mr. and Mrs. Stuart and Shelly Hanfling
ELGIN, IL

Mr. Louis Berkowitz
FAIRFIELD, CT

Dr. and Mrs. Gary and Marlene Price
FORT MYERS, FL

Eugene and Marjorie Lipsky
LEAWOOD, KS

In memory of Rivka Sara bat Efraim Fishel Gejerman
LOS ANGELES, CA

In memory of Mr. Isidor Blumenthal
MADISON, NJ

Mr. and Mrs. Y. K. Cohen
MILWAUKEE, WI

In memory of Shmuel Leib ben Avraham Dovber
NEWTON, MA

Mr. and Mrs. Neil and Hedy Hoffman
NEWTOWN, PA

In honor of Mrs. Maxine Finkel
NORTHEAST PORTLAND, OR

In memory of Meyer Goldberg
ORINDA, CA

Mr. Robert Sacks
S. FE, NM

In memory of Dr. Louis Cohen
SKOKIE, IL

In memory of those who came before us
SOUTH LAKE TAHOE, CA

The Hellman Memorial Chapels
SPRING VALLEY, NY

Mr. Mark Eichner
VENICE, FL

In memory of Dr. Arthur Conn
VIENNA, VA

In memory of Rabbi Levi Deitsch
VIENNA, VA

Kosins Family Foundation
WEST BLOOMFIELD, MI

Jackson, Chasen and Ilan
WESTMINSTER, CO

DEDICATED TO

Lee and Patti Schear

Dayton, Ohio

JLI is indebted and deeply grateful for their partnership in bringing Torah study to all corners of the world and honors their exemplary commitment to Jewish literacy, Am Yisrael, and Eretz Yisrael.

In the merit of the Torah study by thousands of students worldwide, may they be blessed with good health, happiness, *nachat* from their loved ones, and success in all their endeavors.

Foreword

"NATIONS SHALL GO BY YOUR LIGHT, AND KINGS BY THE GLOW OF YOUR RADIANCE."

—ISAIAH 60:3

"All the great conceptual discoveries of the intellect," wrote British historian Paul Johnson, "seem obvious and inescapable once they have been revealed, but it requires a special genius to formulate them for the first time." Humanity therefore remains deeply indebted to Judaism, he insisted, for formulating the many original values that today "constitute the basic moral furniture of the human mind."

The Torah broke radically with the social and political worldviews of the ancient civilizations. It articulated an entirely new order that has gradually yielded disproportionate influence on the emergence of modern society and contemporary universal values. Ancient civilizations often left a record of their history in material things. By contrast, what we know about the Jews in ancient times flows mostly from the ideas they taught and the impact those ideas had on other civilizations.

American historian Max I. Dimont noted that it took sixteen hundred years for Europe to realize that her literature, science, and architecture had their roots in Grecian civilization—and it may well require a couple hundred more until she acknowledges that many of the spiritual, moral, ethical, and ideological roots of Western civilization are embedded in Judaism.

Judaism's Gifts to the World is an in-depth exploration of key values and ideas that have become universal norms. The historical narrative of the unlikely transition of Jewish ideals from rejection to adoption, and from the timeworn tomes of a marginalized nation to socially transformative global appeal, is closely examined in the six lessons of this course.

Beyond fascinating, these studies are highly instructive for the present. For, as long as humanity hopes to fine-tune its advance, Judaism's gifts will keep on giving.

THE ROHR JEWISH LEARNING INSTITUTE (JLI)

Endorsements

"*Judaism's Gifts to the World* provides important insights into our current world. It is unfashionable today to delve into the history and meaning of words, like 'reasonability,' 'purpose,' 'trust,' and 'sanctity of life' but they lay at the heart of our democracy. Our nation is comprised of millions of individual citizens whose goals in life simply cannot be understood without the basic values rooted in Judaism."

KENNETH R. FEINBERG

Special Master, September 11th Victim Compensation Fund; Lecturer, Columbia University School of Law

"With its new course, *Judaism's Gifts to the World*, the Rohr Jewish Learning Institute offers a tremendous opportunity to explore the biblical foundations of values, like a day of rest and the sanctity of all life, that undergird our modern worldview. Well done!"

PAMELA S. NADELL

Patrick Clendenen Chair in Women's and Gender History, American University; Author, *America's Jewish Women: A History from Colonial Times to Today*

"The Rohr Jewish Learning Institute has created an instructive and deeply reflective course, inviting participants to engage thoughtfully with compelling Jewish texts written through the ages. *Judaism's Gifts to the World* is a timely recognition and celebration of how the Jewish faith has contributed to the history of ideas, and a welcome opportunity for individuals and communities to reflect on these values today."

ALISON GRAY

Director of Studies and Biblical Tutor, Westminster College, University of Cambridge

"There can be no doubt that the Jewish contribution to the civilizations of the West and the world is immense. At a time when noxious critics would doubt that contribution, or deny it altogether, the Jewish Learning Institute has offered a timely reminder of the many gifts the Jewish tradition has bestowed. *Judaism's Gifts to the World* is a gift of its own, providing a scintillating course in the history of ideas and culture by leading experts from around the globe."

DARRIN M. MCMAHON

Mary Brinsmead Wheelock Professor of History, Dartmouth College; Co-editor, *Modern Intellectual History*

"The Judaic and Hebraic elements in the development of Western civilization are basic and significant. It is a worthy task to introduce students in this course to the ways in which biblical and Jewish thought have interacted with and influenced other civilizations and cultures over the centuries. The material in *Judaism's Gifts to the World* should be of interest to Jews and non-Jews alike. I wish you much success in your endeavor."

IRA ROBINSON

Chair, Jewish Studies; Director, Institute for Canadian Jewish Studies, Concordia University

"Today many people take the Hebrew Bible and its message for granted. JLI's new course, *Judaism's Gifts to the World*, is a timely and well-conceived effort to remind us of how revolutionary the Hebrew Bible was within the Ancient Near East. At the heart of this revolution was the proclamation of one G-d who cares for His people as well as for all of His Creation. This G-d was, and continues to be, worshipped with prayers and other rituals. But—of equal, if not greater importance—we humans show our love of G-d through our interactions with and respect for other humans. In this course, students will learn how Jewish thinkers identified and enhanced the practical implications of belief in G-d through a system of ethical and meaningful actions. These lessons of the Hebrew Bible are equally relevant today, once we truly understand them. *Judaism's Gifts to the World* is exactly the learning opportunity we need."

LEONARD GREENSPOON

Klutznick Chair in Jewish Civilization, Creighton University

"The Rohr Jewish Learning Institute continues its tradition of contributing to the modern world through the teaching of Jewish values. For many who identify with and take pride in Western society and culture, the course, *Judaism's Gifts to the World*, will be an eye-opener by way of its explication of a series of Judaism's basic values and their contemporary relevance."

CHAIM I. WAXMAN

Professor Emeritus of Sociology and Jewish Studies, Rutgers University; Chair, Department of Behavioral Sciences, Hadassah Academic College, Jerusalem, Israel

"There is no way one can understand Western civilization without understanding the sweep of Jewish history and Jewish values. And it is arguable, as well, that one cannot understand Jewish history without placing it within the context of Western civilization. The Rohr Jewish Learning Institute's *Judaism's Gifts to the World* is an admirable effort to explore the relationship between Jewish and Western values. In these unsettled times, with the increase of anti-Semitism worldwide, the recognition of this reciprocity is ever more vital."

MARSHALL J. BREGER

Professor of Law, Columbus School of Law, The Catholic University of America

"*Judaism's Gifts to the World* not only gives students the unique opportunity to think about the relevance of Judaism to being an American or being a proud member of Western civilization; it also gives them an opportunity to think about how the ancient past relates to the present moment in time."

MENACHEM FEUER

Instructor, Israel and Golda Koschitsky Center for Jewish Studies, York University; Instructor, Jewish Studies, University of Waterloo

"As some seek to destroy the very notion of true historical narratives, along comes the Rohr Jewish Learning Institute to set the record straight in at least one critically important area of epistemology. The role that Jewish thought played in shaping Western civilization has been under-researched and hence underrated for too long. This unique course has the potential to help reconstruct our world as we understand it."

YECHIEL M. LEITER

Senior Fellow, Kohelet Policy Forum
President and CEO, Veresta-Group

"Having taught courses in comparative religion for two decades, I have come to recognize the importance of fostering an appreciation for the contributions of Judaism to Western civilization. With *Judaism's Gifts to the World,* JLI offers a resource not only for the general public seeking an education in Judaism, but also for cultural or religious Jews seeking true insight into their rich heritage."

JONATHAN WEIDENBAUM

Humanities professor, School of Liberal Arts, Berkeley College

"JLI's course, *Judaism's Gifts to the World*, promises to be an easily accessible, powerful learning experience on the enormous positive influence of Judaism on world culture. The way the course brings abstract philosophical concepts into everyday life is brilliant and most effective."

JEROME YEHUDA GELLMAN

Professor Emeritus, Department of Philosophy, Ben-Gurion University; Honorary Professor, Australian Catholic University

Contents

Lesson 1

NO MAN AN ISLAND

THE BONDS AND RESPONSIBILITIES OF SOCIETY

Unemployed men at Volunteers of America soup kitchen in Washington D.C., c. 1934–39. (Everett Historical/Shutterstock.com)

Ancient societies focused on self-survival and self-promotion, with the unfortunate left by the wayside. This was not seen as cruel or uncaring until the Torah introduced the radical concept of social responsibilities—such as assisting the needy and providing jobs—as a moral obligation of civilization and its individual members. It took centuries for the idea to infiltrate the rest of humanity, in a process that is far from complete. The Torah remains a powerful source of inspiration for social change.

Exercise 1.1

If you had the ability to create a perfect society, what would be the values and attitudes about life that you would instill in this society?

TEXT 1

JOHN ADAMS, TO FRANÇOIS ADRIAAN VAN DER KEMP, 16 FEBRUARY 1809, *THE WORKS OF JOHN ADAMS* (BOSTON: LITTLE, BROWN AND COMPANY, 1854), VOL. 9, PP. 608–609

I will insist that the Hebrews have done more to civilize Men than any other Nation. If I were an Atheist and believed in blind eternal Fate, I should Still believe that Fate had ordained the Jews to be the most essential Instrument for civilizing the Nations. If I were an Atheist of the other Sect, who believe or pretend to believe that all is ordered by Chance, I Should believe that Chance had ordered the Jews to preserve and propagate, to all Mankind the Doctrine of a Supreme intelligent wise, almighty Sovereign of the Universe, which I believe to be the great essential Principle of all Morality and consequently of all Civilization.

JOHN ADAMS
1735–1826

Second president of the United States and political theorist. Adams, a Boston lawyer and public figure, was an active and influential leader in the American Revolution and helped Thomas Jefferson draft the Declaration of Independence. Adams served 2 terms as George Washington's vice president before being elected president.

Exercise 1.2

Write down an instance in which you saw someone in need and helped them. Why did you help them?

Write down an instance in which you saw someone in need and did not help them. Why didn't you help them?

TEXT 2

GENESIS 6:13–14, 22

וַיֹּאמֶר אֱלֹקִים לְנֹחַ, קֵץ כָּל בָּשָׂר בָּא לְפָנַי כִּי מָלְאָה הָאָרֶץ חָמָס מִפְּנֵיהֶם וְהִנְנִי מַשְׁחִיתָם אֶת הָאָרֶץ. עֲשֵׂה לְךָ תֵּבַת עֲצֵי גֹפֶר, קִנִּים תַּעֲשֶׂה אֶת הַתֵּבָה, וְכָפַרְתָּ אֹתָהּ מִבַּיִת וּמִחוּץ בַּכֹּפֶר . . .

וַיַּעַשׂ נֹחַ כְּכֹל אֲשֶׁר צִוָּה אֹתוֹ אֱלֹקִים כֵּן עָשָׂה.

G-d* said to Noah, "I have decided to put an end to all people, for the earth is filled with robbery because of them, and I am destroying them from the earth. Make for yourself an ark of gopher wood; make rooms in it, and coat it with pitch inside and out." . . .

Noah did everything just as G-d commanded him.

* Throughout this book, "G-d" and "L-rd" are written with a hyphen instead of an "o" (both in our own translations and when quoting others). This is one way we accord reverence to the sacred divine name. This also reminds us that, even as we seek G-d, He transcends any human effort to describe His reality.

Building the Ark, James Jacques Joseph Tissot, gouache on board, c. 1896–1902. (The Jewish Museum, New York)

TEXT 3

GENESIS 18:20–21, 23–24

וַיֹּאמֶר ה', זַעֲקַת סְדֹם וַעֲמֹרָה כִּי רָבָּה. וְחַטָּאתָם כִּי כָבְדָה מְאֹד. אֵרְדָה נָּא וְאֶרְאֶה הַכְּצַעֲקָתָהּ הַבָּאָה אֵלַי עָשׂוּ, כָּלָה . . .

וַיִּגַּשׁ אַבְרָהָם וַיֹּאמַר, הַאַף תִּסְפֶּה צַדִּיק עִם רָשָׁע. אוּלַי יֵשׁ חֲמִשִּׁים צַדִּיקִם בְּתוֹךְ הָעִיר, הַאַף תִּסְפֶּה וְלֹא תִשָּׂא לַמָּקוֹם לְמַעַן חֲמִשִּׁים הַצַּדִּיקִם אֲשֶׁר בְּקִרְבָּהּ.

G-d said to Abraham, “The outcry from Sodom and Gomorah is so great and their sin so grievous that I will go down and see if what they have done is as bad as the outcry that has reached me. If it is, I will destroy them.” . . .

Abraham approached and said to G-d, “Will You even destroy the righteous with the wicked? What if there are fifty righteous people in the city; will You destroy it and not spare the place for the sake of the fifty righteous people who are in it?”

TEXT 4

GENESIS 18:18–19

וְאַבְרָהָם הָיוֹ יִהְיֶה לְגוֹי גָּדוֹל וְעָצוּם וְנִבְרְכוּ בוֹ כֹּל גּוֹיֵי הָאָרֶץ. כִּי יְדַעְתִּיו לְמַעַן אֲשֶׁר יְצַוֶּה אֶת בָּנָיו וְאֶת בֵּיתוֹ אַחֲרָיו וְשָׁמְרוּ דֶּרֶךְ ה' לַעֲשׂוֹת צְדָקָה וּמִשְׁפָּט.

Abraham will surely become a great and powerful nation, and all nations on earth will be blessed through him. For I love Abraham because he instructs his children and his household to follow the path of G-d by doing charity and justice.

***Professor Lawrence Schiffman** discusses charity and righteousness in the Bible and Dead Sea Scrolls:*

MYJLI.COM/GIFTS

TEXT 5

MIDRASH, *TANA DEVEI ELIYAHU RABAH* 11

כָּל יִשְׂרָאֵל עֲרֵבִים זֶה לָזֶה. וּלְמָה הֵן דּוֹמִים, לִסְפִינָה שֶׁנִּקְרַע בָּהּ בַּיִת אֶחָד. אֵין אוֹמְרִים נִקְרַע בָּהּ בַּיִת אֶחָד, אֶלָּא כָּל הַסְּפִינָה נִקְרְעָה כֻּלָּהּ.

All Jews are responsible for each other. We are like a ship where a hole has been ruptured in one room. It cannot be said that one room has been ruptured; the entire ship is ruptured.

TANA DEVEI ELIYAHU

A Midrashic work, sometimes referred to as *Seder Eliyahu*. Midrash is the designation of a particular genre of rabbinic literature usually forming a running commentary on specific books of the Bible. This work deals with the divine precepts, their rationales, and the importance of knowledge of Torah, prayer, and repentance. The work is divided into 2 sections *(sedarim): Eliyahu Rabah* and *Eliyahu Zuta*.

TEXT 6

DEUTERONOMY 15:7–8

כִּי יִהְיֶה בְךָ אֶבְיוֹן מֵאַחַד אַחֶיךָ בְּאַחַד שְׁעָרֶיךָ בְּאַרְצְךָ אֲשֶׁר ה' אֱלֹקֶיךָ נֹתֵן לָךְ, לֹא תְאַמֵּץ אֶת לְבָבְךָ וְלֹא תִקְפֹּץ אֶת יָדְךָ מֵאָחִיךָ הָאֶבְיוֹן.

כִּי פָתֹחַ תִּפְתַּח אֶת יָדְךָ לוֹ וְהַעֲבֵט תַּעֲבִיטֶנּוּ דֵּי מַחְסֹרוֹ אֲשֶׁר יֶחְסַר לוֹ.

If there will be a needy person among you, one of your brothers in one of your cities in your land that your G-d is giving you, you shall not harden your heart, and you shall not close your hand to your needy brother.

Rather, you shall open your hand to him and give him enough to supply what he lacks.

Gedenke der Armut (Think of the Poor), Alphons Bodenmüller, oil on wood, 1879.

Figure 1.1

Mitzvot of Helping the Poor

MITZVAH	DEFINITION	SOURCE
Pe'ah	When harvesting produce, a corner of the field should be left unharvested for the poor to take from. The rabbis ruled that the size of the leftover corner should be no less than one-sixtieth of the entire field.	Leviticus 19:9, 23:22; *Mishneh Torah*, Laws of the Gifts for the Poor 1–3
Leket	When gathering the harvested produce into bundles, any produce that falls should be left there for the poor to take.	Leviticus 19:9, 23:22; *Mishneh Torah*, Laws of the Gifts for the Poor 4:1–14
Shichechah	When gathering produce from the field, any produce that was forgotten and left behind in the field should remain there for the poor to take.	Deuteronomy 24:19; *Mishneh Torah*, Laws of the Gifts for the Poor 5
Peret	Any grapes that fall to the floor while the vine is being picked should be left there for the poor.	Leviticus 19:10; *Mishneh Torah*, Laws of the Gifts for the Poor 4:15–16
Olelot	The small bunches of grapes should be left behind on the vine for the poor to take.	Leviticus 19:10; Deuteronomy 24:21; *Mishneh Torah*, Laws of the Gifts for the Poor 4:17–27
Maaser Ani	During the third and sixth years of the seven-year cycle, one-tenth of all produce should be given to the poor.	Deuteronomy 14:28–29, 26:12; *Mishneh Torah*, Laws of the Gifts for the Poor 6

***Professor Adam Chodorow** analyzes the similarities and differences between Jewish charity and secular tax law:*

MYJLI.COM/GIFTS

TEXT 7

RABBI SHLOMO BEN ADERET, *RESPONSA* 3:380

עֲנִיֵּי הָעִיר מְרוּבִּין וְהַמְזוֹנוֹת בְּיוֹקֶר עַל כֵּן נָפְלָה הַקְטָטָה בֵּין הָעֲשִׁירִים. כִּי הָעֲשִׁירִים הַגְדוֹלִים אוֹמְרִים יְחַזְרוּ עַל הַפְּתָחִים וְנִתֵּן לָהֶם כֻּלָּנוּ פַּת בְּכָל יוֹם כְּדֵי שֶׁיִתְפַּרְנְסוּ בּוֹ, כִּי גַם הָעֲשִׁירִים הַבֵּינוֹנִיִּים הַדִין נוֹתֵן שֶׁיִתְּנוּ לְכָל הָעֲנִיִּים בְּכָל יוֹם פַּת כָּמוֹנוּ.

וְהַבֵּינוֹנִיִּים טוֹעֲנִין שֶׁאֵין הַדִין נוֹתֵן כֵּן אֶלָּא שֶׁיֵשְׁבוּ בְּבָתֵּיהֶם וְלֹא יְחַזְרוּ עַל הַפְּתָחִים כִּי אַחֵינוּ בְּשָׂרֵנוּ הֵם וְתִהְיֶה פַּרְנָסָתָם מוּטֶלֶת עַל הַצִּבּוּר וְנִפְרַע כֻּלָּנוּ לְפִי הָעוֹשֶׁר . . . הוֹדִיעָנוּ הַדִין עִם מִי.

There are many poor people in the city, and the cost of living is high. A dispute has arisen between the well-off members of the community: The wealthy upper class argues that the poor should go collecting door-to-door, and we will all give them food every day to sustain them because the middle class is also obligated to feed the poor just as we are.

The middle class disagrees and says that the poor should not be made to go out and beg because they are our brethren. They argue that the sustenance of the poor is a communal obligation, and all must contribute toward this in accordance with their wealth. . . . Please let us know which side is correct.

RABBI SHLOMO BEN ADERET (RASHBA) 1235–1310

Medieval halachist, Talmudist, and philosopher. Rashba was born in Barcelona, Spain, and was a student of Nachmanides and Rabbi Yonah of Gerona. He was known as *El Rab d'España* ("the Rabbi of Spain") because of his fame as a rabbinical authority. More than 3,000 of his responsa are extant, dealing with varied questions on halachah and religious philosophy, addressed to him from Spain, Portugal, Italy, France, Germany, and even from Asia Minor. Among his numerous students were the Ritva, Rabbeinu Bechaye, and the Re'ah.

Is there an obligation to provide tsedakah *to all who ask?* ***Rabbi Yitzchak Breitowitz*** *addresses this question:*

MYJLI.COM/GIFTS

Exercise 1.3

Study Texts 8a–c with a partner, and then answer the Question for Discussion that follows.

TEXT 8a

MAIMONIDES, *MISHNEH TORAH,* LAWS OF THE GIFTS FOR THE POOR 10:8, 10

פָּחוּת מִזֶּה הַנּוֹתֵן צְדָקָה לָעֲנִיִּים וְלֹא יָדַע לְמִי נָתַן וְלֹא יָדַע הֶעָנִי מִמִּי לָקַח, שֶׁהֲרֵי זוֹ מִצְוָה לִשְׁמָהּ . . . וְקָרוֹב לָזֶה הַנּוֹתֵן לְתוֹךְ קוּפָּה שֶׁל צְדָקָה . . .

פָּחוּת מִזֶּה שֶׁיֵּדַע הֶעָנִי מִמִּי נָטַל וְלֹא יֵדַע הַנּוֹתֵן כְּגוֹן גְּדוֹלֵי הַחֲכָמִים שֶׁהָיוּ צוֹרְרִים הַמָּעוֹת בִּסְדִינֵיהֶן וּמַפְשִׁילִין לַאֲחוֹרֵיהֶן וּבָאִין הָעֲנִיִּים וְנוֹטְלִין כְּדֵי שֶׁלֹּא יִהְיֶה לָהֶן בּוּשָׁה.

A high form of charity is to give to the poor without the givers knowing to whom they give and without the recipients knowing from whom they receive. For this is performing a mitzvah solely for the sake of Heaven. . . . Giving to a charity fund is similar to this mode of charity. . . .

A lesser level than this is when the givers do not know to whom they give, but the poor know their benefactors. For example, the sages used to tie coins into cloths and throw them behind their backs so that the poor would be able to come and take the coins out of the cloths without being ashamed.

RABBI MOSHE BEN MAIMON (MAIMONIDES, RAMBAM) 1135–1204

Halachist, philosopher, author, and physician. Maimonides was born in Córdoba, Spain. After the conquest of Córdoba by the Almohads, he fled Spain and eventually settled in Cairo, Egypt. There, he became the leader of the Jewish community and served as court physician to the vizier of Egypt. He is most noted for authoring the *Mishneh Torah,* an encyclopedic arrangement of Jewish law, and for his philosophical work, *Guide for the Perplexed.* His rulings on Jewish law are integral to the formation of halachic consensus.

TEXT 8b

TALMUD, BAVA BATRA 8B

וְהָא כְּתִיב "וּפָקַדְתִּי עַל כָּל לוֹחֲצָיו", (יִרְמְיָה ל, כ) וְאָמַר ר' יִצְחָק בַּר שְׁמוּאֵל בַּר מַרְתָא מִשְּׁמֵיהּ דְּרַב, וַאֲפִילוּ עַל גַּבָּאֵי צְדָקָה.

לֹא קַשְׁיָא. הָא דְּאָמִיד, הָא דְּלָא אָמִיד.

כִּי הָא דְּרָבָא אַכְפְּיֵהּ לְרַב נָתָן בַּר אַמִי וְשָׁקִיל מִינֵיהּ אַרְבַּע מֵאָה זוּזֵי לִצְדָקָה.

Is it really true that collectors for the communal charity fund may seize contributions? But doesn't the verse state, "I will punish all that oppress them" (JEREMIAH 30:20), and Rabbi Yitschak bar Shmuel bar Marta expounded in the name of Rav, "G-d will mete out punishment even to charity collectors"? [If charity collectors are permitted to compel people to contribute charity, why are they counted among Israel's oppressors?]

This is not a difficulty. When the contributors are wealthy and have not contributed what they are capable of, the collectors may seize money from them. However, when the contributors are not wealthy and the collectors are seizing more than they are capable of giving, the collectors are termed "oppressors of Israel."

This right to compel the wealthy to contribute is illustrated in the case of Rava, who seized four hundred dinars from Rabbi Natan bar Ami for charity.

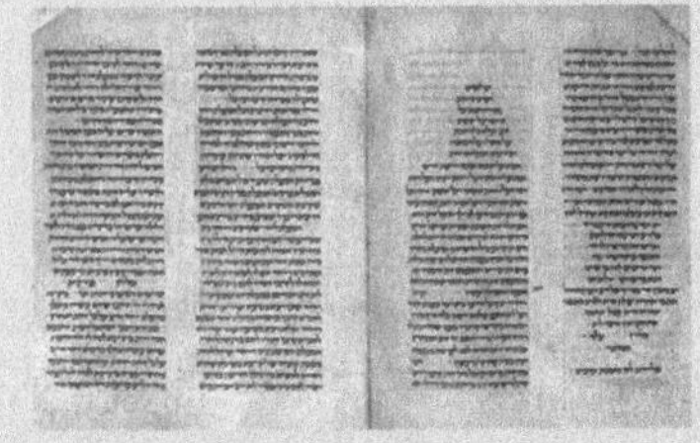

BABYLONIAN TALMUD

A literary work of monumental proportions that draws upon the legal, spiritual, intellectual, ethical, and historical traditions of Judaism. The 37 tractates of the Babylonian Talmud contain the teachings of the Jewish sages from the period after the destruction of the 2nd Temple through the 5th century CE. It has served as the primary vehicle for the transmission of the Oral Law and the education of Jews over the centuries; it is the entry point for all subsequent legal, ethical, and theological Jewish scholarship.

TEXT 8c

TALMUD, KETUVOT 66B–67A

אָמַר לָהּ: בִּתִּי מִי אַתְּ? אָמְרָה לוֹ: בַּת נַקְדִּימוֹן בֶּן גּוּרְיוֹן אֲנִי. אָמַר לָהּ . . .
וְנַקְדִּימוֹן בֶּן גּוּרְיוֹן לֹא עָבַד צְדָקָה? וְהָתַּנְיָא, אָמְרוּ עָלָיו עַל נַקְדִּימוֹן בֶּן גּוּרְיוֹן כְּשֶׁהָיָה יוֹצֵא מִבֵּיתוֹ לְבֵית הַמִּדְרָשׁ כְּלֵי מֵילָת הָיוּ מַצִּיעִין תַּחְתָּיו וּבָאִין עֲנִיִּים וּמְקַפְּלִין אוֹתָן מֵאַחֲרָיו . . .
כִּדְבָעֵי לֵיהּ לְמֵיעֲבַד לֹא עֲבַד. כִּדְאָמְרִי אִינְשֵׁי, לְפוּם גַּמְלָא שִׁיחְנָא.

Rabbi Yochanan ben Zakai met the daughter of Nakdimon ben Gurion. [In their conversation, she told him that her father had not been charitable.] . . .

But didn't Nakdimon ben Gurion give charity? Indeed, a *beraita* states that people would say about Nakdimon ben Gurion that when he would leave his home to go to the study hall, his attendants would spread fine woolen garments underneath him for him to walk on, and he would allow the poor to follow him and take the expensive garments for themselves. . . .

Although Nakdimon gave much charity, in proportion to his wealth he did not give as much as he should have. As the saying goes, the burden is set according to the strength of the camel.

QUESTION FOR DISCUSSION

Based on Texts 8a–c, how do you think Rabbi Shlomo ben Aderet would have ruled?

TEXT 9

LANCELOT ADDISON, *THE PRESENT STATE OF THE JEWS* (LONDON: J.C. FOR WILLIAM CROOKE, 1675), PP. 213–214**

Those who have observed that the Jews have no beggars seem not well informed of the manner of their alms and their way of providing for the poor.

For it is true that we may not reckon these people among beggars, as that word usually implies seeking relief from house to house. For though among the Jews in Barbary there is great store of needy persons, yet they are supplied for in a manner which much conceals (to men of other religions) their poverty. For the wealthier take care to provide for them, and very much glorify their religion upon this very score, that they live under its profession in a more mutual charity of alms than either the Moor or Christian; both of which I have heard upbraiding their common beggars with great insult.

And it cannot be denied that the Jews' manner of relieving their poor is proper and commendable.

LANCELOT ADDISON
1632–1703

Writer and clergyman. Lancelot Addison was educated at Queen's College, Oxford, and served 7 years as chaplain of the garrison at Tangiers, Morocco. While in North Africa, he became interested in the customs and behaviors of the Jews and wrote a book titled *The Present State of the Jews.*

Mr. Kenneth Feinberg, *special master of the September 11th Victim Compensation Fund, discusses how his Jewish upbringing influenced his communitarian work:*

MYJLI.COM/GIFTS

** With minor updates to the archaic English.

TEXT 10

MAIMONIDES, *MISHNEH TORAH*, LAWS OF THE GIFTS FOR THE POOR 10:7

> מַעֲלָה גְדוֹלָה שֶׁאֵין לְמַעֲלָה מִמֶּנָּה זֶה הַמַּחֲזִיק בְּיַד יִשְׂרָאֵל שֶׁמָּךְ, וְנוֹתֵן לוֹ מַתָּנָה אוֹ הַלְוָאָה אוֹ עוֹשֶׂה עִמּוֹ שׁוּתָּפוּת אוֹ מַמְצִיא לוֹ מְלָאכָה כְּדֵי לְחַזֵּק אֶת יָדוֹ עַד שֶׁלֹּא יִצְטָרֵךְ לַבְּרִיּוֹת לִשְׁאוֹל.

The highest form of charity, exceeded by none, is that of a person who assists poor Jews by providing them with a gift or a loan, or making a business partnership with them, or by finding them employment—supporting them so that they will not come to need other people's help.

TEXT 11

NUMBERS 33:54

> וְהִתְנַחַלְתֶּם אֶת הָאָרֶץ . . . לְמִשְׁפְּחֹתֵיכֶם. לָרַב תַּרְבּוּ אֶת נַחֲלָתוֹ וְלַמְעַט תַּמְעִיט אֶת נַחֲלָתוֹ.

You shall give the land as an inheritance to your families. . . . A large family shall be given a larger inheritance, and a smaller family should receive a smaller inheritance.

TEXT 12a

LEVITICUS 25:25–28

> כִּי יָמוּךְ אָחִיךָ וּמָכַר מֵאֲחֻזָּתוֹ, וּבָא גֹאֲלוֹ הַקָּרֹב אֵלָיו, וְגָאַל אֵת מִמְכַּר אָחִיו. וְאִישׁ כִּי לֹא יִהְיֶה לוֹ גֹּאֵל, וְהִשִּׂיגָה יָדוֹ וּמָצָא כְּדֵי גְאֻלָּתוֹ. וְחִשַּׁב אֶת שְׁנֵי מִמְכָּרוֹ, וְהֵשִׁיב אֶת הָעֹדֵף לָאִישׁ אֲשֶׁר מָכַר לוֹ, וְשָׁב לַאֲחֻזָּתוֹ.
>
> וְאִם לֹא מָצְאָה יָדוֹ דֵּי הָשִׁיב לוֹ, וְהָיָה מִמְכָּרוֹ בְּיַד הַקֹּנֶה אֹתוֹ עַד שְׁנַת הַיּוֹבֵל. וְיָצָא בַּיֹּבֵל וְשָׁב לַאֲחֻזָּתוֹ.

If your fellow becomes poor and sells some of his inherited property, his nearest relative shall come and redeem his relative's sale. If there is no one to redeem it for him but he later prospers and gains sufficient means to redeem it himself, he shall calculate the value of the years for which the land had been sold and refund the balance to the man to whom he sold it. He can then return to his inheritance.

But if he cannot afford to repay the buyer, what was sold shall remain in the buyer's possession until the jubilee year. Then, in the jubilee year, the land shall revert to the possession of its ancestral owner.

TEXT 12b

RABBI YOSEF OF ORLEANS, *BECHOR SHOR*, LEVITICUS 25:29

הַקָדוֹשׁ בָּרוּךְ הוּא לֹא הִקְפִּיד אֶלָא בְּקַרְקַע שֶׁחַיוּת הָאָדָם תְּלוּיָה בּוֹ, כְּגוֹן שָׂדֶה וְכֶרֶם וְכָל קַרְקַע שֶׁעוֹשֶׂה פֵּירוֹת. שֶׁאֵין הַקָדוֹשׁ בָּרוּךְ הוּא רוֹצֶה דְלִפְסְקוּהָ לְחַיוּתֵיהּ, וּלְכָךְ אָמַר שֶׁלֹא תִמָכֵר לִצְמִיתוּת.

G-d established the jubilee laws of the return of land because one's livelihood depends on the possession of fields that generate produce. G-d doesn't want a person to be left without a means of livelihood and therefore instituted that land cannot be sold forever.

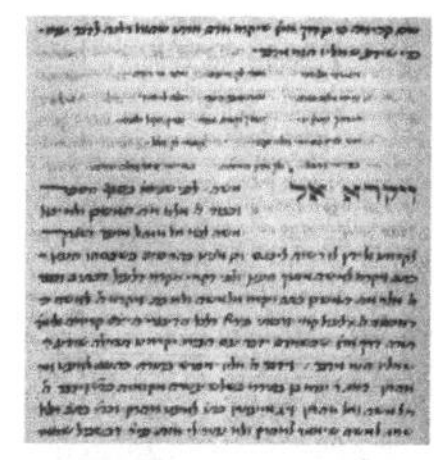

RABBI YOSEF OF ORLEANS
12TH CENTURY

Bible and Talmud commentator. Rabbi Yosef of Orleans, also known as Rabbi Yosef Bechor Shor, was a student of the preeminent French Tosafist Rabbeinu Tam. His Talmudic insights are quoted in *Tosafot*, and he is best known for *Bechor Shor*, his commentary on the Bible.

TEXT 13

LEVITICUS 25:23

וְהָאָרֶץ לֹא תִמָּכֵר לִצְמִתֻת, כִּי לִי הָאָרֶץ. כִּי גֵרִים וְתוֹשָׁבִים אַתֶּם עִמָּדִי.

The land shall not be sold permanently because the land is Mine, and you reside in My land as temporary dwellers and residents.

TEXT 14

RABBI YAAKOV BEN ASHER, *ARBAAH TURIM*, *YOREH DE'AH* 247

וְאַל יַעֲלֶה בְּלִבּוֹ עֵצָה לוֹמַר, אֵיךְ אֲחַסֵר מָמוֹנִי לִיתְּנוֹ לַעֲנִיִּים. כִּי יֵשׁ לוֹ לָדַעַת שֶׁאֵין הַמָּמוֹן שֶׁלוֹ, אֶלָּא פִּקָּדוֹן לַעֲשׂוֹת בּוֹ רְצוֹן הַמַּפְקִיד. וְזֶה רְצוֹנוֹ, שֶׁיְּחַלֵּק לַעֲנִיִּים מִמֶּנוּ.

Do not say, "Why should I deplete my funds by giving of them to the poor?" Understand that the money is not truly yours but is a trust from G-d that must be administered in accordance with the wishes of the trust's owner. G-d's wish is that you disburse from the trust to the poor.

RABBI YAAKOV BEN ASHER (*TUR*, BAAL HATURIM) C. 1269–1343

Halachic authority and codifier. Rabbi Yaakov was born in Germany and moved to Toledo, Spain, with his father, the noted halachist Rabbi Asher, to escape persecution. He wrote *Arbaah Turim ("Tur")*, an ingeniously organized and highly influential code of Jewish law. He is considered one of the greatest authorities of halachah.

***Rabbi Lord Jonathan Sacks** explains how* tsedakah *is a gift for the giver:*

MYJLI.COM/GIFTS

Charity box, unknown artist, brass/other metals, Israel, c. 1920. (Minneapolis Institute of Art)

TEXT 15a

PIETER W. VAN DER HORST, "ORGANIZED CHARITY IN THE ANCIENT WORLD: PAGAN, JEWISH, CHRISTIAN," *JEWISH AND CHRISTIAN COMMUNAL IDENTITIES IN THE ROMAN WORLD* (LEIDEN, NETHERLANDS: BRILL PUBLISHERS, 2016), PP. 116–133

In Greek culture . . . the well-to-do were never expected to support and help the poor. . . . The Greek word *philantropia* never has the sense of our modern philanthropy; one is *philantropos* towards one's own people, parents and other family members, and guests or strangers, not towards the poor. . . . For exhortation to give alms to the poor, one looks in vain to Greek and Roman literature. Greek moralists do not admonish people to concern themselves about the fate of the poor, except incidentally when someone had been unexpectedly hit with a great catastrophe. To be sure, generosity (*eleutheriotes*) was praised as a virtue, but the poor were never singled out as its object, it was always directed to humans in general. . . .

When Greek literature speaks about the joy of giving to others, it has nothing to do with altruism but only with the desired effect of giving, namely honour, prestige, fame and status. Honour is the driving motive behind most of Greek beneficence, and it is for this reason that the Greek word *philotimia* (love of honor, also *philodoxia*) could develop the meaning of "generosity, beneficience," not directed towards the poor but to fellow

PIETER W. VAN DER HORST
1946-

Scholar and author. Professor van der Horst specializes in early Christian literature and the Jewish and Hellenistic context of early Christianity. He is a member of the Royal Netherlands Academy of Arts and Sciences and professor emeritus in the faculty of theology at Utrecht University in the Netherlands.

humans in general, especially those from whom one could reasonably expect a gift in return. . . . It is stated in all its simplicity by Hesiod, "Give to him who gives but do not give to him who does not give (in return)."

***Rabbi Simon Jacobson** discusses which political party better represents the Jewish value of* tsedakah*:*

MYJLI.COM/GIFTS

TEXT 15b

WILL AND ARIEL DURANT, *THE STORY OF CIVILIZATION*, VOL. 3 (NEW YORK: SIMON AND SCHUSTER, 1944), P. 71

Charity found little scope in this frugal life. Hospitality survived as a mutual convenience at a time when inns were poor and far between; but the sympathetic Polybius reports that "in Rome no one ever gives away anything to anyone if he can help it"—doubtless an exaggeration.

WILL DURANT
1885–1981

Historian and philosopher. Will Durant is best known for his 11-volume series, *The Story of Civilization*, written in collaboration with his wife, Ariel Durant. They were awarded the Pulitzer Prize for general nonfiction in 1968 and the Presidential Medal of Freedom in 1977.

ARIEL DURANT
1898–1981

Historian and writer. Ariel Durant coauthored the 11-volume series *The Story of Civilization* with her husband, Will Durant. They were awarded the Pulitzer Prize for general nonfiction in 1968 and the Presidential Medal of Freedom in 1977.

TEXT 16

MAIMONIDES, *COMMENTARY TO THE MISHNAH, ETHICS OF THE FATHERS* 3:15

כְּשֶׁיִּתֵּן הָאָדָם לְמִי שֶׁרָאוּי אֶלֶף זְהוּבִים בְּבַת אַחַת . . . לֹא יַעֲלֶה בְּיָדוֹ מִדַּת הַנְּדִיבוּת בְּזֶה הַמַּעֲשֶׂה הָאֶחָד הַגָּדוֹל כְּמוֹ שֶׁמַּגִּיעַ לְמִי שֶׁהִתְנַדֵּב אֶלֶף זְהוּבִים בְּאֶלֶף פְּעָמִים וְנָתַן כָּל זְהוּב מֵהֶם עַל צַד הַנְּדִיבוּת.

מִפְּנֵי שֶׁזֶּה כָּפַל מַעֲשֵׂה הַנְּדִיבוֹת אֶלֶף פְּעָמִים וְהִגִּיעַ לוֹ קִנְיָן חָזָק, וְזֶה פַּעַם אַחַת לְבַד הִתְעוֹרְרָה נַפְשׁוֹ הִתְעוֹרְרוּת גְּדוֹלָה לְפֹעַל טוֹב וְאַחַר כַּךְ פָּסְקָה מִמֶּנּוּ.

Three Jewish philanthropists discuss the dynamics of giving and getting:

MYJLI.COM/GIFTS

The single act of giving one thousand gold coins to a worthy recipient . . . does not cultivate in the benefactor the same spirit of generosity as does distributing one thousand gold coins on one thousand separate occasions.

In the latter instance, the benefactor acts generously one thousand times, thereby firmly implanting this trait in his or her personality. In the former instance, the individual is only inspired on one occasion, after which the inspiration dissipates.

Vintage Rosh Hashanah Greeting card depicting the practice of giving extra charity during the auspicious month of Elul.

Exercise 1.4

Who do you know that may be in need of help?

What action can you take over the following week to help them?

KEY POINTS

1 Responsibility for others, as exemplified by our forefather Abraham, is a basic principle in the Torah that animates many *mitzvot*.

2 In Jewish law, charity is both an individual as well as communal imperative. Jewish law maintains that (a) the dignity of the poor must be preserved; (b) people may be compelled to contribute; and (c) the wealthier people are, the more they must contribute. The combination of these principles results in the traditional Jewish practice of providing for the poor through the payment of a tax to a communal charity fund.

3 The highest form of charity is to prevent someone from falling into need. The jubilee laws that guaranteed land ownership for all Jews in the Land of Israel served this purpose.

4 The Torah approach to charity functions on two levels: preventing poverty and caring for the poor. Within both of these levels, individual as well as communal efforts are required.

5 The underlying Torah theory of charity is that all of our material possessions ultimately belong to G-d. We hold them as a trust on G-d's behalf and must use them to benefit the needy in accordance with His instructions.

6 The ancient world, including the great Greek and Roman civilizations, did not adopt the Jewish value of caring for others and did not practice charity. The personal mandate to help the needy reached the world after the Christians adopted it.

7 The now universal concept of structuring the economy to minimize poverty can be traced from the mitzvah of the jubilee year, to seventeenth-century Hebraists, and all the way to Thomas Jefferson and the founding fathers of the United States.

Appendix

TEXT 17a

PETRUS CUNAEUS, PETER WYETZNER (TRANSLATOR), *THE HEBREW REPUBLIC* (JERUSALEM: SHALEM PRESS, 2006), PP. 3 AND 15

For your inspection, most illustrious Members of States, I offer a republic—the holiest to have existed in the world, and the richest in examples for us to emulate. It is entirely in your interest to study closely this republic's origins and growth, because its creator and founder was not some man sprung from mortal matter, but immortal G-d Himself—He whose worship, and whose pure service, you have adopted and now protect. You will see what it was, in the end, that preserved the Hebrew citizens for so long in an almost innocent way of life, stirring up their courage, nurturing their harmonious coexistence, and reining in their selfish desires. . . .

There is an excellent author, esteemed by the world, named Rabbi Moses ben Maimon; he successfully collected the Talmud's teachings . . . in that divine work he calls *Mishneh Torah.* I could never say anything so grand about this author that his virtues would not outshine it. . . . In this book I will often call on him to testify, as he is the most distinguished of witnesses.

PETRUS CUNAEUS
1586–1638

Hebraist scholar and author. Petrus Cunaeus was a Dutch political and Hebraist scholar. He is best known for *The Hebrew Republic,* in which he upholds the Torah and the ancient Jewish system of government as the model for the ideal republic.

TEXT 17b

PETRUS CUNAEUS, IBID., P. 17

But come let me describe the usefulness of the agrarian law, which I said Moses had set forth. . . . It was in the best interests of the Republic that the greed of a few men could not disrupt the arrangement of properties that had been so well assigned and distributed, for the wealthier man usually drives the poorer one off his property, and as he makes great inroads into lands for which he has no use, he cuts other men off from their basic necessities. This is why changes of regimes tend to occur from time to time—there is no question that a state in which most of the citizens have been stripped of their ancestral property, and so hope and pray that their fortunes be reversed, is full of its own enemies. Because they hate their current circumstances, these men are eager for a kind of change; and they tolerate this unpleasant state of affairs only as long as necessary.

TEXT 18

THOMAS JEFFERSON, "FROM THOMAS JEFFERSON TO JOHN ADAMS, 28 OCTOBER 1813," U.S. NATIONAL ARCHIVES

The artificial aristocracy is a mischievous ingredient in government, and provision should be made to prevent it's ascendancy. . . .

At the first session of our legislature after the Declaration of Independance, we passed a law abolishing entails. And this was followed by one abolishing the privilege of Primogeniture, and dividing the lands of intestates equally among all their children, or other representatives. These laws, drawn by myself, laid the axe to the root of Pseudo-aristocracy. And had another which I prepared been adopted by the legislature, our work would have been complete. It was a Bill for the more general diffusion of learning. This proposed to divide every county into wards of 5. or 6. miles square, like your townships; to establish in each ward a free school for reading, writing and common arithmetic.

THOMAS JEFFERSON
1743–1826

Founding Father and U.S. president. Virginia native Thomas Jefferson was an American statesman who was the primary author of the U.S. Declaration of Independence. After the Revolution, Jefferson served as governor of Virginia, in various cabinet positions, and then as the 3rd president of the United States.

Additional Readings

HOW TZEDAKA-CHARITY IS DIFFERENT FROM ALL COMMANDMENTS

BY RABBI NACHUM AMSEL

Of the 613 in Judaism, the Mitzvah of *Tzedaka*-charity is unique in certain attributes, Jewish law, and other anomalies connected with it. This makes *Tzedaka* the most unusual of all of the commandments. Three of the remarkable aspects of *Tzedaka* will be examined in this chapter.

Performing a mitzvah-commandment for an ulterior motive

In describing the verse instructing the Jew to give ten percent of produce to the poor, the Torah repeats in the verse the verb for tithing: "*Aser Ta'aser.*"[1] The Talmud often gives a deeper explanation when any "unnecessary" addition or repetition of a word occurs in a verse. On this verse, the Talmud states that one should tithe to the poor *for the purpose* of becoming rich.[2] Since the letters of tithing and wealth are identical (*Ayin, Shin/Sin, Resh*), the verse can then be read, "Tithe so that you can attain wealth." This seems to imply that one's motivation in giving charity in Judaism is not to please G-d or follow His commands, but rather, in order that G-d reward monetarily the person fulfilling this commandment, and he receive back from G-d much more than was donated. This notion seems to contradict the overarching attitude towards serving G-d and performing commandments: a person should act as a servant (to G-d) without expectation of reward.[3] And yet, the Talmud clearly says that one's motivation in giving *Tzedaka* can be for material gain and expected wealth.

The idea of ulterior motives in giving *Tzedaka* becomes even more pronounced in G-d's own words to the people through the prophet Malachi.[4] G-d tells the Jews that if they bring the tithe, they can test G-d through this act and G-d promises that great wealth will follow. Thus, the verse actually encourages Jews to test G-d in performing this Mitzvah. Based on this unusual verse, the Talmud states in several places that if a person conditions his *Tzedaka* donation upon G-d's response that his son will be cured of serious sickness and live, or upon his achieving the World to Come, then this person is considered a fully righteous individual.[5]

This implies that a person can withhold giving the promised charity until one's son is healed and if the son's health does not improve, a person's promise to give *Tzedaka* is no longer obligatory. If a person were to condition performance of any other Mitzvah based on this kind of "deal" with G-d, it would be considered improper, blasphemous, and contrary to Jewish law. For example, if a man were to say "I will only put on Tefillin after G-d makes me a rich man," or a woman were to say "I will keep the Shabbat only once G-d gives me five healthy children," that would be considered heretical! And yet, with regard to the singular commandment of *Tzedaka*, that is not only acceptable, but the person is considered wholly righteous! It is totally legitimate, for example, to condition giving *Tzedaka* to an institution only if the building will be named in memory of one's parents. Why should this be so? The very notion of "commandment" is based on the notion that G-d commands and Jews obey,

RABBI NACHUM AMSEL

Scholar and educator. Rabbi Amsel earned his rabbinical ordination and a doctorate in education from Yeshiva University. He is the director of education at the Destiny Foundation and the author of *The Jewish Encyclopedia of Moral and Ethical Issues*.

without questioning, without demanding, and without making any contract or exchange. How can we then understand this unusual notion in the case of *Tzedaka*? What makes giving charity so different from all other commandments that allows its performance to be conditional and violate the general principle of "serving the Master without expecting reward?"

The Rabbis and commentaries have struggled to try to explain why conditional charity in Judaism is permitted and even welcomed, while conditional performance of any other Mitzvah is forbidden. But before any explanations are attempted, it is important to point out that the power of *Tzedaka* is a stronger cosmic and spiritual force than any other Mitzvah.

The power of Tzedaka as a cosmic force

In describing the ten strongest "forces" in the world, Rabbi Judah goes through each one, such as the hardness of a rock, but also then describes another force that is stronger and overcomes the first force.[6] Thus, iron can cut the rock, fire can melt the iron, water quenches the fire, etc. Near the end of the list, he mentions the force of death, which overcomes everything that is living. But the most powerful force in the world, says Rabbi Judah, is *Tzedaka*, charity. Only *Tzedaka* can overcome that most powerful force of death, as it says two separate times in Proverbs[7] that *Tzedaka* can save a person from death. Concerning no other commandment does it say in Scripture that its performance will protect a person from the decree of death. Thus, the verses and Talmud already hint that the act of *Tzedaka* is quite extraordinary and inherently different from all other commandments and actions in the world.

Several reasons why and how Tzedaka is different from all other commandments

Various explanations have tried to elucidate a rationale for why conditional *Tzedaka* is acceptable, permitted, and even encouraged in Judaism:

1. The Satmar Rebbe compares the Jew accumulating wealth in this world to the worker in the field that produces fruits.[8] The Torah permits the worker to eat from those fruits that he is picking, as long as the worker is working and remains in the field.[9] Maimonides requires as a part of Jewish law that the owner give food to his worker while performing this task.[10] But this Jewish law does not apply to a worker performing any other task in the field (such as fence building) or after a particular task is complete. The Jew in the physical world, says the Satmar Rebbe, is similarly working for G-d in "His field" (the world) to accumulate funds in order to give some of them to *Tzedaka*. As long as the Jew is engaged in this work, he too is permitted to use these *Tzedaka* funds for his own benefit—i.e., he can receive something for giving them away, just as the worker can use what he is picking for his benefit. Thus, a Jew can "control" these earned charity funds by making conditions for how they are spent.
2. G-d promises to always take care of the downtrodden in society, and at the same time, commands Jews to help the downtrodden and give to them.[11] Therefore, the act of giving *Tzedaka* fulfills both obligations at the same time—G-d's and each Jew's. Since this is the only Mitzvah which accomplishes both goals in the same act, *Tzedaka* is unique, and G-d allows Jews to make giving conditional.
3. Judaism is a lifestyle that is supposed to be pleasant and not painful.[12] G-d understands how difficult it is to work in this world, to acquire funds, and to provide for one's family's needs, saying that this task is more difficult than childbirth, more difficult than bringing the ultimate salvation, and just as difficult as G-d splitting the Sea of Reeds.[13] To ask someone to then part with some of this money (even though everything belongs to G-d ultimately in any case) can be a very painful commandment. Thus, to ease the pain, G-d allows a person to make the giving of these accumulated funds to others conditional.
4. It is true that the Talmud cites the person who gives *Tzedaka* conditionally as being righteous, and the verse in Malachi seems to approve of testing G-d in this area. However, this concept is not brought down in Jewish law in the classic books of Halacha. Perhaps, then, this act is not encouraged in practice. If we look at the two specific

conditions that are approved in the Talmud for giving *Tzedaka* conditionally—"my son will live" and "I will attain the World to Come"—these both involve life and death situations. Perhaps conditional *Tzedaka* is permitted only when life itself is at stake, in the same manner that all commandments may be violated in order to save a life (except for three).[14]

5. The Talmud tells us that helping the poor and downtrodden is in the spiritual DNA of each Jew (which is evidenced by the high percentage of Jews giving charity today, even those who are not necessarily observant, and also by Jewish involvement in many organizations helping the downtrodden).[15] Rashi states that because of this predisposition of Jews, even when the stated condition by the potential giver is not fulfilled, the Jew still wishes to give that *Tzedaka* in any case and will donate the funds. [16] The Talmud also seems to make this distinction between Jews who would ultimately give the *Tzedaka* in any case, and some non-Jews who would use permitted conditional charity giving merely to obtain riches.[17]
6. In a similar vein, Meiri says that in a situation in which the stated provision for giving is not fulfilled, many Jews view this as G-d denying them because they are not worthy, and would then give the *Tzedaka* in any event.[18]
7. P'nai Yehoshua explains that the specific language in the Talmud describes the person who gives conditionally as "righteous," but does not use the word "pious" (*Chasid*) to describe this person. That is because although it might be within a person's *right* to give conditionally, it is *not* the proper Jewish way of giving *Tzedaka*.[19]
8. Rabbi Yechezkel Landau distinguishes between the Mitzvah of *Tzedaka* and every other Mitzvah in the Torah. Concerning all other actions, the intent (to perform that deed for G-d) is crucial and an important part of the commandment. But with charity, the intention is not truly important. The only thing that really counts is that the poor person is helped. Thus, intention, while it is an extra benefit, is not necessary in the case of *Tzedaka*, as long as the money gets to the needy individual. Therefore, even if on condition, the Mitzvah is fulfilled, as long as the act is completed.[20]

With all of the above explanations trying to rationalize how and why *Tzedaka* is different in regard to testing the Almighty, the Chinuch, a post-Talmudic commentary, reiterates that it is forbidden to test G-d in one's actions in this world. He then continues to state categorically that the one exception to this rule is *Tzedaka*, regarding which one's giving can indeed be provisional upon G-d's compliance with a certain condition the giver specifies. While Chinuch gives several reasons for this exception (many of them cited above), he clearly permits this behavior for this Mitzvah.[21]

Given all the above arguments, sources, and statements, Jewish law follows the Chinuch, even though this idea remains counterintuitive to the system of commandments. *Tzedaka* is an extremely powerful force in the world, writes *Shulchan Aruch*. And while it is generally forbidden to test G-d and do a Mitzvah conditionally, Rema states that the tithing for *Tzedaka* is the one area where a Jew can test G-d and give conditionally.[22]

Priorities in Tzedaka

In virtually every other area in which the Jew is mandated to give something from his or her possessions, each Jew has the flexibility in choosing which individual to give to. For example, regarding the gifts of produce that went to the Kohen-Priest or Levite, each Jew could decide which Kohen or Levite to give it to.[23] Similarly, concerning fines that went to the Kohen in the Temple, the offending Jew could decide which specific Kohen to give to.[24] When an Israelite brought a sacrifice to the Temple, and certain parts of the animal were forbidden to be eaten by the Israelite but permitted to the Kohen, the person who brought the sacrifice decided which Kohen would receive those parts of the animal due to him.[25]

Even regarding the poor in ancient times, dispersement of what we today would call "*Tzedaka*-charity" was relatively straightforward. In an agrarian society, the Torah mandates that one corner of the field had to be left for the poor people to collect on their own, usually at night, in order not to publically embarrass them.[26] Even when dispersal was done during the day, there were set times for the poor to come to each field, and all of the poor gathered and collected the produce at one time together.[27] In those years when there was an additional tithe given to the poor (years one, two, four, and five of the seven-year cycle), the poor gathered and divided the produce among them (if received in the field). If given from the home, the owner could decide which poor person to give the produce to.[28] It was a simple and very orderly system of *Tzedaka*.

Today, on the other hand, we no longer speak about distributing produce to the poor. Rather, we give money. Since we have much more disposable income, the system has changed radically, making the giving of *Tzedaka* one of the most difficult commandments to fulfill properly; the laws about whom to give, which institution gets Jewish *Tzedaka* first, or which group of poor people has precedence, can confuse even a Torah scholar. The sources within Jewish law seem contradictory, unlike most other areas of Halacha.

The amount that should be given seems straightforward. The *Code of Jewish Law* rules that a certain small amount once a year fulfills the bare minimum, but it is considered miserly.[29] An average Jew gives ten percent of his or her income after basic living expenses. The maximum one may give is twenty percent. However, knowing exactly how to disperse the funds and to whom, seems very confusing, making it a very difficult commandment to fulfill.

Numerous statements in Jewish law about the "most important" Tzedaka

Part of the confusion about how to properly satisfy the obligation to donate funds in the Jewish community is that there are numerous statements in Jewish law, each stating that "this cause" or "this institution" is the most important and takes priority over everything else in the distribution of *Tzedaka*. They are:

1. Both Maimonides and *Shulchan Aruch* state that the *most important* Mitzvah in apportioning charity funds is to redeem those who were kidnapped.[30] This takes precedence over the hungry poor. Moreover, even if money was collected for a specific holy purpose—while normally it is not permitted to use this money for other purposes—one can divert these funds to redeem captives without first asking the donors.
2. The *most important Tzedaka*, states *Shulchan Aruch* in a different place, is to donate funds to poor single girls so they can have enough money to get married.[31]
3. In the next paragraph, the same *Shulchan Aruch* states that some believe that donating to the community synagogue is more important than poor girls and is *the greatest reason for giving charity* in the Jewish community.[32]
4. Then *Shulchan Aruch* quotes another opinion that says that donating money to enable poor boys to learn Torah is *the highest form of Tzedaka*.[33]
5. OR, continues *Shulchan Aruch*, donating to the poor who are sick is *the highest Tzedaka*.[34]

So we are left wondering which need is indeed the most pressing. If a person has limited funds for *Tzedaka* donations, which cause takes precedence above all others—redeeming captives or supporting the synagogue, poor girls needing to get married or poor boys needing to learn Torah? Or is the most essential need to donate to the sick poor people so that they can regain their health (since there were no hospitals or medical insurance in Talmudic times or when *Shulchan Aruch* was written)?

In order to answer these questions, we have to introduce additional factors that are also "important" and take precedence in giving *Tzedaka*, which may at first confuse the reader even more. However, only then will we be able to resolve the conflicting needs and determine a hierarchy of giving *Tzedaka* monies in Jewish law.

You and your family come first

The verse speaks about when poverty exists "within you" or "within your community."[35] Based on this verse and the Talmudic discussion, Rema in the *Code of Jewish Law* rules that you come first.[36] If you are poor, then you come before anyone else and you give to yourself first, in order to escape poverty. *Mishna Berurah* commentary, however, is quick to add that it is forbidden to rationalize in this area and be lenient with your own needs in order to give yourself more funds than you are actually entitled to.[37] You are only permitted to give yourself enough funds for subsistence and to remove yourself from abject poverty before you are obligated to begin giving to others.

If any person extends his or her hand to receive charity, even a non-Jew must give this person some small amount at the minimum.[38] Even if a Jew possesses relatively little for himself or herself, he or she must never turn away a person putting out his or her hand for charity.[39] Since, according to strict Jewish law, a parent's obligation to feed one's children ends at the age of six (at that time most young children worked and earned income), paying for one's children's food and Torah learning fulfills the *Tzedaka* obligation.[40] This is based on the Talmudic passage that speaks about some *Tzedaka* that is fulfilled day and night,[41] which Rashi explains refers to children, who need to be taken care of and have their needs paid for at every moment.[42] Then *Shulchan Aruch* continues with a list of priorities in giving *Tzedaka*. One's relatives come before other people in need. This is followed by the poor of one's community, which takes precedence over the poor of other communities. However, the poor of the Land of Israel are of equal status with the poor of your community.[43]

Man vs. woman

The Mishna states that, if everything else is equal, a man takes precedence over a woman when it comes to life and returning lost objects, while a woman takes precedence over a man when it comes to clothing needs and the redeeming of a captive.[44] And yet, elsewhere the Talmud states that when it comes to needy orphans, the woman always takes precedence over a man because a man can more easily obtain employment and secure funds.[45] *Sefer Be'er Sheva* resolves the apparent contradiction and says that in both areas of food and clothing, a woman always takes precedence over a man if their situation is equal.[46]

Different types of Tzedaka and distinctions within the different types

Until now, we have been comparing "apples" and "oranges." While it is true that all the cases above are situations in the Jewish community that require monetary donations to resolve them, there is little similarity between a captive whose life is in danger and the needs of a synagogue, which are both different from a poor person needing funds in order to live. Thus, say the Rabbis, we must first separate between categories that require community or personal funds, but may not even be considered *Tzedaka* in the technical sense, and then define which need indeed takes precedence. Then we must analyze, differentiate, and determine who takes precedence within each category (such as poverty) and determine precedence (relatives, men and women, etc.).

First and foremost, says Chochmat Adam, we must differentiate between situations when life is in danger or potential danger.[47] This need always comes before anything else. This may include the need to pay a tax to the ruthless king (in a society where failure to pay taxes would result in death), taking care of a sick poor person who may die, and certainly redeeming a captive, whose life is always considered in danger. Beit Yosef (author of *Shulchan Aruch*) states that taking care of the synagogue (which was and often still is the main center of Jewish life in the community) takes precedence over all *Tzedaka* needs for the poor, but may be referring to life and death situations there as well.[48]

What to do with conflicts in priorities

Rav Moshe Shternbuch was asked about a particular case involving legitimate contributions: giving money for a couple to get married or giving funds to a Yeshiva so that it can teach Torah. He then says that it is important to examine the details of each case individually, as there can be vast differences within each category and even within the obligation to help a bride and groom. There is a big difference, for example, between a bride who does not even have any money to pay for the simplest wedding dress and food for guests at the wedding, and a couple who needs money to purchase a three-room apartment. Similarly, there is a vast difference between the needs of a Yeshiva that is trying to build a new wing and another Yeshiva that cannot pay teachers' salaries and may have to close. Thus, determining precedence, even within categories, depends on how dire the situation is in each case. He then quotes the Vilna Gaon on the verse "You shall not close your hand to the poor."[49] When a person closes his or her hand and looks at one's fingers, they all appear to be the same length. It is only when the hand is opened that a person realizes that each finger is of a different length. Thus, the Torah is telling us not to close our hands to the poor and see each situation as equal. Rather, we are obligated to open our hands and see that each finger, situation, is of different length, need, and then we will be able to determine if the situation of the couple who wants to get married is more dire than the situation of the Yeshiva or vice versa. If, after careful examination, the two situations seem identical in need, says Rav Shternbuch, then the Torah needs of the many come before the needs of the individual couple.[50]

Rabbi Moshe Feinstein was asked a similar question.[51] A person's relative can afford to get married but needs money to then sit and learn Torah for a year or two after marriage. At the same time, a poor person needs money for food and sustenance now, but it is not a matter of life and death. Does the small financial need of the relative take precedence over the more immediate need of the poor person who is a stranger? Rabbi Feinstein determines that the financial hardships do not have to be identical in order to favor the relative. Since the financial needs of a relative come before the needs of a poor stranger, even if the needs of the stranger are more dire (but not life-threatening), the general rule that a relative takes precedence stands.

It is clear that even when the general rules of precedence of *Tzedaka* are laid out, when there arises a specific case, doubt, or conflict, a Rabbi should be consulted to determine the correct thing to do according to Judaism.

Final priorities according to one modern decisor

Rabbi Asher Weiss discusses each category outlined above and each priority at length, and then tries to simplify the process by outlining a clear list of rules regarding priorities in giving. He first analyzes all of the statements and categories quoted above as "the most important *Tzedaka*." He concludes that supporting Torah learning takes precedence over supporting poor that are sick. But supporting the poor person who is sick takes precedence over supporting the synagogue, which takes precedence over supporting the poor in general.[52]

Rabbi Weiss then lists the six categories of *Tzedaka* support in order of importance:

1. *Anything that involves possible loss of life is the first priority.* This includes sick poor people who may die and captives who need to be redeemed.
2. *Supporting the learning of Torah is the next priority.* This includes supporting a *Beit Midrash*, a house of Jewish learning, and buying any needed Torah books. (Undoubtedly, he would include in this category the recent phenomenon of the tuition crisis whereby many observant parents today cannot afford to send their children to Yeshivot. Donations to enable these students to be enrolled in day schools would be included in this priority.)
3. *Poor who are ill are the next priority.* This includes not only medical expenses, but also all other expenses necessary to get them back to health.
4. *Building and maintaining a synagogue is the next priority.* However, Rabbi Weiss mentions that the Vilna Gaon and others disagreed with this priority.
5. *Marrying off orphans.* He says that with the enormous expenses today for a wedding and beginning a family, this priority may apply to any poor that cannot afford to get married.
6. *Sustaining the poor of the Jewish people.* The priority and order of precedence within this category should be followed according to the hierarchy outlined by the *Shulchan Aruch* as explained above.

Giving Tzedaka to the poor on Purim

There is another very strange aspect of giving *Tzedaka*. Even though there is a commandment to give to the poor the entire year, on Purim day (the fourteenth of Adar, or the fifteenth of Adar in Jerusalem) there is a special commandment to give to the poor. This is indeed a very strange Mitzvah. We find no other commandment regarding which there is a general commandment to do it all year long, and then an identical, additional commandment to perform on one specific day of the year. While we know that *Matzah* is specific to Pesach, and *Lulav* is specific to Sukkot, honoring one's mother and father is a year-round, everyday commandment. Thus in Judaism, there is no additional Mother's Day or Father's Day to honor one's parents on one specific day. Yet it seems that this is indeed the case with *Tzedaka*. In addition to the everyday Mitzvah, there is a specific commandment to give to the poor on Purim! Why would the Rabbis add an identical Mitzvah, and identical action, again on Purim day? And then we must query: is the Mitzvah on Purim indeed identical in all its laws and *Halachot* to the Mitzvah of giving to the needy the rest of the year? And if this is *not* a Mitzvah of *Tzedaka* on Purim, what else could it be?

The Megillah itself describes the custom to give gifts to the poor on Purim.[53] The Talmud quantifies the obligation as two gifts to two poor people.[54] This is codified in Jewish law—i.e., two gifts must be given to two poor people.[55] The question is if this Mitzvah is unique to Purim and separate from the general commandment to give *Tzedaka*, or if it is an additional obligation of charity. What could be the difference?

There could be several important distinctions. If this Purim commandment is part of the general commandment to give *Tzedaka*, then while a poor person is also obligated to give *Tzedaka* from that which was given to him,[56] this poor person may do it but once a year, on any day of the year. He would not have to do this on Purim. However, if this were a commandment that is part of the Purim Mitzvot and not related to *Tzedaka* per se, then the poor person would also have to give something to another poor person on this day.

Similarly, if this Purim Mitzvah were part of *Tzedaka*, then all of the laws related to *Tzedaka* (the priorities regarding who receives it, for example, as cited above) would be in force. But if this is a unique Purim Mitzvah, then the recipients and priorities may be different from those of "normal" *Tzedaka*. So which is it, a commandment of *Tzedaka* or a unique Purim commandment?

Maimonides seems to leave no doubt. He states that the purpose of giving monies to the poor on Purim is specifically to make joyous the heart of the poor, as well as orphans, widows, and converts.[57] Thus, the funds they receive will add to their Purim joy. This is clearly not related to the general commandments to give funds to the needy, but rather, a unique Purim Mitzvah.

Shiblei HaLeket, on the other hand, clearly states that the funds given to the poor on Purim are considered part of the commandment of *Tzedaka*.[58] But clearly, his view is in the minority.

The Jerusalem Talmud says that unlike the recipients of *Tzedaka* the rest of the year, one need not examine closely the specific situation and need of the poor person you give to on Purim.[59] Rather, anyone who puts out his or her hand to take money on Purim should be immediately given. Ritva elucidates this passage and says that the laws of priorities of *Tzedaka* that apply all year to the giving to the poor do not apply on Purim, and that this is not a Mitzvah of *Tzedaka*, but rather a commandment to make the poor happy on Purim.[60] The *Code of Jewish Law* reflects this attitude as well and states that a Jew is supposed to give to anyone who extends his or her hand on Purim, even to a non-Jew (where this is the local custom).[61] Clearly, Jewish law and all of these opinions demonstrate that giving to the poor on Purim is a special Mitzvah not connected to usual *Tzedaka*.

It is for this reason that Bayit Chadash writes that a poor person must also fulfill this Mitzvah specifically on Purim day. Even though the rest of the year the poor person fulfills his *Tzedaka* Mitzvah by giving to another poor person just once a year, since this practice on Purim is not related to *Tzedaka*, the indigent must also perform this Mitzvah specifically on Purim day.[62]

This view is also echoed by *Turei Zahav*.[63] Therefore, while it may seem that giving money to the poor on Purim is a fulfillment of *Tzedaka*-charity, similar to the rest of the year, the overwhelming majority of commentaries view this act as a unique Mitzvah to make the poor happy on Purim, and the normal rules of *Tzedaka* do not apply.

Endnotes

1 Deuteronomy 14:22
2 *Ta'anit* 9a
3 Mishna *Avot* 1:3
4 Malachi 3:10

5 *Rosh Hashana* 4a, *Bava Batra* 10b, *Pesachim* 8a
6 *Bava Batra* 10b
7 Proverbs 10:2, 11:4
8 Quoted in "Priorities in Tzedaka," Rabbi Moshe Goldberger, 2007, pp. 41–42
9 Deuteronomy 23:25
10 Maimonides, *Hilchot Sechirut* 12:1
11 Exodus 22:21–22, Deuteronomy 24:19, Deuteronomy 15:11
12 Proverbs 3:17
13 *Pesachim* 118a
14 *Kesef Mishne* on Maimonides, *Hilchot Tefillin*, chapter 10
15 *Yevamot* 79a
16 Rashi commentary on *Rosh Hashana* 4a, s.v. "*Kahn beYisrael*"
17 *Bava Batra* 10b
18 Meiri commentary on *Rosh Hashana* 42
19 Pnai Yehoshua commentary on *Rosh Hashana* 42
20 *Derushai Tzelach, Ahavat Tziyon*, tenth address
21 *Sefer HaChinuch*, Mitzvah 424
22 *Shulchan Aruch, Yoreh De'ah* 147:4
23 Bartenura commentary on Mishna *Demai* 6:3
24 Bartenura commentary on Mishna *Challah* 1:9
25 Tosefta *Pe'ah* 2:13; *Shulchan Aruch, Yoreh De'ah* 61:28
26 Leviticus 23:22, Deuteronomy 24:19
27 Maimonides, *Hilchot Matnot Aniyim* 21:17
28 Maimonides, *Hilchot Matnot Aniyim* 6:7, 9, 10, 12
29 *Shulchan Aruch, Yoreh De'ah* 249:1
30 Maimonides, *Hilchot Matnot Aniyim* 8:10; *Shulchan Aruch, Yoreh De'ah* 252:1
31 *Shulchan Aruch, Yoreh De'ah* 249:15
32 *Shulchan Aruch, Yoreh De'ah* 249:16
33 *Shulchan Aruch, Yoreh De'ah* 249:16
34 *Shulchan Aruch, Yoreh De'ah* 249:16
35 Deuteronomy 15:7
36 Rema on *Shulchan Aruch, Yoreh De'ah* 61:28
37 *Mishna Berurah* commentary on *Shulchan Aruch, Orach Chaim* 156:2
38 *Tur, Yoreh De'ah* 251
39 Rema on *Shulchan Aruch, Yoreh De'ah* 249:4
40 *Shulchan Aruch, Yoreh De'ah* 251:3
41 *Ketuvot* 50a
42 Rashi commentary on *Ketuvot* 50a
43 *Shulchan Aruch, Yoreh De'ah* 251:3
44 *Horayot* 3:7
45 *Ketuvot* 67a
46 *Sefer Be'er Sheva* commentary to *Horayot* 13a
47 *Chochmat Adam* 145:8
48 *Beit Yosef* on *Tur, Yoreh De'ah* 149
49 Deuteronomy 15:7
50 *Responsa Teshuvot Vehanhagot* I:567
51 *Responsa Igrot Moshe, Yoreh De'ah* I:144
52 *Minchat Asher, Parshat Re'ah* 21
53 Esther 9:22
54 *Megillah* 7a
55 *Shulchan Aruch, Orach Chaim* 69 4:1
56 *Shulchan Aruch, Yoreh De'ah* 248:1
57 Maimonides, *Hilchot Megillah* 2:16–17
58 *Shiblei HaLeket* 202
59 Jerusalem Talmud, *Megillah* 5a
60 Ritva commentary on (Babylonian) *Megillah* 7a
61 *Shulchan Aruch, Orach Chaim* 694:3
62 Bach on *Tur, Orach Chaim* 694:1
63 Taz on *Shulchan Aruch* 694:1

The Encyclopedia of Jewish Values (Jerusalem: Urim Publications, 2015), pp. 145–153

Lesson 2

Abraham Contemplates the Stars, engraving for *Die Bücher das Bibel (The Books of the Bibel)*, Vol. 7, Ephraim Moses Lilien, 1908.

DISCOVERING ONE

THE EXTRAORDINARY IMPACT OF MONOTHEISM

As a young man, Abraham, the Jewish people's original Patriarch, defied his pagan surroundings and began to introduce humanity to the concept of one G-d—the Creator and Director of the universe. This cornerstone of the Jewish faith gradually spread throughout civilization, bringing drastic changes not only to the global religious landscape but also to the way humanity views and approaches life.

QUESTION FOR DISCUSSION

Is monotheism significant only to your "religious views" and "religious life," or would you say that belief in exclusively one G-d also impacts your feelings about life in general? In what way?

Greek astronomer at the observatory of Alexandria, Egypt, engraving for Camille Flammarion's *Astronomie Populaire: Description générale du ciel*, Paris, 1880.

TEXT 1a

MAIMONIDES, *MISHNEH TORAH*, LAWS OF IDOLATRY 1:2

וּפָשַׁט דָּבָר זֶה בְּכָל הָעוֹלָם לַעֲבֹד אֶת הַצּוּרוֹת בַּעֲבוֹדוֹת מְשֻׁנּוֹת זוֹ מִזּוֹ וּלְהַקְרִיב לָהֶם וּלְהִשְׁתַּחֲווֹת.

וְכֵיוָן שֶׁאָרְכוּ הַיָּמִים, נִשְׁתַּכַּח הַשֵּׁם הַנִּכְבָּד וְהַנּוֹרָא מִפִּי כָּל הַיְקוּם וּמִדַּעְתָּם וְלֹא הִכִּירוּהוּ, וְנִמְצְאוּ כָּל עַם הָאָרֶץ הַנָּשִׁים וְהַקְּטַנִּים אֵינָם יוֹדְעִים אֶלָּא הַצּוּרָה שֶׁל עֵץ וְשֶׁל אֶבֶן וְהַהֵיכָל שֶׁל אֲבָנִים שֶׁנִּתְחַנְּכוּ מִקַּטְנוּתָם לְהִשְׁתַּחֲווֹת לָהּ וּלְעָבְדָהּ וּלְהִשָּׁבַע בִּשְׁמָהּ. וְהַחֲכָמִים שֶׁהָיוּ בָּהֶם, כְּגוֹן כֹּהֲנֵיהֶם וְכַיּוֹצֵא בָּהֶן, מְדַמִּין שֶׁאֵין שָׁם אֱלוֹהַּ אֶלָּא הַכּוֹכָבִים וְהַגַּלְגַּלִּים שֶׁנַּעֲשׂוּ הַצּוּרוֹת הָאֵלּוּ בִּגְלָלָם.

Thus, idolatrous beliefs spread throughout the world. People would worship images in all sorts of strange ways and offer sacrifices to them and bow down to them.

As the years passed, the true G-d was forgotten from the minds of all people, and they gave Him no recognition. The common people knew only the images of wood or stone and the temples of stone—which they had been raised, from their youth, to bow down to and worship and in whose name they took oaths. Even the priests and wise people among them believed that there is no god other than the stars and planets, for whose sake they had made those images.

RABBI MOSHE BEN MAIMON (MAIMONIDES, RAMBAM) 1135–1204

Halachist, philosopher, author, and physician. Maimonides was born in Córdoba, Spain. After the conquest of Córdoba by the Almohads, he fled Spain and eventually settled in Cairo, Egypt. There, he became the leader of the Jewish community and served as court physician to the vizier of Egypt. He is most noted for authoring the *Mishneh Torah*, an encyclopedic arrangement of Jewish law, and for his philosophical work, *Guide for the Perplexed*. His rulings on Jewish law are integral to the formation of halachic consensus.

TEXT 1b

MAIMONIDES, *GUIDE FOR THE PERPLEXED* 3:29

יָדוּעַ כִּי אַבְרָהָם אָבִינוּ עָלָיו הַשָּׁלוֹם גָּדַל בְּאוּמַּת הצאב"ה, וְשִׁטָתָם שֶׁאֵין שָׁם אֱלוֹהַּ כִּי אִם הַכּוֹכָבִים. וְכַאֲשֶׁר אוֹדִיעֲךָ בַּפֶּרֶק הַזֶּה סִפְרֵיהֶם הַמְצוּיִם עַתָּה בְּיָדֵינוּ אֲשֶׁר תּוּרְגְמוּ לְלָשׁוֹן הָעֲרָבִי, וְדִבְרֵי יְמֵיהֶם הָעַתִּיקִים, וַאֲגַלֶּה לְךָ שְׁטוּתֵיהֶם וְשִׂיחוֹתֵיהֶם כְּפִי שֶׁנֶּאֶמְרוּ בָּהֶם, יִתְבָּאֵר לְךָ מֵהֶם אוֹמְרָם בְּפֵירוּשׁ כִּי הַכּוֹכָבִים הֵם הָאֱלוֹהַּ, וְשֶׁהַשֶּׁמֶשׁ הִיא הָאֱלוֹהַּ הַגָּדוֹל. וְכָךְ אָמְרוּ גַּם יֶתֶר שִׁבְעַת הַכּוֹכָבִים אֱלוֹהוּת, אֶלָּא שֶׁשְּׁנֵי הַמְּאוֹרוֹת יוֹתֵר גְּדוֹלִים . . . וּלְפִיכָךְ הָיוּ כָּל הצאב"ה בְּדֵעָה שֶׁהָעוֹלָם קַדְמוֹן, כִּי הַשָּׁמַיִם לְדַעְתָּם הֵם הָאֱלוֹהַּ . . .

וְעַל פִּי אוֹתָם הַהַשְׁקָפוֹת שֶׁל הצאב"ה הֶעֱמִידוּ אֶת הַצְּלָמִים לְכּוֹכָבִים, צַלְמֵי הַזָּהָב לַשֶּׁמֶשׁ, וְצַלְמֵי הַכֶּסֶף לַיָּרֵחַ, וְחָלְקוּ אֶת הַמַּתָּכוֹת וְהָאַקְלִימִים לְכּוֹכָבִים, וְאָמְרוּ אַקְלִים פְּלוֹנִי אֱלוֹהוֹ הַכּוֹכָב הַפְּלוֹנִי, וּבָנוּ הַהֵיכָלוֹת וְהֶעֱמִידוּ בָּהֶם הַצְּלָמִים, וְדִימוּ כִּי כּוֹחוֹת הַכּוֹכָבִים שׁוֹפְעִים עַל אוֹתָם הַצְּלָמִים, וְאָז יְדַבְּרוּ אוֹתָם הַצְּלָמִים וְיָבִינוּ וְיַשְׂכִּילוּ, וִינַבְּאוּ אֶת בְּנֵי אָדָם, כְּלוֹמַר: הַצְּלָמִים, וְיוֹדִיעוּ לִבְנֵי אָדָם תּוֹעַלִיּוֹתֵיהֶם.

It is well known that our patriarch Abraham was brought up among the Sabeans, who believed that there is no divine being except the stars. In this chapter, I will survey their books and ancient chronicles that have been translated into Arabic, and I will depict their foolish beliefs and statements according to those books. You will see that they regard the stars as deities, and the sun as the chief deity. They believe that all seven stars and planets are gods, but the sun and the moon are greater than the rest. . . . The Sabeans thus believed that the universe had always existed because they believed the celestial beings to be gods.

In accordance with these Sabean theories, they erected images corresponding to the celestial beings—golden images to the sun, silver images to the moon, and so on. Moreover, they associated various metals and climates with the powers of the planets, saying that certain planets are the gods of certain climatic zones. They built temples and placed images in them. They believed that the stars sent forth their influence upon these images, enabling these images to think, comprehend, communicate, and prophetically inform human beings concerning what is good for them.

TEXT 1C

RABBI LORD JONATHAN SACKS, *A LETTER IN THE SCROLL* (NEW YORK: FREE PRESS, 2009), PP. 66–69

Just as there were many stars and planets and countless species of animals, so there were many gods. They fought, struggled, and established hierarchies of dominance, slowly establishing order out of chaos.

We have many records of those ancient times, and though the names of the gods change—depending on whether we speak of Mesopotamia, Egypt, Canaan or ancient Greece—the stories are remarkably similar. The god of the sky does battle with the god of the sea, and

RABBI LORD JONATHAN SACKS
1948–

Former chief rabbi of the United Kingdom. Rabbi Sacks attended Cambridge University and received his doctorate from King's College, London. A prolific and influential author, his books include *Will We Have Jewish Grandchildren?* and *The Dignity of Difference.* He received the Jerusalem Prize in 1995 for his contributions to enhancing Jewish life in the Diaspora, was knighted and made a life peer in 2005, and became Baron Sacks of Aldridge in 2009.

out of his victory establishes dry land, usually over the dead body of his slain victim. The god of the lightning and rain impregnates the goddess of the earth, and thus crops grow and the land brings forth its produce. There is no sharp distinction between nature, the animals, the gods, and mankind. . . . In the stories they told about them, [the gods] are usually personifications of the forces of nature—the sun, the sea, the wind, the rain. . . .

The ancient world was one in which order was constantly threatened by chaos, at times in the form of floods and droughts, at others by war from invading tribes. Through the stories they told, they explained to themselves why this is so. Disturbances here reflect more ultimate struggles elsewhere, between the gods. . . . If the god of the sky won his battle with the sea, there would be no floods that year. If the god of rain successfully mated with the goddess of the soil, the harvest would be good. . . . Humanity, in its various gradations, is replaceable.

*Is there a relationship between monotheism and morality? **Rabbi Yitzchak Breitowitz** explains:*

MYJLI.COM/GIFTS

Exercise 2.1

Considering the pagan beliefs described in Texts 1a–1c, indicate with a √ or an X which of the following attributes would apply to any of the gods they believed in.

Attribute	
1. The One and Only	
2. Precedes and transcends all of nature	
3. Nonmaterial	
4. Omnipotent	
5. Creates ex nihilo	
6. In exclusive control of everything	
7. Creates benevolently	
8. Just and righteous	
9. Creates purposefully	
10. Cares about the happenings in the universe	
11. Holds humankind in high regard	

TEXT 2

MIDRASH, *BEREISHIT RABAH* 39:6

מָשָׁל לְאֶחָד שֶׁהָיָה עוֹבֵר מִמָּקוֹם לְמָקוֹם, וְרָאָה בִּירָה אַחַת דוֹלֶקֶת. אָמַר, "תֹּאמַר שֶׁהַבִּירָה הַזוֹ בְּלֹא מַנְהִיג"?! הֵצִיץ עָלָיו בַּעַל הַבִּירָה, אָמַר לוֹ: אֲנִי הוּא בַּעַל הַבִּירָה.

כָּךְ לְפִי שֶׁהָיָה אָבִינוּ אַבְרָהָם אוֹמֵר: "תֹּאמַר שֶׁהָעוֹלָם הַזֶה בְּלֹא מַנְהִיג?!" הֵצִיץ עָלָיו הַקָּדוֹשׁ בָּרוּךְ הוּא וְאָמַר לוֹ: אֲנִי הוּא בַּעַל הָעוֹלָם . . . הֱוֵי: "וַיֹּאמֶר ה' אֶל אַבְרָם" . . . (בְּרֵאשִׁית יב, א).

A parable: A man was traveling from one place to another and encountered a well-lit palace. He said, "Is it possible that this palace has no master?"

The owner of the palace looked out and said, "I am the master of the palace."

Similarly, our father Abraham said, "Is it fathomable that this world has no master?"

G-d looked out and said to him, "I am the Master of the universe." . . . This is the background behind, "G-d said to Abraham . . ." (GENESIS 12:1).

BEREISHIT RABAH

An early rabbinic commentary on the Book of Genesis. This Midrash bears the name of Rabbi Oshiya Rabah (Rabbi Oshiya "the Great"), whose teaching opens this work. This Midrash provides textual exegeses and stories, expounds upon the biblical narrative, and develops and illustrates moral principles. Produced by the sages of the Talmud in the Land of Israel, its use of Aramaic closely resembles that of the Jerusalem Talmud. It was first printed in Constantinople in 1512 together with 4 other Midrashic works on the other 4 books of the Pentateuch

TEXT 3

MAIMONIDES, *GUIDE FOR THE PERPLEXED* 3:29

וְכַאֲשֶׁר גָּדַל עַמּוּדוֹ שֶׁל עוֹלָם, וְנִתְבָּרֵר לוֹ שֶׁיֵּשׁ שָׁם אֱלוֹ-הַ נִבְדָּל, לֹא גּוּף וְלֹא כֹּחַ בְּגוּף, וְשֶׁכָּל אֵלֶּה הַכּוֹכָבִים וְהַגַּלְגַּלִּים - מַעֲשָׂיו, וְהֵבִין אַפְסוּת אוֹתָם הַהֲבָלִים הָהֵם אֲשֶׁר נִתְחַנֵּךְ עֲלֵיהֶם, הֵחֵל לִסְתּוֹר שִׁטָתָם וּלְבָאֵר הֶפְסֵד הַשְׁקָפוֹתֵיהֶם, וּפִרְסֵם הַפָּכָם, וְקָרָא "בְּשֵׁם ה' אֵ-ל עוֹלָם" (בְּרֵאשִׁית כא, לג) - קְרִיאָה הַכּוֹלֶלֶת מְצִיאוּת ה' וְחִדּוּשׁ הָעוֹלָם מֵאִתּוֹ יִתְבָּרֵךְ.

What's so harmful about idolatry? Three contemporary scholars address this:

MYJLI.COM/GIFTS

As Abraham, the "Pillar of the World," matured, it became clear to him that there is a Divine Being Who is abstract, neither a body nor a force residing in a body, and that all the planets and the stars are His doing. He understood the worthlessness of the nonsense with which he had been raised, and he began to disprove their beliefs and demonstrate the fallacy of their outlook. He publicly taught otherwise and "called in the name of the G-d of the world" (GENESIS 21:33), proclaiming the existence of G-d and His Creation of the universe.

Exercise 2.2

The following passages are segments of the story of Creation as related in the first chapter of Genesis. As you read these passages, try to identify—from what *is* said and what *is not* said—how Judaism views G-d and His act of Creation. Then enter your findings in the chart that follows.

GENESIS, CHAPTER 1

In the beginning, G-d created heaven and earth. . . . And G-d said, "Let there be light." And there was light. G-d saw that the light was good, so G-d separated between the light and the darkness. G-d called the light "day," and the darkness He called "night." And there was evening, and there was morning: day one.

. . . G-d said, "Let there be luminaries in the expanse of the heavens to separate between the day and the night, and they shall be for signs and for appointed seasons and for days and for years. And they shall be for luminaries in the expanse of the heavens to give light on the earth." And it was so. G-d made the two great luminaries: the greater luminary to rule by day and the lesser luminary to rule at night, accompanied by the stars. And G-d placed them in the expanse of the heavens to give light on the earth, to rule by day and at night, and to separate between the light and the darkness. And G-d saw that it was good. And there was evening, and there was morning, a fourth day.

. . . G-d said, "Let us make man in our image, in our likeness, and they shall rule over the fish of the sea and the birds of the sky, over the animals and all of the earth, and over all the creatures that move along the ground." And G-d created man in His image, in the image of G-d He created him; male and female he created them.

G-d blessed them and said to them, "Be fruitful and multiply, fill the earth and subdue it. Rule over the fish of the sea and the birds of the sky and over all of the beasts that tread upon the earth." And G-d said, "See, I give you every seed-bearing plant on the face of the entire earth and every tree that has seed-bearing fruit; they shall be yours for food. . . ." And it was so.

And G-d saw all that He had made, and behold, it was very good. And it was evening and it was morning, the sixth day.

Considering the passages from Genesis, indicate with a √ or an X in the middle column which of the following statements could be said about G-d. In the next column, indicate which words in the verse (or which ideas that are absent from the narrative) make some of these points clear to us.

	√/X	WORDS FROM TEXT
1. The One and Only		
2. Precedes and transcends all of nature		
3. Nonmaterial		
4. Omnipotent		
5. Creates ex nihilo		
6. In exclusive control of everything		
7. Creates benevolently		
8. Just and righteous		
9. Creates purposefully		
10. Cares about the happenings in the universe		
11. Holds humankind in high regard		

TEXT 4

RABBI LORD JONATHAN SACKS, *A LETTER IN THE SCROLL* (NEW YORK: FREE PRESS, 2009), P. 73

The account of creation in the first chapter of Genesis is stunningly original, quite unlike any other in antiquity. . . . There are no contending forces, no battles of the gods, no capricious spirits. G-d speaks, and the universe comes into being. G-d is not in nature but above it, transcending it and ordering it according to His word. Nature has no will, or set of wills of its own. . . . This was an immense intellectual leap. . . . If G-d created the world, then it is, in principle, intelligible. The mists of irrationality have been dispelled.

TEXT 5

VIKTOR FRANKL, *MAN'S SEARCH FOR MEANING* (BOSTON: BEACON PRESS, 2006), P. 101

He who has a *why* to live for can bear with almost any *how*.

VIKTOR EMIL FRANKL
1905–1997

M.D., PhD, founder of logotherapy. Frankl was professor of neurology and psychiatry at the University of Vienna Medical School. During World War II, he spent 3 years in various concentration camps, including Theresienstadt, Auschwitz, and Dachau. Frankl was the founder of the psychotherapeutic school called logotherapy. Frankl authored 39 books, which have been published in 38 languages. His most famous book, *Man's Search for Meaning*, has sold over 9 million copies in the U.S. alone.

TEXT 6

HUSTON SMITH, *THE RELIGIONS OF MAN* (NEW YORK: HARPER AND ROW, 1958), P. 229

The G-d of the Jew possessed none of these traits which, in greater or lesser degree, characterized the gods of their neighbors. It is here that we come to the supreme achievement of Jewish thought . . . in the character it ascribed to the G-d it discovered to be One. The Greeks, the Romans, the Syrians, and most of the other Mediterranean peoples would have said two things about their gods' characters. First, the gods tend to be amoral; second, toward man they are preponderantly indifferent. The Jews reversed the thinking of their contemporaries on both points. Whereas the gods of Olympus tirelessly pursued beautiful women, the G-d of Sinai watches over the widows and orphans.

HUSTON CUMMINGS SMITH
1919–2016

Philosopher and scholar. Dr. Smith was a professor of philosophy at MIT. He was regarded as one of the world's most influential figures in religious studies and authored at least 13 books on the world's religions and philosophies.

When the Rebbe reached out to Dr. Viktor Frankl, as told by ***Rabbi Yaakov Biderman:***

MYJLI.COM/GIFTS

TEXT 7

HENRI FRANKFORT, *THE INTELLECTUAL ADVENTURE OF ANCIENT MAN* (CHICAGO: UNIVERSITY OF CHICAGO PRESS, 1977), P. 366

Throughout the Mesopotamian texts we hear overtones of anxiety, which seem to express a haunting fear that the unaccountable and turbulent powers may at any time bring disaster to human society.

HENRI FRANKFORT
1897–1954

Egyptologist and archaeologist. Born into a Dutch Jewish family, Frankfort became a leading scholar in the fields of archaeology and cultural anthropology, especially on the religious systems of the ancient Near East. He authored many books and articles on these subjects.

Illustration of Abraham smashing his father's idols, from the *Herlingen Haggadah*, 1725. (The Braginsky Collection)

TEXT 8a

RABBI BACHYA IBN PAKUDAH, *DUTIES OF THE HEART*, CHAPTER 2

כִּי הָאָדָם כַּאֲשֶׁר יֵדַע עַל זוּלָתוֹ שֶׁהוּא מְרַחֵם וְחוֹמֵל עָלָיו, בּוֹטֵחַ בּוֹ, וְנַפְשׁוֹ נִרְגַּעַת עָלָיו בְּמַה שֶּׁיַּטִּיל עָלָיו מֵעִנְיָנָיו . . . שֶׁיִּהְיֶה אוֹתוֹ שֶׁבָּטַח עָלָיו חָזָק, בִּלְתִּי מְנוּצָּח נֶגֶד רְצוֹנוֹ, וְלֹא יִמְנַע בַּעֲדוֹ מוֹנֵעַ מִלְּמַלֵּא צְרָכָיו. לְפִי שֶׁאִם יִהְיֶה חָלָשׁ לֹא יִתָּכֵן הַבִּטָּחוֹן עָלָיו אַף עַל פִּי שֶׁנִּתְבָּרְרָה חֶמְלָתוֹ וְהַשְׁגָּחָתוֹ, מִפְּנֵי הַמְּנִיעוּת הַדְּבָרִים מִמֶּנּוּ עַל הָרוֹב . . . שֶׁיִּהְיֶה זֶה שֶׁבּוֹטְחִים עָלָיו בְּתַכְלִית הַטּוֹב וּבְתַכְלִית הַחֶסֶד . . .

הֲרֵי מִי שֶׁנִּתְקַבְּצוּ בּוֹ כָּל אֵלֶּה . . . וְחוֹבָה עַל מִי שֶׁיֵּדַע אֶת זֶה לִבְטוֹחַ עָלָיו, וְיֵרָגַע עָלָיו בְּנִגְלֵהוּ וּבְסִתְרוֹ וְלִבּוֹ וְאֵבָרָיו, וְיִתְמַסֵּר לִרְצוֹנוֹ, וִיקַבֵּל מִשְׁפָּטוֹ בְּרָצוֹן, וְיַחְשׁוֹב עָלָיו טוֹב בְּכָל מִשְׁפָּטָיו וּפְעָלָיו.

When you know that there are people who have compassion and pity for you, you will trust them and be at peace in all matters upon which you depend on them . . . provided that they are strong, undefeatable, and cannot be prevented from fulfilling what is requested of them. But if they are weak, they cannot be relied upon, even if it is clear that they are compassionate and caring, due to the many areas in which they are restricted. . . . In addition, you must be certain that they are absolutely generous and kind. . . .

Now, if people were to have all these traits . . . it would behoove those who know this to place their trust in them, and to be totally at peace, internally and externally, in their hearts and limbs, and to be faithful to them, and to accept and favorably regard all their judgments and actions.

RABBI BACHYA IBN PAKUDAH
11TH CENTURY

Moral philosopher and author. Ibn Pakudah lived in Muslim Spain, but little else is known about his life. *Chovot Halevavot (Duties of the Heart)*, his major work, was intended to be a guide for attaining spiritual perfection. Originally written in Judeo-Arabic and published in 1080, it was later translated into Hebrew and published in 1161 by Judah ibn Tibbon, a scion of the famous family of translators. Ibn Pakudah had a strong influence on Jewish pietistic literature.

Psychological optimism or theological optimism? ***Rabbi Mendel Kalmenson*** *addresses this:*

MYJLI.COM/GIFTS

TEXT 8b

RABBI BACHYA IBN PAKUDAH, *DUTIES OF THE HEART*, INTRODUCTION TO THE GATE OF TRUST

אַךְ תּוֹעֶלֶת הַבִּטָּחוֹן . . . מֵהֶן - מְנוּחַת הַלֵּב מִן הַדְּאָגוֹת הָעוֹלָמִיּוֹת . . .
וְהוּא בְּהַשְׁקֵט וּבִבְטְחָה וּבְשַׁלְוָה בָּעוֹלָם הַזֶּה, כְּמוֹ שֶׁכָּתוּב (יִרְמְיָה יז, ז):
"בָּרוּךְ הַגֶּבֶר אֲשֶׁר יִבְטַח בַּה' וְהָיָה ה' מִבְטַחוֹ".

The benefits of trust in G-d . . . include tranquility of the heart in the face of worldly worries. . . . The one who has trust finds serenity, security, and peacefulness within this world. As it is written, "Blessed is the man who trusts in G-d; G-d will be his reassurance" (JEREMIAH 17:7).

***Natan Sharansky** reveals the secret of his endurance in Soviet prison in this exclusive interview with JLI:*

MYJLI.COM/GIFTS

Israeli soldier praying, 30 November, 2011. (Israel Defense Forces)

TEXT 9

RABBI LORD JONATHAN SACKS, "THE BIRTH OF HOPE (BECHUKOTAI 5779)," RABBISACKS.ORG

Hope is one of the very greatest Jewish contributions to Western civilization, so much so that I have called Judaism "the voice of hope in the conversation of humankind." In the ancient world, there were tragic cultures in which people believed that the gods were at best indifferent to our existence, at worst actively malevolent. The best humans can do is avoid their attention or appease their wrath. In the end, though, it is all in vain. We are destined to see our dreams wrecked on the rocks of reality. . . .

The great tragedians were Greek. Biblical Hebrew did not even contain a word that meant "tragedy" in the Greek sense. Modern Hebrew had to borrow the word: hence, *tragedia*. . . .

Hope is not unknown in such cultures, but it is what Aristotle defined as "a waking dream," a private wish that things might be otherwise.

***Rabbi Simon Jacobson** explains why hope and purpose are critical gifts of Judaism:*

MYJLI.COM/GIFTS

Exercise 2.3

1 Recall an experience you've had in which, after a period of doubt, things turned out unexpectedly well.

2 Now, if you can, recall the feelings and thoughts you had before the unexpectedly good results.

3 Think of a concern that you are presently facing. How might the past experience that you just thought about, coupled with the teachings about trust that we just examined, be used to change your current feelings?

TEXT 10

MIDRASH, *EICHAH RABAH* 3:8

מֶלֶךְ שֶׁנִכְנַס לִמְדִינָה, וְהָיוּ עִמוֹ דֻכָּסִין וְאִפַּרְכִין וְאִיסְטְרַטִילוּטִין . . . חַד אֲמַר: אֲנָא נָסֵיב דֻכָּסִין לְגַבִּי. וְחַד אֲמַר: אֲנָא נָסֵיב אִפַּרְכִין לְגַבִּי. וְחַד אֲמַר: אֲנָא נָסֵיב אִיסְטְרַטִילוּטִין לְגַבִּי.

הָיָה פִּקֵחַ אֶחָד לְשָׁם. אֲמַר: אֲנָא נָסֵיב לְמַלְכָּא . . .

כֵּן עוֹבְדֵי כּוֹכָבִים, מֵהֶן עוֹבְדִין לַחַמָּה, וּמֵהֶן עוֹבְדִין לַלְּבָנָה, וּמֵהֶן עוֹבְדִין לְעֵץ וָאֶבֶן. אֲבָל יִשְׂרָאֵל אֵינָן עוֹבְדִין אֶלָּא לְהַקָדוֹשׁ בָּרוּךְ הוּא. הֲדָא הוּא דִכְתִיב: "חֶלְקִי ה' אָמְרָה נַפְשִׁי" (אֵיכָה ג, כד), שֶׁאֲנִי מְיַחֵד אוֹתוֹ שְׁתֵּי פְּעָמִים בְּכָל יוֹם, וְאוֹמֵר: "שְׁמַע יִשְׂרָאֵל ה' אֱלֹהֵינוּ ה' אֶחָד" (דְבָרִים ו, ד).

An analogy: A king entered a province accompanied by dukes, prefects, and commanders. . . . One person said, "I am taking a duke as my patron." Another said, "I am taking a prefect as my patron." And still another said, "I am taking a commander as my patron."

One clever individual was there among them who said, "I am taking the king. . . ."

So it is with the nations of the world: Some of them worship the sun, some worship the moon, and some of them worship wood and stone. But Israel serves none other than G-d Himself.

This is the intent of the verse, "'G-d is my portion,' says my soul" (LAMENTATIONS 3:24), whose Oneness I proclaim twice each day, "Hear, O Israel, the L-rd is our G-d, the L-rd is One" (DEUTERONOMY 6:4).

EICHAH RABAH

A Midrashic text on the Book of Lamentations, produced by the sages of the Talmud in the Land of Israel. Its language closely resembles that of the Jerusalem Talmud. It was first printed in Pesaro, Italy, in 1519, together with 4 other midrashic works on the other 4 *megilot*.

TEXT 11

RABBI MENACHEM MENDEL OF LUBAVITCH, *DERECH MITSVOTECHA*, P. 138A

וְכַךְ הָיָה נִשְׁמַע הַלָּשׁוֹן מִמּוֹרֵינוּ וְרַבֵּינוּ נִשְׁמָתוֹ עֵדֶן בִּדְבֵיקוּתוֹ, שֶׁהָיָה אוֹמֵר בָּזֶה הַלָּשׁוֹן:

אִיךְ ווִיל זֶע גָאר נִיסְט. אִיךְ ווִיל נִיט דַאיין גַן עֵדֶן. אִיךְ ווִיל נִיט דַאיין עוֹלָם הַבָּא כוּלִי. אִיךְ ווִיל מֶער נִיט אַז דִיךְ אַלֵיין.

When our master and teacher [Rabbi Shne'ur Zalman of Liadi] would enter a state of spiritual ecstasy, he would be heard exclaiming:

"I want nothing at all! I don't want Your Paradise. I don't want Your World to Come. I want nothing but You alone."

RABBI MENACHEM MENDEL OF LUBAVITCH (*TSEMACH TSEDEK*) 1789–1866

Chasidic rebbe and noted author. The *Tsemach Tsedek* was the third leader of the Chabad Chasidic movement and a noted authority on Jewish law. His numerous works include halachic responsa, Chasidic discourses, and kabbalistic writings. Active in the communal affairs of Russian Jewry, he worked to alleviate the plight of the cantonists, Jewish children kidnapped to serve in the Czar's army. He passed away in Lubavitch, leaving seven sons and two daughters.

TEXT 12

RABBI SHNE'UR ZALMAN OF LIADI, *TANYA*, CHAPTER 44

כִּי זֶה כָּל הָאָדָם וְתַכְלִיתוֹ, לְמַעַן דַעַת אֶת כְּבוֹד ה' וִיקָר תִּפְאֶרֶת גְדוּלָּתוֹ, אִישׁ אִישׁ כְּפִי אֲשֶׁר יוּכַל שְׂאֵת, כְּמוֹ שֶׁכָּתוּב בְּרַעֲיָא מְהֵימְנָא פַּרְשַׁת בֹּא (מב, ב), "בְּגִין דְיִשְׁתְּמוֹדְעוּן לֵיהּ".

This is the whole raison d'être of man: to come to know the glory of G-d and the splendid majesty of His greatness, each person according to their capacity. As is written in the *Zohar* (2, 42B), [G-d's creation of the world is] "so that humanity may know Him."

RABBI SHNE'UR ZALMAN OF LIADI (ALTER REBBE) 1745–1812

Chasidic rebbe, halachic authority, and founder of the Chabad movement. The Alter Rebbe was born in Liozna, Belarus, and was among the principal students of the Magid of Mezeritch. His numerous works include the *Tanya*, an early classic containing the fundamentals of Chabad Chasidism, and *Shulchan Aruch HaRav*, an expanded and reworked code of Jewish law.

Exercise 2.4

On a scale of 1–10, ask yourself: How often do I contemplate G-d being the Creator of the entire universe, including myself and all aspects of my life?

How might I specifically benefit if I thought about this more often, perhaps on a regularly scheduled basis?

What is preventing me from making regular meditation about the Creator a part of my routine?

What steps can I take to make this practice more a part of my routine?

KEY POINTS

1 Beyond Judaism's direct influence on the world's major religions, elements of the Jewish concept of monotheism have greatly influenced modern thinking in general.

2 The pagans believed that the various forces of nature were gods, each vying for dominance, and all indifferent to humankind.

3 Abraham spread the belief in the one, nonmaterial, benevolent G-d Who created the world and humanity for a dignified purpose.

4 Knowing that the entire universe was created intentionally by G-d brings us to the realization that the world in general, and our lives in particular, have a purpose. Meaning and purpose give us motivation and happiness in our lives.

5 We can be optimistic when we realize that G-d has exclusive control over all that transpires in the universe and that He is interested in our benefit and good.

6 Recognizing and contemplating G-d's oneness and greatness is not only a means to an end but is humankind's goal in and of itself.

Appendix

TEXT 13

MIDRASH, *BEREISHIT RABAH* 38:13

תֶּרַח עוֹבֵד לִצְלָמִים וּמוֹכֵר הָיָה. חַד זְמַן נָפֵיק לַאֲתַר, הוֹשִׁיב לְאַבְרָהָם מוֹכֵר תַּחְתָּיו. הֲוָה אָתֵי בַּר אֵינָשׁ בָּעֵי דְיִזְבַּן, וַהֲוָה אָמַר לֵיהּ: בַּר כַּמָּה שְׁנִין אַתְּ?

וַהֲוָה אָמַר לֵיהּ: בַּר חַמְשִׁין אוֹ שִׁיתִּין.

וַהֲוָה אָמַר לֵיהּ: וַי לֵיהּ לְהַהוּא גַבְרָא דְהוּא בַּר שִׁיתִּין וּבָעֵי לְמִסְגַד לְבַר יוֹמָא, וְהָיָה מִתְבַּיֵּישׁ וְהוֹלֵךְ לוֹ.

חַד זְמַן, אֲתַת חַדָא אִיתְּתָא טְעִינָא בִּידָהּ חַדָא פִּינָךְ דְסֹלֶת. אָמְרָה לֵיהּ, הֵא לָךְ, קָרֵב קוֹדָמֵיהוֹן.

קָם, נְסֵיב בּוּקְלָסָא בִּידֵיהּ, וְתַבַּרְהוֹן לְכוּלְהוֹן פְּסִילַיָא, וִיהַב בּוּקְלָסָא בִּידָא דְרַבָּה דַהֲוָה בֵּינֵיהוֹן.

כֵּיוָן דַאֲתָא אֲבוּהָ אֲמַר לֵיהּ: מַאן עָבֵיד לְהוֹן כְּדֵין?

אֲמַר לֵיהּ: מַה נִכְפּוּר מִינָךְ! אֲתַת חַדָא אִיתְּתָא, טְעִינָא לָהּ חַדָא פִּינָךְ דְסוֹלֶת, וַאֲמָרַת לִי: הֵא לָךְ, קָרֵיב קוֹדָמֵיהוֹן, קָרֵיבְת לְקֳדָמֵיהוֹן, הֲוָה דֵין אָמַר: אֲנָא אֵיכוֹל קַדְמָאי, וְדֵין אָמַר: אֲנָא אֵיכוֹל קַדְמָאי. קָם הָדֵין רַבָּה דַהֲוָה בֵּינֵיהוֹן, נְסַב בּוּקְלָסָא וְתַבְּרִינוּן.

אֲמַר לֵיהּ: מָה אַתָּה מַפְלֶה בִּי, וְיָדְעִין אִינוּן?!

אֲמַר לֵיהּ, וְלֹא יִשְׁמְעוּ אָזְנֶיךָ מַה שֶׁפִּיךָ אוֹמֵר?!

Terach was an idol manufacturer. Once he had to travel somewhere, and he left Abraham in charge of his store. When someone would come in to buy idols, Abraham would ask, "How old are you?"

They would reply, "Fifty or sixty."

Abraham would then respond, "Woe to him who is sixty years old and wants to worship something made today!" Ashamed, the customer would leave.

One time, a woman entered carrying a dish filled with flour. She said to him, "Here you go; offer it before them."

Abraham arose, took a club in his hands, and broke all of the idols, and then he placed the club in the hands of the largest idol among them.

When his father returned, he asked, "Who did all of this?"

Abraham replied, "I cannot conceal this from you. A woman came bearing a dish of flour and told me to offer it before them. As I did so, they each began to say, 'I will eat first,' while the others said, '*I* will eat first.' The biggest one rose, took a club, and smashed the rest of them."

Terach said, "Do you think you can trick me? Do these idols have any cognition?!"

To which Abraham replied, "Do your ears hear what your mouth is saying?!"

TEXT 14

TALMUD, SOTAH 10A–10B

וַיִּקְרָא שָׁם בְּשֵׁם ה' אֵ-ל עוֹלָם (בְּרֵאשִׁית כא, לג). אָמַר רֵישׁ לָקִישׁ, אַל תִּיקְרֵי וַיִּקְרָא אֶלָּא וַיַּקְרִיא; מְלַמֵּד שֶׁהִקְרִיא אַבְרָהָם אָבִינוּ לִשְׁמוֹ שֶׁל הַקָּדוֹשׁ בָּרוּךְ הוּא בְּפֶה כָּל עוֹבֵר וָשָׁב. כֵּיצַד? לְאַחַר שֶׁאָכְלוּ וְשָׁתוּ, עָמְדוּ לְבָרְכוֹ. אָמַר לָהֶם, וְכִי מִשֶּׁלִּי אֲכַלְתֶּם? מִשֶּׁל אֱלֹקֵי עוֹלָם אֲכַלְתֶּם! הוֹדוּ וְשַׁבְּחוּ וּבָרְכוּ לְמִי שֶׁאָמַר וְהָיָה הָעוֹלָם.

"And he called there [*vayikra*] on the name of the L-rd, G-d of the universe" (GENESIS 21:33). Reish Lakish said, "Do not read this word literally as '*vayikra*—and he called' but rather as '*vayakri*—and he caused others to call.' This teaches that Abraham, our forefather, caused the name of G-d to be called out in the mouths of all passersby. How so? After his guests ate and drank, they arose to bless him. He said to them, 'But did you eat from what is mine? Rather, you ate from the food belonging to the G-d of the world. Give thanks, praise, and bless the One Who spoke and the world came into being!'"

Additional Readings

ACCEPTANCE

BY RABBI SHAIS TAUB

Two Plus Two Is Four

When I was a teenager, my father, who is a psychologist, asked me, "Do you know the difference between a psychotic and a neurotic?" I said that I didn't. "A psychotic," he proceeded to explain, "is someone who thinks that two plus two equals five. A neurotic knows that two plus two equals four . . . *and can't stand it!*"

Little did I realize at the time that my father had transmitted to me an important spiritual principle. What psychologists call *neurosis*, and philosophers might call *hubris*, the folks in recovery call *playing G-d*. Whether we look through the lenses of psychology, religion, philosophy, or recovery, there seems to be a general agreement to at least one aspect of human happiness and health. Certain things are what they are. Fighting them, as such, is altogether unproductive, arrogant, silly, and even tragic—like Don Quixote tilting at windmills. Well-adjusted people just don't declare war against the fact that two plus two is four.

In recovery, major emphasis is placed on practicing "acceptance." Acceptance almost sounds like a high-falutin clinical term, but it really just means to relax and get over the fact that things may not always be just as you want them to be—and that's fine. Another big word in recovery is *serenity*, which means pretty much the same thing.

Worry, anxiety, anger, dread—these are all highly unspiritual qualities. We're supposed to stay above the fray and be calm and tranquil.

RABBI SHAIS TAUB

Chabad rabbi and author. Rabbi Taub is a teacher of Chabad philosophy and Jewish mysticism and wrote the JLI course *Soul Maps*, based on the teachings of the *Tanya*, the foundational text of Chabad philosophy. He is also an expert in addiction recovery and wrote the best-selling book, *G-d of Our Understanding: Jewish Spirituality and Recovery from Addiction.*

On the other hand, the human being uniquely possesses free choice to make decisions and take actions. G-d gave us the ability not just to accept the status quo but also to make positive change.

So which is it? Which is the more desirable trait? Taking decisive action, or accepting "facts" as they are?

Of course, the answer is both. Or, more accurately, it depends.

It depends on what we're dealing with. Some things call for acceptance, and other things call for action.

Which leaves us with the $64,000 Question.

How do we know which things to accept and which things to change?

The Serenity Prayer

Perhaps the most famous words associated with recovery are the words of Serenity Prayer. In just a few brief lines, the prayer encapsulates the great conundrum of which we speak:

> *G-d, grant me the serenity to accept the things I cannot change, the courage to change the things I can, and the wisdom to know the difference.*

I'm going to go on a sort of tangent for a moment, but since it's something that I am asked about so often, I would like to talk about the origins of the Serenity Prayer. In my experience, it is very common for Jewish people in recovery to wonder whether it's ideal or even okay for them to say this prayer. So, let's put our discussion of the prayer's content on hold for a bit and talk about its history.

For the record, the Serenity Prayer was first used in connection with recovery in 1942, when the staff at AA headquarters in New York saw it included, without attribution, in a newspaper obituary. "Never had we seen so much AA in so few words," cofounder Bill Wilson would later write.

To this day, there are still many theories about the prayer's true authorship. As Wilson wrote, "No one can tell for sure who first wrote the Serenity Prayer. Some say it came from early Greeks; others think it was from the pen of an anonymous English poet; still others claim it was written by an American Naval officer. . . ."

It is generally accepted that the prayer was composed—at least in its current and most famous version—by the American theologian Reinhold Niebuhr, who is said to have written the prayer for a sermon he gave in the 1930s, though Niebuhr himself admitted that he could never be certain whether or not he unconsciously adapted the prayer from some other source. "It may have been spooking around for years, even centuries," Niebuhr told AA's magazine, *The Grapevine*, in 1950.

At any rate, what is germane to our discussion is that the prayer is not known to appear anywhere in any denomination's liturgy. It seems that it is just an old idea that has been passed around in different forms throughout the years, and that Niebuhr, who was a Christian, is the one who drafted—or at least made famous—the version that is popular today. In that sense, I can't see much of a difference between a Jew's reading the Serenity Prayer and reading the words "In G-d we trust" on an American dollar bill.

Now, let's return to our main discussion. We were faced with a question: What needs to be accepted, and what needs to be changed?

The Serenity Prayer doesn't seem to give us the answer, it just confirms that there is a legitimate question.

Now an easy (but all together unsatisfying) answer would be to say that this is precisely *why* the Serenity Prayer is a *prayer*. Since we have no way of knowing what must be accepted and what must be changed, we ask G-d to give us wisdom and let us know. But as I said, that answer doesn't do it for me.

I think that there are some general guidelines that we can learn that can help us to know when we need the serenity to accept things and when we need the courage to make a change. I also think that it is lack of understanding about this distinction that gives rise to the frequently hysterical disapproval of how acceptance and serenity are practiced in recovery.

Everything Is in the Hands of Heaven

The Jewish view on this matter is clear. The Talmud says, "Everything is in the hands of Heaven except for one's awe of Heaven."

It is an unequivocal statement. It's black and white. G-d controls reality, every bit of it. We control our attitude, every bit of it. In other words, everything that *happens* to us is up to G-d, but the way we *feel* about it is up to us.

In this light, it is clear that "the things we cannot change" means every aspect of objective reality while that which we must have the courage to change is just one thing—how we view the reality. In other words, all we can change is our opinion about G-d and the job that He is doing running the world, but we cannot run the world.

It is worthwhile to note that the sages employed the term "*awe* of Heaven" to describe the perceptions we choose. Why specifically awe? Why not, say, love?

Because awe is the other side of the same coin as courage. The more we fear G-d, the less we fear things that are finite and fleeting, and hence, the more equipped we are to handle life as it comes. If we are in awe of G-d, then we are not overwhelmed by the world.

When he was five years old, the Ba'al Shem Tov became an orphan. Just before his father passed, he told his son, "Yisrolik [the diminutive of the Ba'al Shem Tov's given name], fear nothing but G-d alone." This is a deep concept. There is a lot of meaning hidden in these words.

As we have noted in an earlier chapter, Judaism believes in G-d who is all-powerful and always in control. Knowing that one's life is entirely in G-d's hands should logically inspire one to feel the utmost reverence of Him. Equally important is the corollary to the awe of Heaven—a *lack of awe* of things that we can't control anyway.

If one believes that G-d is in absolute control, then one will not erroneously attribute power to any other beings. In other words, the Ba'al Shem Tov's father gave him the formula for serenity and courage. "Fear nothing." How? By fearing "G-d alone."

The eleventh-century Jewish philosopher Rabbi Bachya ibn Pakuda expressed the same concept quite succinctly in his classic *Duties of the Heart*:

> *When a person feels that one created entity has the ability to help him or harm him without the permission of the Creator, then his heart will turn away from fear of them or hope in these things and will trust in the Creator alone.*

In other words, the more one acknowledges that G-d's power is absolute, the more one is relieved of emotional dependence upon all kinds of transitory conditions. One who relies only on G-d will never be afraid of any fact of his or her own life. Awe of heaven is the flipside of and corollary to serenity, contentment, and freedom.

To once again quote Ibn Pakuda:

> *He will be happy with whatever G-d brings him. . . . He will not desire anything that G-d has not chosen for him and will want only what G-d wants for him. . . . In worldly matters, he will not prefer one condition over another nor desire to be in any other condition than the one he is in.*

Material vs. Spiritual

Another way of viewing this same formula is by classifying all matters as either material or spiritual. The "everything" that is "in the hands of Heaven" refers to the material conditions of our lives, while the "except for the awe of Heaven," which is in *our* hands, refers to our spiritual state over which we have been granted free will. In other words, I don't have power over the conditions G-d puts me in, but I do have the power to make moral decisions regardless of those conditions. As the Talmud says, already from the time that a child is conceived, it is decreed from Heaven whether that child will be "strong or weak, wise or foolish, rich or poor. And yet," says the Talmud, "righteous or wicked is *not* decreed, for . . . 'All is in the hands of Heaven except for one's awe of Heaven.'"

There's an old Chasidic expression, "The goat's job is to give milk. The goatherd's job is to take care of her." What this means is that we "goats" only have to do one thing; we have to fulfill the mission that G-d has given us. The "Goatherd" takes care of the rest. And just like a goat doesn't worry about the goatherd's responsibilities, neither should we waste our time figuring out how G-d should run the world. As I heard one recovering addict put it nicely, "I try to do G-d's work; *not* G-d's job." When we stay focused on *our* duties—our spirituality—and stay out of G-d's business—our physicality—things seem to work out best.

A story is told about a young and gifted Torah scholar who met with the first Chabad Rebbe, Rabbi Schneur Zalman, in a private audience. The Rebbe told him, "Spirituality and physicality are essentially opposites. A superior quality of the physical is a deficiency of the spiritual. In material matters, being happy with one's lot is the greatest of virtues. But in spiritual matters, being happy with one's lot is the worst deficiency there can be."

In light of what we have already explained, this makes perfect sense. Since material matters are really out of our hands, then it makes no sense to lament over what we think we are lacking in that area. To the contrary, because G-d is in control and will always give us what's best for us, then the healthiest and most rational disposition to have regarding these things is contentment and gratitude. But when it comes to our spiritual condition, what kind of person we are and how hard we are working on our growth, we have no reason to ever be satisfied. There is always something more that we can do. Indeed, it is truly the *only* thing we can do.

People, Places, and Things

To one who is not in recovery, "people, places, and things" sounds like an English grammar lesson on nouns, but to Twelve-Steppers, the reference is an immediately recognizable spiritual axiom. "People, places, and things" is essentially recovery-speak for "All is in the hands of Heaven except for one's awe of Heaven." What am I powerless over? People, places, and things. What is in G-d's hands? People, places, and things. What do I have to stop being stressed out about and trying to control? People, places, and things.

The exact origin of this now ubiquitous turn of phrase is unknown, at least to me, but a similar expression is used in a personal story entitled "Acceptance Was the Answer" in later editions of the Big Book:

When I am disturbed, it is because I find some person, place, thing, or situation—some fact of my life—unacceptable to me, and I can find no serenity until I accept that person, place, thing or situation as being exactly the way it is supposed to be at this moment. Nothing, absolutely nothing happens in G-d's world by mistake. Until I could accept my alcoholism, I could not stay sober; unless I accept life completely on life's terms, I cannot be happy. I need to concentrate not so much on what needs to be changed in the world as on what needs to be changed in me and in my attitudes. (p. 417)

A Final Word on Faith

It's unfortunate that so many people misunderstand the idea of acceptance and confuse it with timidity or meekness when that is so much the opposite of the truth. Any recovering addict can tell you that the self-reliance of active addiction is a life of terror, but the G-d-reliance of recovery is a life of courage.

Another assumption is that acceptance makes us passive. The irony is that it is a *lack* of acceptance that paralyzes us in our lives and cuts us off from growth. I think it may safely be said that even from a very rational and clinical standpoint, the less energy we expend on things that are not our business, the more energy we have to live our lives contentedly and effectively. And although one can debate whether there is an underlying spiritual truth that governs the distinction between the two, for most addicts in recovery, it seems to work best to accept that we're talking plain and simple about relying on G-d.

There are many reasons that we may be prejudiced against faith. Perhaps we have been jaded by experiences, or maybe we suffer from intellectual pride. But the proof, as they say, is in the pudding. The power and the strength drawn from "letting go and letting G-d" can be seen in every miraculous story of personal recovery. Reliance on G-d is not a liability but the greatest possible asset. As a former self-avowed agnostic in the program once told me, "At first I thought the G-d thing was a crutch. Turns out that it's stilts."

As we wrap up this small chapter on a very large concept, I'd like to quote an excerpt from the Big Book that I am also moved to include here not only for the relevance of its subject but also for the beauty of its prose:

We trust infinite G-d rather than our finite selves. We are in the world to play the role He assigns. Just to the extent that we do as we think He would have us, and humbly rely on Him, does He enable us to match calamity with serenity.

We never apologize to anyone for depending upon our Creator. We can laugh at those who think spirituality the way of weakness. Paradoxically, it is the way of strength. The verdict of the ages is that faith means courage. All men of faith have courage. They trust their G-d. We never apologize for G-d. Instead we let Him demonstrate, through us, what He can do. (p. 68)

G-d of Our Understanding (Jersey City, N.J.: Ktav Publishing House, Inc., 2011), ch. 18

THE GENESIS OF IDOLATRY AND THE GUARDIANS OF MONOTHEISM

RABBI REUVEN CHAIM KLEIN

Adam, the First Monotheist

Judaism teaches that early humans, including Adam, were monotheists. In fact, the Midrash relates that when Hashem created Adam, all of Creation thought that he was their creator. They came to prostrate themselves before him. However, Adam rebuffed their advances and said, "You came to bow to me? Let me and you go together and coronate He who created all of us."[1]

Mankind started out as believers in One G-d because Man was able to experience Hashem through Creation in a way that later people were unable to do. In other words, Judaism accepts monotheism as the eternal truth and shuns polytheism as a later corruption of that truth. This follows an epistemological axiom formulated by Tertullian (155–240) who wrote, *Id esse verum quodcunque primum, id esse adulterum quodcunque posterius* ("Truth always comes first, and error always comes later"). In our case, monotheism came first, and polytheism came later. Idolatry is thus "the result of a devolution from a primordial monotheism."[2]

Adam's Winter Holiday

Although Adam was very well-aware of the One G-d, he inadvertently laid the groundwork for one element of pagan culture. The Talmud writes that after Adam sinned by eating the forbidden fruit of the Tree of Knowledge, he noticed that the days began to grow shorter and shorter. He thought that this was Divine punishment for his sin, so he spent eight days fasting and praying in repentance. When the winter solstice arrived and the days began to grow longer again, Adam realized that the days' length naturally varies seasonally, so he made an eight-day festival. The next year, he celebrated all sixteen days.[3]

The Talmud remarks that Adam established these winter holidays with the proper intention of thanking Hashem, but the pagans later misappropriated those holidays for idolatrous purposes. Thus, Adam unwittingly established the holidays that later became the Roman holidays of Saturnalia and Calends,[4] and later, the Christian holidays of Christmas and New Year's Day.[5]

Although the Romans and Christians entered the world stage thousands of years after Adam, idolatry made its unfortunate debut far sooner, in the times of Adam's grandson Enosh.

The Idolaters' Mistake

Maimonides (1105–1204) writes that in the days of Adam's grandson Enosh, mankind made a grave mistake which begat the descent toward idolatry. When Hashem created the world, He created the stars and other celestial bodies and placed them in lofty positions, bestowing much honor upon them. Because of this, people mistakenly reasoned that just as a king wishes his subjects to honor those who stand before him, Hashem wants humankind to glorify and honor those who make Him great and honor Him. Thus, they concluded, Hashem's will demands that the stars and celestial bodies be praised, glorified, and honored because they are His servants.[6]

As this idea developed, people began to worship the stars and celestial bodies. Besides verbally praising and glorifying them, people built sanctuaries honoring the stars, offered sacrifices to them, and bowed to them. All of this was done in order to fulfill what they wrongly perceived as Hashem's will.[7] Eventually people forgot about Hashem's role in Creation, and these trends gave way to full-fledged idolatry.[8]

RABBI REUVEN CHAIM KLEIN

Rabbi Klein studied at the Mir Yeshiva in Jerusalem and has published papers in several journals, including the *Journal of Halacha and Contemporary Society* (New York) and *Jewish Bible Quarterly* (Jerusalem).

Based on this, R. Sher proposes that the innovators of idol worship did not personally practice it. They were intelligent enough to continue worshipping Hashem as man had done since time immemorial. However, they erred in how to present the matter to the masses. They felt that the masses were not intelligent enough to comprehend worshipping Hashem, so they taught the masses to worship His servants in the form of the celestial bodies, and through such worship to eventually forge a connection to Hashem. Those who introduced this idea did not realize that with the passing of time, the masses would eventually forget about Hashem altogether.[9]

Early Idolaters Believed in G-d

Maimonides notes that those who understand idol worship's origins acknowledge that the early idolaters believed in Hashem. That is, the early idolaters did not claim that the stars that they worshipped were the creators of the universe. Rather, they claimed that although Hashem had created the universe, He wanted mankind to worship the stars.

Similarly, Radak explains that the meaning of the Psalmist's statement, *From the rising of the sun to its setting, Hashem's name* is *praised* (Ps. 103:3), is that the entire world population recognized Hashem—even those who also worshipped idolatry. Humanity collectively agreed that Hashem was the Unique One. Their mistake was that they imagined that His will was for them to worship the stars. The prophet Jeremiah already noted this phenomenon when preaching the futility of idol worship:

> *There is none like You, O Hashem. You are great and Your name is great in might. Who does not fear you, O King of the Nations? For it befits You because among all the wise men of the nations and in all their kingdoms, [it is known that] there is none like You. They are uniformly foolish and stupid, the [idolatrous] vanities for which they are punished are [but] wood. Beaten silver is brought from Tarshish and gold from Uphaz, the work of an artisan and the hands of a smith; blue and purple are their vestments, all the work of "wise men." And Hashem the G-d is truth, He is the Living G-d and the Eternal King, from His anger the earth quakes, and nations cannot bear His wrath. (Jer. 10:6–10)*

Enosh's Generation

Although the Bible does not explicitly record the development of idolatry in Enosh's time, it alludes to it with an enigmatic passage related to Enosh's birth: *Then [people] began* (הוחל) *to call in Hashem's name* (Gen. 4:26). Targum pseudo-Jonathan and Targum Neofiti explain that this refers to the fact that in Enosh's time, people began to err by worshipping idols and calling their idols "G-d."[10]

Others render this verse differently, but preserve the same basic meaning. For example, Rashi (1040–1105) understands that the verse reads, *Then, to call in Hashem's name became profane* (הוחל).[11] That is, people began to profane Hashem's name[12] by applying it to other entities and worshipping them instead of Him.[13] Rashi explains that they called people and objects "G-d," while Radak (1160–1235) adds that they also called the celestial bodies "G-d."[14]

However, a third group of commentators, including R. Avraham Ibn Ezra (1092–1176),[15] explain that *Then [people] began to call in Hashem's name* refers to the advent of prayer, not to the establishment of idolatry. Radak cites this explanation and develops it. Prior to Enosh's time, people thought that whatever was Divinely decreed for them could not change, so they viewed prayer as futile. However, in Enosh's time, people realized that prayer had the ability to change their destiny, so they began to pray to Hashem in times of need. In stark contrast to the view that idolatry developed in Enosh's time,[16] these commentators understand that whatever occurred in Enosh's time was a positive development.[17]

R. Yitzchak Luria (1534–1572), better known as Arizal, explains that *to call* in *Hashem's name* refers to His various names and the names of angels, which the idolaters of Enosh's generation invoked in order to force their desired results.[18]

Was Enosh Himself an Idolater?

Maimonides notes that Enosh himself is included among those who made the mistake which led to idolatry. Nachmanides suggests that Enosh did not begin to worship idols until his grandfather Adam's death (when Enosh was 695 years old!).[19] From this passage, it seems that Nachmanides agrees with Maimonides that Enosh worshipped idols. Interestingly, R. Menachem Tziyyoni writes that Enosh was the chief idolater.[20]

However, R. Yehudah ha-Levi mentions Enosh when delineating the names of historically important individuals in his epic work *Kuzari*.[21] R. Yehudah Muscato (1530–1593) derives from this that R. Yehudah ha-Levi understood that Enosh was not an idolater.[22] However, R. Yisrael of Zamosc (1700–1772) rejected this contention,[23] and argues that *Kuzari* does not necessarily disagree with Maimonides.[24]

R. Yaakov Kamenetsky asks why tradition associates idolatry with the "Generation of Enosh," if according to Nachmanides, idolatry began well into Enosh's life, at a time when several subsequent generations had already been begat.[25]

The Ambiguity of Enosh's Generation

R. Nissim of Gerona (1315–1376) argues that the Torah did not explicitly elaborate on how idolatry developed because the original idolaters did not mean to rebel against Hashem. In other words, the Torah did not wish to openly condemn the early idolaters, because their goals were noble.[26] R. Nissim writes that because the Torah was not explicit, commentators like Ibn Ezra were free to mistakenly understand that the Torah means that in Enosh's time the concept of prayer was invented, while really it was idolatry that was introduced.[27]

R. Gedalia Ibn Yachya (1515–1587) offers a fusion of these two approaches: Enosh was the first person to form images as intermedia through which people would be roused to pray to Hashem.[28] Thus, Ibn Yachya takes the idea that prayer began in Enosh's time and links it to the start of idolatry (or, more precisely, iconism).

Idolatry Begins

One Medieval source relates a story about people's first forage into fashioning and worshipping idols.

> *The people of Enosh's generation came to him and asked him, "What is your father's name?"*
> *Enosh answered, "Seth."*
> *Then, they asked him, "What is your father's father's name?"*
> *Enosh said, "Adam."*
> *Then, they asked, "And what was Adam's father's name?"*
> *Enosh replied, "He did not have a father. Hashem created him as a lifeless figure from the ground and breathed a living spirit into him."*
> *They asked, "How did He create him?"*
> *To this, Enosh responded by taking a clump of dirt and fashioning the form of a man. A demonic spirit entered its body, giving it life. All the people exclaimed, "This is our G-d!" and began to worship it.*[29]

Early Kabbalists such as R. Elazar of Worms (1176–1238)[30] and R. Menachem Tziyyoni (circa. early 14th century)[31] relay a tradition that in Enosh's generation, people traversed the entire world gathering gold, silver, and precious gems in order to erect idols all over the world, on mountains, and on hilltops. They used witchcraft to bring the celestial bodies to Earth in order to somehow serve them in the way that those bodies were understood to serve Hashem. Similarly, *Sefer ha-Yashar* writes that in Enosh's days, people made idolatrous images of copper, bronze, wood, and stone.[32]

Classical Historians on the Beginning of Idolatry

Although tradition traces the invention of idolatry to Enosh's time, various historians have attempted to date it to the times of different early Biblical figures. As we will see below, the idolatrous Sabian cult traced its origins to Adam's son Seth. The Roman philosopher Porphyry (234–305 CE) wrote that Sanchuniathon (apparently an ancient Phoenician writer) discussed the idolatrous practices of the early Phoenicians, and implied that idolatry itself started with the Phoenicians. Sidon, the patriarch of the Phoenicians, was Canaan's firstborn son (Gen. 10:15), thus implicating Canaan and his family with the advent of idolatry. Similarly, the Christian writer Antoine Augustin Calmet (1672–1757) noted that several writers attributed idolatry's origin to Ham (son of Noah) and/or Ham's son Canaan.

However, Calmet rejected these opinions, first arguing that Terah and Nahor were the first idolaters.[33] Calmet also rejected Epiphanius of Salamis' (310–403 CE) view that Serug was the first to introduce idolatry and Hellenism; while two generations later, the craft of image-making with clay and pottery was conceived by Serug's grandson, Terah.[34] Calmet argued that there is no Biblical allusion to Serug's role in the advent of idolatry.[35] Ultimately, Calmet sided with the traditional Jewish view that idolatry began in Enosh's generation.[36]

The Bible writes that Tubal-Cain invented the smelter used for forging metals like copper and iron (Gen. 4:22). Based on this, *The Book of Biblical Antiquities*—a work wrongly ascribed to Philo Judaeus of Alexandria (25 BCE–50 CE), but likely written during his lifetime by somebody else—recorded that in Tubal-Cain's time, people began to use that new technology for forming idols and worshipping them.[37] According to pseudo-Philo's account, generations later, at the time that Haran fathered Lot (Gen. 11:27), humanity began to engage in stargazing and divination, and people would give their sons and daughters to the fire (as sacrifices). However, as pseudo-Philo told it, Serug and his descendants *resisted* this trend and remained steadfast in their conviction to Hashem.[38] This tradition not only denies Serug's role in the beginning of idolatry, but actually singles him and his family out as early defenders of monotheism.

Historical Development of Idolatry

In short, while tradition understands that idolatry began in Enosh's time, other sources date the beginning of idolatry differently. R. Chananiah Elchanan Chai Cohen suggests reconciling most of these sources by arguing that idolatry really started in the time of Seth and Enosh, i.e., when Seth fathered Enosh. In Seth's time, idolatry originally began as the worship of existing concepts and components of nature (i.e., the sun and the moon). Later, Enosh, who was born and raised in an idolatrous atmosphere, became the first person to construct images/idols for the purpose of idolatry. After all idolaters were wiped out in the Deluge,[39] idolatry was later restored by Noah's son Ham and Ham's son Canaan. According to this theory, Seth, Enosh, Ham, and Canaan all had a hand in the development of idolatry and, in one way or another, could be said to be its inventor.

Nonetheless, throughout this entire period, man always recognized Hashem as the "prime mover" in existence, and only worshipped other entities as "secondary forces" that were understood to be subservient to Hashem. However, as idolatry became more prevalent and prominent, humanity steadily focused less and less on Hashem. This continued until the rise of Nimrod, under whose dominion Hashem was completely forgotten and the sun became the complete focus of all worship.[40]

R. Moshe Schick (1807–1879) takes a slightly different approach: He understands that after all the idolaters died in the Deluge, the world was free from idolatry for approximately 340 years—until it was reintroduced in Nimrod's time by the builders of the Tower of Babel.[41]

Endnotes

1 *Pirkei de-Rabbi Eliezer* (ch. 11). See also *Bereishis Rabbah* §17:4 which, *inter alia*, tells of Adam's penetrating insight in his ability to give G-d His name. R. Nosson Tzvi Finkel (1849–1927), known as the Alter of Slabodka, derives from this Midrashic source that Adam was not only able to immediately intuit Hashem's existence, but to realize His complete dominion over all of Creation (see also *Nefesh ha-Chaim* 1:6).

Yet, despite Adam's great intellect, he perceived only a small portion of the infinite knowledge available to man. The more he sought out Hashem, the more he was able to understand Him. Hashem thus prohibited Adam from engaging in "idolatry" (TB *Sanhedrin* 57 a). The Alter explains that here "idolatry" refers to a change in focus of one's intellectual pursuits. In other words, should Adam ever become satisfied with his relatively limited knowledge of Hashem and refrain from continuing to seek out more, this would be conceptually similar to idolatry whereby one changes the focus of one's worship from Hashem to a different entity. See *Ohr ha-Tzafon, Shemos* (Jerusalem, 1968), pp. 61; 208; and Y. Cohen (ed.), *Sichos ha-Saba mi-Slabodka*, vol. 2 (Jerusalem, 2009), pp. 908–909.

2 A. Brill, *Judaism and Other Religions: Models of Understanding* (Palgrave Macmillan, 2010), p. 34. This, of course, stands in contrast with Wellhausen's model of an evolutionary progression from polytheism to monotheism. He argued that, *au contraire*, man started off with a crude, polytheistic system of belief and only slowly graduated to the more-developed, monotheistic model. These two models and the history of their reception are documented by Kaufmann 1960:153; 221–223, Halbertal 1992:121, and Stroumsa 2010:51–52; 89; 104. See also J. P. Rosenblatt, *Renaissance England's Chief Rabbi: John Selden* (Oxford University Press, 2006), p. 81.

3 TB *Avodah Zarah* 8a and JT *Avodah Zarah* 1:2.

4 Calends was a monthly festival which marked the beginning of every calendar month, but when the Sages discuss Calends, they refer specifically to the holiday at the start of January.

5 The Babylonian Talmud explains that Saturnalia was observed before the winter solstice and Calends afterwards. However, when the Mishnah *(Avodah Zarah* 1:2) mentions these two pagan holidays, it lists Calends before Saturnalia—implying that Calends preceded Saturnalia. *Tosafos Yom Tov* (ad loc.), R. Menachem Meiri *(Beis ha Bechira* to TB *Avodah Zarah* 8a), and Maharsha (ad loc.) align the Mishnah with the Babylonian Talmud by explaining that *historically* Adam established the holiday which came to be known as Calends before he established the holiday which would later become Saturnalia; but in terms of their dates on the calendar, Saturnalia always preceded Calends. However, the Jerusalem Talmud writes the opposite; that is, that Calends was observed before the winter solstice and Saturnalia afterwards (see *Yefeh Einaim* to TB *Avodah Zarah* 6a who addresses this).

6 Various Christian scholars, especially in the 17th century, used Maimonides' account of the history of idolatry as a basis for their own assessment of the topic. For a survey of such sources, see Stroumsa 2010:91–98.

7 However, see *Bereishis Rabbah* §23:7 and *Sefer ha-Yashar* (Tel Aviv, 1955), p. 9, which clearly characterize the introduction of idolatry in Enosh's time as a rebellion against Hashem. Moreover, R. Nissim disagrees with Maimonides and understands that the early idolaters were not merely fools, they were wicked. A more thorough discussion of the ideologies behind early idolatry will appear in Volume II.

8 Maimonides, Laws of *Avodah Zarah* 1:1.

9 LSM, pp.181–182; 184–186.

10 Sforno (to Gen. 4:26) also understands that הוחל means "began," but explains the verse slightly differently. He explains that *[people] began to call* in *Hashem's name* means that the righteous men of that generation needed to publicly preach about G-d in order to oppose the views of idolaters, who by then had begun worshipping idolatry.

11 Radak *(Sefer ha-Shorashim* s.v. חלל and commentary to Gen. 4:26) explains that הוחל can either mean "begin" or "profane."

12 Alternatively, the Tosafists in *Daas Zekeinim* (ad loc.) explain that the people of Enosh's generation profaned Hashem's name by swearing falsely in His name.

13 See *Tosafos,* Nachmanides, Rashba, and Ran (to TB *Shavuos* 29a) and Rashba (to TB *Nedarim* 25a) who all explain that the idolaters in Enosh's time applied the Tetragrammaton to their gods. However, as we shall discuss concerning Micah's idol (Chap. 4.16), some authorities understand that the Tetragrammaton cannot be applied to anyone but Hashem.

14 R. Shimon Lavie (1485–1586) expands on this idea in his work *Kesem Paz,* vol. 1 (Livorno, 1795), pp. 162a; 170a. See also *Midrash Tanchuma (Noach* §18), which explains that in Enosh's time people began to worship stars and constellations as idols.

15 Rashbam, Abarbanel, and possibly Targum Onkelos also adopt this approach.

16 See *Gur Aryeh* who explains why the other commentators assume that the verse in question refers to a negative development. R. Avraham ben Shlomo explains (Ratzabi 1947:277) that in Enosh's time, people *stopped* praying. He reads the verse as: *Then, to call in Hashem's name [i.e., to pray] became profane [i.e., socially unacceptable].*

17 One Tosafistic source relates a tradition that sacrifices to Hashem were reinstituted in Enosh's time. Cain had killed Ebel in a jealous rage because Hashem had accepted Ebel's sacrifices and not his own. This resulted in a hiatus on sacrifices, because Seth was too scared to offer sacrifices, lest Cain attack him like he had attacked Ebel. However, once Seth begat Enosh, he felt secure enough to resume offering sacrifices, because he reasoned that if Cain would attack him, Enosh would come to his rescue. Thus, in Enosh's time, sacrifices to Hashem were reinstituted. See Y. Gellis (ed.), *Tosafos ha-Shaleim,* vol. 1 (Jerusalem: Machon Harry Fishel, 1982), p. 171.

Interestingly, R. Menashe Ben-Israel similarly suggests that the Bible's description of Enosh's generation was not meant negatively at all. On the contrary, he proposes that the Bible simply means that Enosh was the first person to actively call out in Hashem's name (i.e., preach to the masses) in the same way that Abraham later did (Lindo 1842:159–160).

18 *Likkutei Torah (Parashas Noach);* see also *Zohar (Bereishis* 56a).

19 Nachmanides to Gen. 2:3.

20 *Tziyyoni* (Lemberg, 1882), p. 7a.

21 *Kuzari* 1:47.

22 In his commentary *Kol Yehudah* to *Kuzari* (ad loc.).

23 In his commentary *Otzar Nechmad* to *Kuzari* (ad loc.).

24 See also *Radal* to *Pirkei de-Rabbi Eliezer* 18:52, and *Divrei Yirmyahu* to Maimonides' Laws of *Avodah Zarah* 1:1. For more sources about whether or not Enosh himself strayed after idolatry, see *Tiferes Tzvi* (to the *Zohar, Bereishis* 56a) by R. Mordechai Spielman (1923–2006).

25 *Emes le-Yaakov* to Gen. 2:3.

26 Alternatively, Nachmanides explains that the Torah does not explicitly note idolatry beginning in Enosh's time in line with its general tendency towards disregarding heretical views through omission in lieu of granting them a semblance of legitimacy through mention (Chavel 1963:170).

27 L. A. Feldman (ed.), *Peirush al ha-Torah-Rabbeinu Nissim* (Jerusalem: Shalem Institute,
1968), p. 70.

28 *Shalsheles ha-Kabbalah* (Jerusalem, 1962), p. 217.

29 See *Peirush ha-Rosh Al ha-Torah* to Gen. 4:26. [This account seems to be at odds with Maimonides' understanding of idolatry's origins; see Volume II.]

30 A. Bromberg (ed.), *Sifrei Rabbi Elazar mi-Germayza,* vol. 2, *Sodi Razi* (Jerusalem, 2004), p. 2.

31 *Tziyyoni* (Lemberg, 1882), p. 7a.

32 *Sefer ha-Yashar* (Tel Aviv, 1955), p. 9.

33 In this, Calmet followed his earlier rejection of Epiphanius' view presented in Calmet's *Commentaire litteral sur tousles livres de Ianden et du nouveau testament, Genesis* (Paris, 1715), p. 125.

34 F. Williams (trans.), *The Panarion of Epiphanius of Salamis* (Brill, 1997), p. 17.

35 A. Calmet, *Commentaire litteral sur tous les livres de l'ancien et du nouveau testament, Book of Wisdom* (Paris, 1726), p. 133.

Epiphanius possibly arrived at his conclusion based on a misunderstanding of a verse in Joshua, *Your forefathers always dwelt "beyond the River"—Terah, the father of Abraham and the father of Nahor—and they served other gods* (Josh. 24:2). The term *the father of Nahor* refers back to Terah, who was the father of both Abraham and Nahor. However, Epiphanius might have misunderstood "Nahor" as a different Nahor—Terah's father (see Gen. 11:23–26). Accordingly, he rendered the verse: *Your forefathers always dwelt "beyond the River;" even Terah, the father of Abraham, and [Serug] the father of*

[Terah's father] Nahor; and they served other gods. Assuming he understood the passage thusly, he saw this as Biblical proof that early idolatry began with Terah and Serug.

36 See A. Calmet, *Commentaire Iitteral sur tous les livres de l'ancien et du nouveau testament, Genesis* (Paris, 1715), p. 53, and A. Calmet, *Histoire universelle, sacree et profane, depuis le commencement du monde jusqu'a nos jours,* vol. 1 (Strasbourg, 1735), p. 11.

37 Orlinsky 1971:78. *The Book of Jerahmeel* (Yassif 2001:119) echoes pseudo-Philo and adds that in Enosh's time, people had begun to call various entities G-d and built temples for them. He notes that in Reu's time, those temples were (miraculously?) destroyed.

38 Orlinsky 1971:86 and Yassif 2001:121. Some scholars note that this account seems to contradict the traditional view that Terah (Abraham's father) was an idolater. However, there is no direct contradiction, because Terah may have joined the idolatry bandwagon despite the rest of his family's iconoclastic stance.

39 Indeed, Gersonides (to Gen. 9:7) writes that antediluvian society sinned, *inter alia,* by engaging in idolatry, and that this sin contributed to the Deluge.

40 *BB,* pp. 6b–10a.

41 *Maharam Shick al ha-Torah* (to Gen. 11:1).

G-d versus gods: Judaism in the Age of Idolatry (Jerusalem: Mosaica Press, Inc., 2018), pp. 33–44

Lesson  3

DIVINE IMAGE

WHO SAYS LIFE IS SACRED?

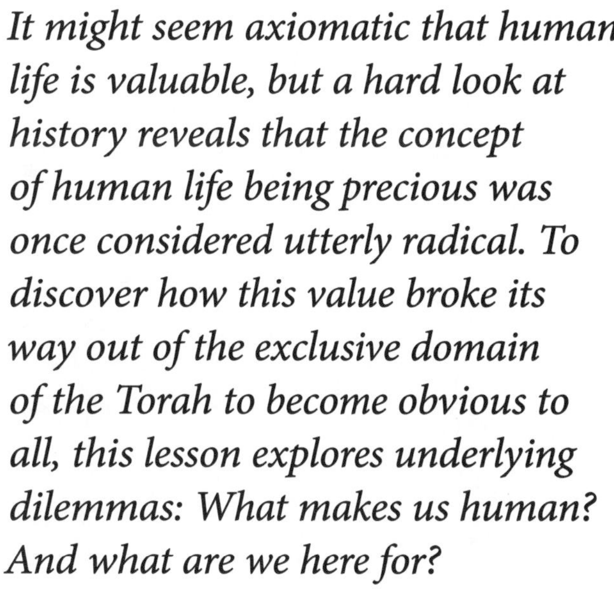

It might seem axiomatic that human life is valuable, but a hard look at history reveals that the concept of human life being precious was once considered utterly radical. To discover how this value broke its way out of the exclusive domain of the Torah to become obvious to all, this lesson explores underlying dilemmas: What makes us human? And what are we here for?

The English mother (detail). Artist unknown, engraving. (Wellcome Collection)

Exercise 3.1

What is it that makes us human?

TEXT 1

GENESIS 1:26—28

וַיֹּאמֶר אֱלֹקִים, "נַעֲשֶׂה אָדָם בְּצַלְמֵנוּ כִּדְמוּתֵנוּ, וְיִרְדּוּ בִדְגַת הַיָּם וּבְעוֹף הַשָּׁמַיִם וּבַבְּהֵמָה וּבְכָל הָאָרֶץ וּבְכָל הָרֶמֶשׂ הָרֹמֵשׂ עַל הָאָרֶץ".

וַיִּבְרָא אֱלֹקִים אֶת הָאָדָם בְּצַלְמוֹ בְּצֶלֶם אֱלֹקִים בָּרָא אֹתוֹ, זָכָר וּנְקֵבָה בָּרָא אֹתָם.

וַיְבָרֶךְ אֹתָם אֱלֹקִים, וַיֹּאמֶר לָהֶם אֱלֹקִים, "פְּרוּ וּרְבוּ וּמִלְאוּ אֶת הָאָרֶץ וְכִבְשֻׁהָ, וּרְדוּ בִּדְגַת הַיָּם וּבְעוֹף הַשָּׁמַיִם וּבְכָל חַיָּה הָרֹמֶשֶׂת עַל הָאָרֶץ".

*What are the implications of being created "in G-d's image"? **Rabbi Simon Jacobson** explains:*

MYJLI.COM/GIFTS

G-d said, "Let us make man in our image, in our likeness. They shall rule over the fish of the sea and the birds of the sky, over the animals and all of the earth, and over all the creatures that move along the ground."

And G-d created man in His image, in the image of G-d He created him; male and female he created them.

G-d blessed them and said to them, "Be fruitful and multiply, fill the earth and subdue it. Rule over the fish of the sea and the birds of the sky and over all of the beasts that tread upon the earth."

TEXT 2

RABBI OVADIAH SEFORNO, GENESIS 1:26

בְּצַלְמֵנוּ, שֶׁהוּא עֶצֶם נִצְחִי וְשִׂכְלִי...

כִּדְמוּתֵנוּ, בְּעִנְיַן הַמַּעֲשִׂיּוֹת, שֶׁיִּדְמֶה בָּם קְצָת לְפַמַּלְיָא שֶׁל מַעְלָה, בְּצַד מַה שֶּׁהֵם פּוֹעֲלִים בִּיְדִיעָה וּבְהַכָּרָה.

אָמְנָם פְּעוּלָּתָם הִיא בִּלְתִּי בְּחִירִיִּית, וּבָזֶה לֹא יִדְמֶה לָהֶם הָאָדָם. וּבִקְצָת יִדְמֶה הָאָדָם לָאֵ-ל יִתְבָּרֵךְ, הַפּוֹעֵל בִּבְחִירָה.

"In our image": This refers to humanity's abstract intelligence. . . .

"In our likeness": This refers to the realm of action. It is saying that the human being, acting with self-awareness and consciousness, somewhat resembles the behavior of the angels.

However, the angels' actions are not voluntary; in this respect, the human being does not resemble them. Rather, in this respect, the human being somewhat resembles G-d, Who acts with free choice.

RABBI OVADIAH SEFORNO
1475–1550

Biblical exegete, philosopher, and physician. Seforno was born in Cesena, Italy. After gaining a thorough knowledge of Talmud and the sciences, he moved to Rome, where he studied medicine and taught Hebrew to the German scholar Johannes Reuchlin. Seforno eventually settled in Bologna, where he founded and directed a yeshiva until his death. His magnum opus is a biblical commentary focused on the simple interpretation of the text, with an emphasis on philology and philosophy.

Figure 3.1

Humanity's Unique Qualities

1	Intelligence
2	Self-consciousness
3	Free Choice

TEXT 3

RABBI MOSHE BEN NACHMAN, GENESIS 1:28

> נָתַן לָהֶם כֹּחַ וּמֶמְשָׁלָה בָּאָרֶץ לַעֲשׂוֹת כִּרְצוֹנָם בַּבְּהֵמוֹת וּבַשְּׁרָצִים וְכָל זוֹחֲלֵי עָפָר, וְלִבְנוֹת, וְלַעֲקוֹר נָטוּעַ, וּמֵהֲרָרֶיהָ לַחְצוֹב נְחוֹשֶׁת, וְכַיּוֹצֵא בָּזֶה. וְזֶה יִכְלוֹל מַה שֶּׁאָמַר "וּבְכָל הָאָרֶץ".

G-d gave humans power and dominion over the earth. They can do as they wish with the animals and the creatures that move along the ground; they can build, uproot, mine copper from the hills, etc. This is all included in the words of the verse, "Over all of the earth."

RABBI MOSHE BEN NACHMAN (NACHMANIDES, RAMBAN), 1194–1270

Scholar, philosopher, author, and physician. Nachmanides was born in Spain and served as leader of Iberian Jewry. In 1263, he was summoned by King James of Aragon to a public disputation with Pablo Cristiani, a Jewish apostate. Though Nachmanides was the clear victor of the debate, he had to flee Spain because of the resulting persecution. He moved to Israel and helped reestablish communal life in Jerusalem. He authored a classic commentary on the Pentateuch and a commentary on the Talmud.

Farmer behind the Plow, Anton Mauve, drawing/brush on paper, c. 1885. (Rijksmuseum, Amsterdam)

TEXT 4

THE REBBE, RABBI MENACHEM MENDEL SCHNEERSON,
SEFER HASICHOT 5751:1, PP. 80–81

די בְּרָכָה און צִיווּי ה' "פְּרוּ וּרְבוּ וּמִלְאוּ אֶת הָאָרֶץ וְכִבְשׁוּהָ" וָועלְכֶע דֶער אוֹיבֶּערְשְׁטֶער הָאט גֶעזָאגְט נָאךְ בְּרִיאַת הָאָדָם . . . אִיז אַ בְּרָכָה כְּלָלִית און אַ צִיווּי כְּלָלִי וָועלְכֶער גִיט אַרוֹיס דֶער תַּפְקִיד וְתַכְלִית פוּן בְּרִיאַת הָאָדָם: עֶר זָאל זִיךְ מֶערְן און אָנְפִילְן און בַּאזֶעצְן דָאס לַאנְד און אִיר אַיינְנֶעמֶען, וּבְלָשׁוֹן הַיָּדוּעַ לַעֲשׂוֹת לוֹ יִתְבָּרֵךְ דִירָה בַּתַּחְתּוֹנִים.

The blessing and divine command, "be fruitful and multiply, fill the earth and subdue it" that G-d gave after the creation of humanity . . . is a general command that expresses the role and purpose of the creation of humankind. Humans were created to multiply, fill, and settle the earth and subdue it—making it into a "dwelling place for G-d."

RABBI MENACHEM MENDEL SCHNEERSON
1902–1994

The towering Jewish leader of the 20th century, known as "the Lubavitcher Rebbe," or simply as "the Rebbe." Born in southern Ukraine, the Rebbe escaped Nazi-occupied Europe, arriving in the U.S. in June 1941. The Rebbe inspired and guided the revival of traditional Judaism after the European devastation, impacting virtually every Jewish community the world over. The Rebbe often emphasized that the performance of just one additional good deed could usher in the era of Mashiach. The Rebbe's scholarly talks and writings have been printed in more than 200 volumes.

TEXT 5

LLOYD DEMAUSE (ED.), *THE HISTORY OF CHILDHOOD*
(LANHAM, MD.: ROWMAN AND LITTLEFIELD, 2006), PP. 25–26

Infanticide of both legitimate and illegitimate children was a regular practice of antiquity. . . .

Children were thrown into rivers, flung into dung-heaps and cess trenches, "potted" in jars to starve to death, and exposed on every hill and roadside, "a prey for birds, food for wild beasts to rend" (EURIPIDES, ION, 504). To

LLOYD DEMAUSE
1931–

Psychohistorian. Lloyd deMause is a leading American scholar of psychohistory, a controversial field that studies the psychological motivations of historical events. DeMause is the founder of *The Journal of Psychohistory* and is best known for his work on the psychological history of childhood and the family.

begin with, any child that was not perfect in shape and size, or cried too little or too much, or was otherwise than is described in the gynecological writings on "How to Recognize the Newborn That Is Worth Rearing," was generally killed. Beyond this, the first-born was usually allowed to live, especially if it was a boy. Girls were, of course, valued little, and the instructions of Hilarion to his wife Alis [1 BCE] are typical of the open way these things were discussed: "If, as may well happen, you give birth to a child, if it is a boy let it live; if it is a girl, expose it.". . .

The killing of legitimate children even by wealthy parents was so common that Polybius blamed it for the depopulation of Greece:

"In our own time the whole of Greece has been subject to a low birth-rate and a general decrease of the population, owing to which cities have become deserted and the land has ceased to yield fruit, although there have neither been continuous wars nor epidemics . . . as men had fallen into such a state of pretentiousness, avarice and indolence that they did not wish to marry, or if they married to rear the children born to them, or at most as a rule but one or two of them. . . ."

Until the fourth century [CE], neither law nor public opinion found infanticide wrong in either Greece or Rome. The great philosophers agreed.

TEXT 6

UGO ENRICO PAOLI, *ROME: ITS PEOPLE, LIFE AND CUSTOMS* (BRISTOL, U.K.: BRISTOL CLASSICAL PRESS, 2004), PP. 250–253

The *ludi circenses* [circus games] consisted of spectacles of very different types; the most usual were the *ludi gladitori* [gladiators], in which well-trained gladiators fought in various ways, each trying to wound or kill his opponent. . . . Gladiators were usually prisoners of war and were trained in barracks run on military lines. . . . The public execution of criminals formed part of the *circences* (circus) when they were thrown *ad bestias* [to the beasts] or put to death in some equally cruel way; as the condemned man had to be tortured to death, there seemed to be no reason for cheating the public, who could never have enough bloodshed, of such a spectacle. . . .

The Romans watched gladiatorial shows . . . almost drunk with the sight of so much bloodshed. "Kill him," they shouted, "beat him, burn him! Why does he meet the sword so timidly? Why didn't he fight more bravely? Why does he die so unwillingly?" In the intervals, impatient voices could be heard, "Now let's have some throats cut to keep the action going."

UGO ENRICO PAOLI
1884–1963

Historian and philologist. Paoli was a professor of classical antiquity and Latin literature at the University of Florence, Italy. His primary interest was the history of ancient legal systems.

TEXT 7

GENESIS 9:5–6

וְאַךְ אֶת דִּמְכֶם לְנַפְשֹׁתֵיכֶם אֶדְרֹשׁ . . . וּמִיַּד הָאָדָם מִיַּד אִישׁ אָחִיו, אֶדְרֹשׁ אֶת נֶפֶשׁ הָאָדָם.

שֹׁפֵךְ דַּם הָאָדָם בָּאָדָם דָּמוֹ יִשָּׁפֵךְ, כִּי בְּצֶלֶם אֱלֹקִים עָשָׂה אֶת הָאָדָם.

For your lifeblood I will demand an accounting. . . . From the hand of each human being, from the hand of each man for that of his brother, I will demand an accounting for the life of another human being.

Whoever sheds human blood shall have his blood shed by man, for G-d made the human in His image.

Watch ***Rabbi Lord Jonathan Sacks*** *lecture on the topic of "Confronting Violence in the Name of G-d":*

MYJLI.COM/GIFTS

Cain and Abel (Brudermord), Lovis Corinth, woodcut, 1919. (National Gallery of Art, Washington, D.C.)

TEXT 8

MECHILTA, EXODUS 20:13

כְּתִיב "אָנֹכִי ה' אֱלֹקֶיךָ" וּכְנֶגְדוֹ "לֹא תִרְצָח", מַגִּיד הַכָּתוּב שֶׁכָּל מִי שֶׁשּׁוֹפֵךְ דָּם, מַעֲלֶה עָלָיו הַכָּתוּב כְּאִלּוּ מְמַעֵט בִּדְמוּת הַמֶּלֶךְ.

מָשָׁל לְמֶלֶךְ בָּשָׂר וָדָם שֶׁנִּכְנַס לַמְּדִינָה, וְהֶעֱמִיד לוֹ אִיקוֹנוֹת וְעָשָׂה לוֹ צְלָמִים וְטָבְעוּ לוֹ מַטְבֵּעוֹת. לְאַחַר זְמַן כָּפוּ לוֹ אִיקוֹנוֹתָיו, שָׁבְרוּ לוֹ צְלָמָיו וּבָטְלוּ לוֹ מַטְבֵּעוֹתָיו וּמִיעֲטוּ בִּדְמוּתוֹ שֶׁל מֶלֶךְ.

כָּךְ, כָּל מִי שֶׁהוּא שׁוֹפֵךְ דָּמִים, מַעֲלֶה עָלָיו הַכָּתוּב כְּאִלּוּ מְמַעֵט בִּדְמוּת הַמֶּלֶךְ, שֶׁנֶּאֱמַר "שֹׁפֵךְ דַּם הָאָדָם בָּאָדָם דָּמוֹ יִשָּׁפֵךְ, כִּי בְּצֶלֶם אֱלֹקִים עָשָׂה אֶת הָאָדָם".

"I am your G-d" is written on one tablet, and the corresponding line on the second tablet is, "Do not murder." The Torah thereby teaches us that one who spills human blood is considered to have reduced the Divine King's image.

This is analogous to a human king who gained rule over a country. Statues of his image were erected, and coins were minted with his image. Sometime later, the people toppled the statues of the king and abolished his currency. By doing so they reduced the image of the king.

Similarly, any person who spills human blood is considered by the Torah to have reduced the Divine King's image, as the verse states, "Whoever sheds human blood shall have his blood shed by man, for G-d made the human in His image."

MECHILTA

A halachic Midrash to Exodus. Midrash is the designation of a particular genre of rabbinic literature usually forming a running commentary on specific books of the Bible. The name "*Mechilta*" means "rule" and was given to this Midrash because its comments and explanations are based on fixed rules of exegesis. This work is often attributed to Rabbi Yishmael ben Elisha, a contemporary of Rabbi Akiva, though there are some references to later sages in this work.

TEXT 9

TACITUS, *THE HISTORIES* (TRANSLATED BY ALFRED JOHN CHURCH AND WILLIAM JACKSON BRODRIBB) (LONDON: MACMILLAN AND CO., 1876), BOOK V

They provide for the increase of their numbers. It is a crime among them to kill any newly-born infant. . . . Hence a passion for propagating their race and a contempt for death.

PUBLIUS CORNELIUS TACITUS
C. 56–117

Senator and historian of the Roman Empire; considered to be one of the greatest Roman chroniclers. The surviving portions of his 2 major works, *The Annals* and *The Histories*, cover an 80-year period of the Roman Empire. Among the events documented are the Jewish-Roman War and the destruction of the Second Temple in Jerusalem.

Watch ***Rabbi Shlomo Yaffe*** *discuss the laws and ethics of war in Judaism:*

MYJLI.COM/GIFTS

QUESTION FOR DISCUSSION

Can killing ever be justified? If yes, when?

Figure 3.2

Do Not Murder

רצח	הרג
R-TS-CH	*H-R-G*
Murder	Kill

TEXT 10

RABBI NAFTALI TZVI BERLIN, *HAAMEK DAVAR*, GENESIS 9:5

> מִיַּד אִישׁ אָחִיו - פֵּירֵשׁ הַקָּדוֹשׁ בָּרוּךְ הוּא: אֵימָתַי הָאָדָם נֶעֱנָשׁ? בְּשָׁעָה שֶׁרָאוּי לִנְהוֹג בְּאַחֲוָה. מַה שֶּׁאֵין כֵּן בִּשְׁעַת מִלְחָמָה וְעֵת לִשְׂנוֹא אָז עֵת לַהֲרוֹג וְאֵין עוֹנֶשׁ עַל זֶה כְּלָל.

The verse states, "From the hand of each man for that of his brother." With this, G-d qualified that man is punished for murder in times of comradery and peace. However, at times of war and conflict, killing is allowed and does not incur punishment.

RABBI NAFTALI TSVI YEHUDAH BERLIN (NETSIV), 1816–1893

Head of the Volozhin yeshiva, Volozhin, Russia. Rabbi Berlin was born in Mir, Russia. He applied himself to his studies and was renowned for his extraordinary diligence. He is recognized for being one of the greatest scholars of his time. In 1854, he became the head of the yeshiva, one of the largest institutions of its kind, which he led for nearly 40 years. He authored several works, including a commentary on the Talmud and halachic responses.

Bouw van de tempel van Salomo (Construction of the Temple of Solomon), Jan Luyken, etching, Amsterdam, 1700. (Rijksmuseum, Amsterdam)

TEXT 11

I CHRONICLES 22:7–10

וַיֹּאמֶר דָּוִיד לִשְׁלֹמֹה: בְּנִי, אֲנִי הָיָה עִם לְבָבִי לִבְנוֹת בַּיִת לְשֵׁם ה' אֱלֹקָי.
וַיְהִי עָלַי דְּבַר ה' לֵאמֹר: דָּם לָרֹב שָׁפַכְתָּ וּמִלְחָמוֹת גְּדֹלוֹת עָשִׂיתָ, לֹא תִבְנֶה
בַיִת לִשְׁמִי כִּי דָּמִים רַבִּים שָׁפַכְתָּ אַרְצָה לְפָנָי. הִנֵּה בֵן נוֹלָד לָךְ הוּא יִהְיֶה
אִישׁ מְנוּחָה וַהֲנִחוֹתִי לוֹ מִכָּל אוֹיְבָיו מִסָּבִיב כִּי שְׁלֹמֹה יִהְיֶה שְׁמוֹ וְשָׁלוֹם
וָשֶׁקֶט אֶתֵּן עַל יִשְׂרָאֵל בְּיָמָיו. הוּא יִבְנֶה בַיִת לִשְׁמִי.

David said to Solomon, "My son, my intention was to build a house for G-d. But the word of G-d came to me, saying, 'You have shed much blood and have fought great wars. You shall not build a house for Me because you have shed much blood on the earth before Me. But you will have a son who will be a man of peace, and I will give him respite from all his enemies on every side. His name will be Solomon, and I will grant Israel peace and quiet during his reign. He is the one who will build a house for Me.'"

***Dr. Henry Abramson** relates the life story of King David:*

MYJLI.COM/GIFTS

TEXT 12

MISHNAH, SHABBAT 6:4

לֹא יֵצֵא הָאִישׁ לֹא בְּסַיִף, וְלֹא בְּקֶשֶׁת, וְלֹא בִּתְרִיס, וְלֹא בְּאַלָּה, וְלֹא בְּרוֹמַח . . . אֵינָן אֶלָּא לִגְנַאי, שֶׁנֶּאֱמַר (יְשַׁעְיָה ב, ד) וְכִתְּתוּ חַרְבוֹתָם לְאִתִּים וַחֲנִיתוֹתֵיהֶם לְמַזְמֵרוֹת, לֹא יִשָּׂא גוֹי אֶל גוֹי חֶרֶב וְלֹא יִלְמְדוּ עוֹד מִלְחָמָה.

A man may not go out on Shabbat with a sword, bow, shield, club, or spear. . . . These weapons are a disgrace for the person, as the verse states, "And they shall beat their swords into plowshares, and their spears into pruning hooks. Nation will not take up sword against nation, nor will they train for war anymore" (ISAIAH 2:4).

MISHNAH

The first authoritative work of Jewish law that was codified in writing. The Mishnah contains the oral traditions that were passed down from teacher to student; it supplements, clarifies, and systematizes the commandments of the Torah. Due to the continual persecution of the Jewish people, it became increasingly difficult to guarantee that these traditions would not be forgotten. Rabbi Yehudah Hanassi therefore redacted the Mishnah at the end of the 2nd century. It serves as the foundation for the Talmud.

TEXT 13

TALMUD, MEGILAH 6A

"וְהָיָה כְּאַלּוּף בִּיהוּדָה וְעֶקְרוֹן כִּיבוּסִי" (זְכַרְיָה ט, ג). אֵלּוּ תְּרֵאַטְרָיוֹת
וְקִרְקְסָיוֹת שֶׁבֶּאֱדוֹם שֶׁעֲתִידִין שָׂרֵי יְהוּדָה לְלַמֵּד בָּהֶן תּוֹרָה בָּרַבִּים.

"The cities of Edom shall be like a chief in Judah, and Ekron shall be like Jebusi [Jerusalem]" (ZACHARIAH 9:7). This refers to the amphitheaters and circuses of Rome, where the princes of Judah are destined to teach Torah publicly.

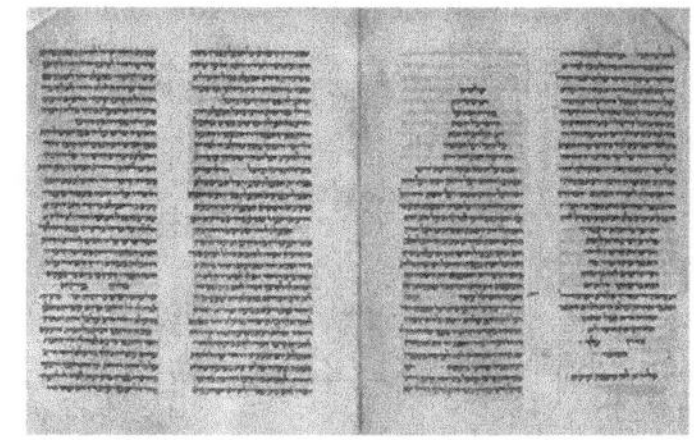

BABYLONIAN TALMUD

A literary work of monumental proportions that draws upon the legal, spiritual, intellectual, ethical, and historical traditions of Judaism. The 37 tractates of the Babylonian Talmud contain the teachings of the Jewish sages from the period after the destruction of the 2nd Temple through the 5th century CE. It has served as the primary vehicle for the transmission of the Oral Law and the education of Jews over the centuries; it is the entry point for all subsequent legal, ethical, and theological Jewish scholarship.

The Isaiah Wall (Andrews & Clark, architects), granite, 1948; located in Ralph Bunche Park at the United Nations, New York.

TEXT 14

THE REBBE, RABBI MENACHEM MENDEL SCHNEERSON,
IGROT KODESH 4, PP. 261–262

רוֹאִים אָנוּ בְּמוּחָשׁ, אֲשֶׁר בְּמִידָה יְדוּעָה וְרַבָּה תְּלוּיֵ הָרוֹשֶׁם מִמְאוֹרְעוֹת חַיֵּי הָאָדָם בְּהָאָדָם עַצְמוֹ בְּאֵיזֶה חֲרִיפוּת הוּא מְקַבְּלָם וְעוֹנֶה (רעֶאַגִירְט) עֲלֵיהֶם.

וּמִי לָנוּ גָדוֹל כָּרַמְבַּ"ם אֲשֶׁר חַיָּיו הַחִיצוֹנִיִּים הָיוּ מְלֵאִים צָרוֹת וְהַרְפַּתְקָאוֹת יִסוּרִים וְאַסוֹנוֹת רַחְמָנָא לִיצְלָן יוֹצְאִים מִן גֶּדֶר הָרָגִיל, וּבְכָל זֶה הַשְׁקָפָתוֹ עַל הַחַיִּים, כְּפִי שֶׁמְבוּאָר בִּסְפָרָיו מוֹרֶה נְבוּכִים, הָיְתָה טוֹבָה בְּיוֹתֵר, אָפְּטִימִיסְטִישׁ בְּלַעַ"ז.

וּלְאִידָךְ גִיסָא רָאִינוּ כַּמָה וְכַמָה אֲנָשִׁים שֶׁבְּחַיֵּיהֶם הַחִיצוֹנִיִּים לִכְאוֹרָה מוּצְלָחִים הֵם, וּבְכָל זֹאת רַק לְעִתִּים רְחוֹקוֹת בְּיוֹתֵר נִרְאֶה בָּהֶם אֵיזֶה שְׂבִיעַת רָצוֹן . . .

וּבִפְרַט בְּעִנְיָנִים שֶׁאֵינָם תְּלוּיִים בִּבְחִירָתוֹ, הֲרֵי בְּוַדַאי נוֹתֶנֶת תּוֹרַת הַחֲסִידוּת הַיְכוֹלֶת לִמְצוֹא בָּהֶם, גַם בְּשֵׂכֶל הָאֱנוֹשִׁי, אֵיזֶה צַד שֶׁל שִׂמְחָה . . .

מוּבָן אֲשֶׁר כָּל הָאָמוּר לְעֵיל אֵינוֹ חַס וְשָׁלוֹם דֶּרֶךְ אֲמִירַת מוּסָר, וְעוֹד יוֹתֵר דאָס אִיז שְׁוֶוער צוּ זָאגְן יֶענֶעם, ווִיסְנְדִיק דוּרְךְ וָואס יֶענֶער אִיז דוּרְכְגֶעגַאנְגֶען, וְלֹא בָּאתִי בָּזֶה אֶלָּא לְהוֹרוֹת לוֹ בְּאֵיזֶה מֵעִנְיָנֵי תּוֹרָתֵנוּ אֲשֶׁר יוּכְלוּ לְהָקֵל עָלָיו אֶת עוֹל הַמַשָׂא וּלְהַרְגִיעַ אֶת רוּחוֹ, עַל כָּל פָּנִים בְּמִקְצָת, עַד אֲשֶׁר יְקוּיַּים בּוֹ הַבְטָחָה . . . אֲשֶׁר ה' הַטוֹב יִתֵּן הַטוֹב וְיָאֵר פָּנָיו אֵלָיו בְּכָל הַמִצְטָרֵךְ לוֹ.

It is clearly apparent that the effect that life's events have on us depend, to a large degree, on our perspective toward them and our reaction to them.

There is no better example for this than Maimonides. Maimonides's life circumstances were filled with extraordinarily distressing events, troubles, tumults, suffering, and tragedies, may G-d protect us. Yet, nevertheless, Maimonide's outlook on life, as expressed in his book *Guide for the Perplexed*, was extremely positive and optimistic.

On the other hand, we see many people whose life circumstances seem successful, yet only very rarely do they show any measure of satisfaction. . . .

When circumstances are beyond our control, it becomes especially vital to tap into Chasidic teachings, which enable the human mind to find some measure of positivity in the undesired circumstance. . . .

My intention with the above is not to reproach you, G-d forbid. In fact, it is difficult to write such things to you, knowing what you have endured. I am only trying to guide you to some Torah concepts that can lessen your burden and assuage your spirit, at least in some measure. This is until the fulfillment of the promise that the good G-d will give you good and will show you His favor in all that you need.

TEXT 15a

GENESIS 39:20–23

וַיְהִי שָׁם בְּבֵית הַסֹּהַר. וַיְהִי ה' אֶת יוֹסֵף וַיֵּט אֵלָיו חָסֶד, וַיִּתֵּן חִנּוֹ בְּעֵינֵי שַׂר בֵּית הַסֹּהַר. וַיִּתֵּן שַׂר בֵּית הַסֹּהַר בְּיַד יוֹסֵף אֵת כָּל הָאֲסִירִם אֲשֶׁר בְּבֵית הַסֹּהַר, וְאֵת כָּל אֲשֶׁר עֹשִׂים שָׁם הוּא הָיָה עֹשֶׂה. אֵין שַׂר בֵּית הַסֹּהַר רֹאֶה אֶת כָּל מְאוּמָה בְּיָדוֹ בַּאֲשֶׁר ה' אִתּוֹ, וַאֲשֶׁר הוּא עֹשֶׂה ה' מַצְלִיחַ.

While Joseph was in prison, G-d was with him; He showed him kindness and granted him favor in the eyes of the prison warden. The warden put Joseph in charge of all of the prisoners, and he was made responsible for all that was done there. The warden paid no attention to anything under Joseph's care because G-d was with Joseph and gave him success in whatever he did.

TEXT 15b

GENESIS 40:6–8

וַיָּבֹא אֲלֵיהֶם יוֹסֵף בַּבֹּקֶר, וַיַּרְא אֹתָם וְהִנָּם זֹעֲפִים. וַיִּשְׁאַל אֶת סְרִיסֵי
פַרְעֹה אֲשֶׁר אִתּוֹ בְמִשְׁמַר בֵּית אֲדֹנָיו לֵאמֹר: "מַדּוּעַ פְּנֵיכֶם רָעִים הַיּוֹם".
וַיֹּאמְרוּ אֵלָיו: "חֲלוֹם חָלַמְנוּ וּפֹתֵר אֵין אֹתוֹ", וַיֹּאמֶר אֲלֵהֶם יוֹסֵף: "הֲלוֹא
לֵאלֹקִים פִּתְרֹנִים סַפְּרוּ נָא לִי".

Joseph came to them in the morning and saw that they were dejected. Joseph asked Pharaoh's officials who were imprisoned with him in his master's house, "Why do you look so sad today?"

"We both had dreams," they answered, "but there is no one to interpret them."

Joseph said to them, "Don't interpretations belong to G-d? Tell me your dreams."

TEXT 16

RABBI YAAKOV TZVI MECKLENBURG, *HAKETAV VEHAKABBALAH*, GENESIS 9:6

נִרְאֶה לִי כִּי יֵשׁ שְׁנֵי אוֹפַנֵּי רְצִיחָה. אִם לְרָעַת הַנִּרְצָח, לִנְקוֹם נִקְמָתוֹ מִמֶּנּוּ, אוֹ לָקַחַת מָמוֹנוֹ וְכַדוֹמֶה. אִם לְטוֹבַת הַנִּרְצַח כְּשֶׁהוּא מְשׁוּקָע בְּצַעַר גָּדוֹל וְיִבְחַר מָוֶת מֵחַיִּים . . .

עַל שְׁנֵי אֵלֶּה דִיבֶּר הַכָּתוּב, עַל הַהוֹרֵג לְרָעַת הַנִּרְצַח . . . יֹאמַר, וּמִיַּד הָאָדָם . . . וְאֶל הַשֵּׁנִי הַנַּעֲשֶׂה לִרְצוֹן הַנִּרְצַח וּלְטוּבָתוֹ אֲשֶׁר גַּם אִישׁ הַמְעוּלֶּה בְּמַדְרֵגָה וְגַם כְּשֶׁהוּא מֵאוֹהֲבֵי הַנִּרְצַח יִדְמֶה כִּי מִצְוָה הוּא עוֹשֶׂה לַהֲמִיתוֹ כְּדֵי לְהַשְׁקִיטוֹ מִצַּעַר, עַל זֶה אָמַר מִיַּד אִישׁ אָחִיו.

There are two forms of murder. One is murder intended for the detriment of the victim, as an act of revenge or in order to take the victim's money or the like. A second form of murder is for the benefit of the other, when someone is overwhelmed with great pain and prefers death to life. . . .

The Torah addresses both of these. Regarding murder for the detriment of the victim . . . the verse says, "From the hand of each human being." . . . The second form of murder, which is committed with the consent of the suffering individual and for his or her benefit, may even be done by a virtuous friend, who may believe that it is in fact a mitzvah. The verse, therefore, says, "From the hand of each man for that of his brother."

RABBI YAAKOV TSVI MECKLENBURG
1785–1865

German rabbi and biblical exegete. Rabbi Yaakov served as rabbi in Königsberg, East Prussia. In 1839, he published *Haketav Vehakabbalah*, an important commentary that often demonstrates the indivisibility of the Written Torah and the Oral Torah.

Watch ***Rabbi Yitzchak Breitowitz*** *discuss Jewish philosophy and law concerning physician-assisted suicide and end-of-life care:*

MYJLI.COM/GIFTS

KEY POINTS

1 The Torah narrative of Creation teaches us that human beings possess a "divine image" that is expressed in our intelligence, self-consciousness, and capacity for free choice. Humanity was given these unique qualities in order to advance civilization and make the world a more G-dly place.

2 In the ancient world, human life was cheap and disposable. Murderous practices such as infanticide, the gladiators' circus, and human sacrifice were widespread and celebrated.

3 The Torah taught that murder is forbidden because the human possesses the "divine image" and to take a life is to reduce G-d's image.

4 The Torah is not pacifist, and it allows killing in self-defense and war. But even necessary violence is despised and was viewed as a stain on King David's record.

5 When other faiths adopted some of the Torah's teachings, much of the world began to appreciate the sacred nature of human life.

6 Our possession of the "divine image" means that we are not bound by fate. We are able to use our intelligence to change our natural circumstances. Even when circumstances cannot be changed, our capacity for free choice allows us to transcend difficult situations by choosing to adopt a different perspective toward them, finding meaning and purpose in every situation.

7 In modern times, many see human life as a personal human right rather than something inherently sacred and valuable. One outcome of this is the movement to legalize physician-assisted suicide for people suffering from terminal illness.

8 The Torah forbids physician-assisted suicide because it views human life as inherently valuable due to the "divine image" we possess. Our divine image gives us the intellectual ability to develop cures for illnesses and the ability to choose to rise above terrible suffering and find meaning in it.

Additional Readings

LIFE AS AN INTRINSIC GOOD
RELIGIOUS REFLECTIONS ON EUTHANASIA

BY RABBI J. DAVID BLEICH

"But your blood of your lives will I require; from the hand of every beast will I require it, and from the hand of man, from the hand of a person's brother, will I require the life of man."[1] This earliest and most detailed biblical prohibition against homicide contains one phrase that is an apparent redundancy. Since the phrase "from the hand of man" pronounces man culpable for the murder of his fellow man, to what point is it necessary for Scripture to reiterate "from the hand of a person's brother will I require the life of man"? Fratricide is certainly no less heinous a crime than ordinary homicide. A nineteenth-century biblical scholar, Rabbi Jacob Zevi Mecklenburg, in his commentary on the Pentateuch, *Ha-Ketav ve-ha-Kabbalah*, astutely comments that, while murder is the antithesis of brotherly love, in some circumstances the taking of the life of one's fellow man may be perceived as indeed being an act of love par excellence.[2] Euthanasia, designed to put an end to unbearable suffering, is born not of hatred or anger but of concern and compassion. It is precisely the taking of life even under circumstances in which it is manifestly obvious that the perpetrator is motivated by feelings of love and brotherly compassion that the Bible finds necessary to brand as murder, pure and simple. Despite the noble intent that prompts such an action, mercy killing is proscribed as an unwarranted intervention in an area that must be governed only by G-d himself. The life of man may be reclaimed only by the Author of life. As long as man is yet endowed with a spark of life—as defined by G-d's eternal law—man dare not presume to hasten death, no matter how hopeless or meaningless continued existence may appear to be in the eyes of a mortal perceiver.

Indeed, there is some cogency to the argument that a dogmatic prohibition against homicide is necessary *only* in order to proscribe euthanasia. The Talmud lays down the rule that a person must allow himself to be put to death rather than take the life of his fellow.[3] *Force majeure* cannot, in good conscience, be advanced as a justification for an act of homicide. This rule constitutes one of only three exceptions to the general principle in Jewish law that preservation of human life, regardless of the quality or duration of the life saved, takes precedence over all other considerations. The other exceptions are based upon hermeneutic modes of biblical exegesis. No such basis exists upon which the rule might be predicated requiring a person to accept martyrdom rather than allowing himself to be coerced to commit an act of murder. The Talmudic justification is that this rule of law is based upon reason alone. It is self-evident that such an act cannot be justified, since, asserts the Talmud, "Why do you think that your blood is sweeter than the blood of your fellow?"[4] That moral judgement is regarded as an *a priori* perception of the human conscience; in effect, it is regarded as a proposition of natural law. It would then follow, *a fortiori*, that man, as a moral creature, is fully capable of recognizing by the light of his own reason that ordinary acts of murder committed for ignoble reasons, or committed wantonly for no reason at all, are heinous in nature. If so, there is no need for a prohibition based upon divine

RABBI DR. J. DAVID BLEICH, 1936–

Expert on Jewish law, ethics, and bioethics. Rabbi Bleich serves as professor of Talmud at the Rabbi Isaac Elchanan Theological Seminary, an affiliate of Yeshiva University, as well as head of its postgraduate institute for the study of Talmudic jurisprudence and family law. A noted author, he is most famous for his 6-volume *Contemporary Halakhic Problems*.

revelation. Revelation is necessary precisely because the act is prohibited even in those situations in which man's moral faculty, if left to its own devices, would not recognize the deed as repugnant, *viz.*, when the taking of human life constitutes an act of euthanasia.

The value of human life is supreme and takes precedence over virtually all other considerations. This attitude is most eloquently summed up in a Talmudic passage regarding the creation of Adam: "Therefore, only a single human being was created in the world, to teach that if any person has caused a single soul to perish, Scripture regards him as if he had caused an entire world to perish; and if any human being saves a single soul, Scripture regards him as if he had saved an entire world."[5] Human life is not a good to be preserved as a condition of other values but as an absolute, basic, and precious good in its own stead. The obligation to preserve life is commensurately all-encompassing.

Accordingly, life with suffering is regarded as being, in many cases, preferable to termination of life and with it elimination of suffering. The Talmud[6] and Maimonides[7] indicate that the adulterous woman who was made to drink "the bitter waters"[8] did not always die immediately. If she possessed other merit, even though guilty of the offense with which she was charged, the waters, rather than causing her to perish immediately, produced a debilitating and degenerative state that led to a protracted termination of life. The added longevity, although accompanied by pain and suffering, was viewed as a privilege bestowed in recognition of meritorious action. Life accompanied by pain is thus viewed as preferable to death. It is this sentiment that is reflected in the words of the Psalmist: "The L-rd had indeed punished me, but He has not left me to die."[9]

This, however, does not necessarily mean that we can understand why life, even when accompanied by suffering, is preferable to elimination of pain through the foreshortening of life. The Talmud[10] presents a remarkable elucidation of the biblical verse "In those days Hezekiah was sick unto death and the prophet, Isaiah the son of Amoz, came to him and said unto him, 'Thus said the L-rd: Command your house, for you shall die and not live.'"[11] The Talmud explains that King Hezekiah correctly understood the redundancy inherent in the phrase "you shall die and not live" as meaning "you shall die in this world and not live in the world to come." Going beyond the scriptural text, the Talmud then relates that Hezekiah demanded to know why he deserved so severe a punishment. The prophet responded, "Because you did not engage in procreation." Thereupon King Hezekiah defended himself in saying, "I saw by means of the holy spirit that unvirtuous children would issue from me." To that excuse Isaiah responded, "What have you to do with the secrets of the All-Merciful? You should have done what you were commanded and let the Holy One, blessed be He, do that which is pleasing to Him."

The principle reflected in this Talmudic exposition is valid with regard to the declining stages of human life no less so than it is for the generation of human life. The meaning and value of human life is a divine mystery. Man is commanded to procreate, to nurture and sustain life, and to preserve the life that has been entrusted to him until it is reclaimed by the Creator of all life. Whether or not man finds value in the life he is commanded to preserve is, in this fundamental sense, irrelevant; man's obligations vis-à-vis sustaining life are not predicated upon his aptitude for fathoming divine secrets.

Man must hearken to the divine command regardless of whether he understands its purpose or fails to do so, and, assuredly, he may not seek to rescind or modify the divine imperative on the plea that he does fathom the divine intent and is capable of independent decision making in effecting its realization. Nevertheless, man is not constrained from endeavoring to ascertain purposes or values reflected in the divine command provided that he does not become guilty of hubris in allowing his intellect to substitute human norms for the divine imperative. The fourteenth-century philosopher and exegete Gersonides authored a commentary on the Bible in which he incorporated a section entitled "*To'aliyot*," literally translated as "Benefits" but best rendered as "Lessons." In these vignettes Gersonides offers a list of moral maxims or values that man may derive from a particular section of Scripture. In doing so, there is no claim that man has plumbed the depths of divine meaning and intent or that he has exhaustively discerned the divine purpose. In much the same manner it is possible to discern a reinforcement of values in the preservation and prolongation of life even when that life appears to be bereft of value in conventional human or social terms. Indeed, centuries ago, the Sages of the Talmud, in an entirely different context, compared the human body to Sacred Writ. Lessons and purposes may be derived from divinely ordained experiences just as they are derived from divinely revealed texts. Paradoxically, although the ultimate meaning or purpose of human life remains a divine mystery, strictures against euthanasia serve manifold purposes, some of which are readily perceived.

1. Human Life and Divine Grandeur

In *Hales v. Petit*, a classic sixteenth-century case in which the interest of the state in prevention of suicide was first articulated, Justice Dyer wrote that suicide is an offence "against the king in that hereby he has lost a subject, and . . . he being the head has lost one of his mystical members."[12] Suicide may be prevented—and punished—by the king because it constitutes interference with his rights as monarch. Anthropomorphic analogies, by their very nature, can never be completely accurate. Nevertheless, in human terms, honor and glory are often found in sheer magnitude. Royal majesty is perceived as a correlate of the number of subjects over whom the monarch reigns. The more citizens in his domain, the greater the king. Thus, to deprive the king of a subject is to diminish his grandeur; to willfully cause the death of a subject of the king is to be guilty of *lèse majesté.*

Although this, too, is a mystery beyond our ken, G-d is the supreme king, whose dominion extends over all of mankind. The more numerous the populace, the greater his grandeur. The loss of even a single life represents a diminution of his kingship. One of the most solemn prayers in the Jewish liturgy is the *Kaddish*, the mourner's prayer. Although recited as memorialization of a loved one, the *Kaddish* contains no reference to the deceased, no hint of reward or punishment, no mention of everlasting life, and no prayer for the repose of the soul of the departed. Its opening phrase, "May His great Name be magnified and sanctified," sets the tenor of the entire prayer as a paean celebrating ultimate universal acceptance of divine sovereignty. Rabbi Meir Shapiro of Lublin explained that the loss of even a single human life represents a diminution of divine sovereignty and hence evokes a prayer expressing the supplicant's yearning for the restoration and enhancement of G-d's glory.[13]

It is difficult enough for us to comprehend any sense in which mere human existence serves to enhance the glory of the Deity. In anthropomorphic terms, we can readily understand that a monarch's power and glory, both real and received, are directly commensurate with the number of able-bodied, healthy, productive subjects over whom he rules. But incremental numbers of aged, nonproductive, ailing subjects hardly enhance royal power or grandeur. Nevertheless, to the extent that the mind can fathom the mystery of human existence, mankind must be perceived as constituting a vast orchestra engaged in a continuous performance in praise of the Creator. In an orchestra, each musician has an assigned role, and those assigned identical or similar roles are arranged in groups. There are separate sections for musicians playing wind, string, and percussion instruments. Not all the musicians and not all sections play at once. Effective rendition of the musical arrangement requires that, at times, some of the musicians remain silent. Yet even when not actually engaged in playing his instrument, every member remains seated with the orchestra and contributes to the visual magnificence of the performance. Similarly, each and every individual has an assigned role in the divine orchestration of mankind. Not every member is called upon to extol the Deity by fulfilling his assigned role continuously. Some, by virtue of their physical condition, may be quiescent; they are silent members of an orchestra that is nevertheless more majestic by virtue of their presence. Even though an individual in a precarious physical condition may not have the capacity to serve G-d in an active sense, nevertheless, his very existence constitutes an act of divine service.

2. Man as the Chattel of G-d

Preservation and prolongation of the life of a comatose patient also serve to impress a significant moral lesson upon the human conscience. Much is said in our day regarding patient autonomy and the right of every individual to be master of his or her own destiny. To be sure, no person enjoys rights over the life of another. Nevertheless, the concept of personal autonomy is flawed if it is understood as embodying the notion that man enjoys a proprietary interest in his own life. Our religious heritage teaches us that G-d is the Creator of man and that he is the Author of both life and death. Thus, even Plato spoke of man as the "chattel of the gods" in denying man's right to foreshorten his own life.[14] Man's interest in his life and in his body are subservient to those of the Creator. It is extremely easy to lose sight of that verity since, in the ordinary course of events, a person's natural desires, self-interest and preservation instinct serve to assure that his natural inclinations coincide with his moral obligation. That is frequently not the case when a person is pain-ridden, debilitated and terminally ill or involved in decision making on behalf of a comatose or nonsentient patient. In such cases, preservation of life does not appear to be at all desirable from a human perspective. But precisely because there is no longer a human will to live does man become cognizant of the fact that he may not make a decision to terminate life because his autonomy is not untrammeled. He is forcibly reminded of the fact that it is the Creator who is the ultimate proprietor of human life—a lesson that man might otherwise be prone to forget.

3. Moral Effect on Health Care Providers

Equally germane in analyzing the purposes reflected in a vitalist policy is an understanding of the negative values it does not allow to take root. In inveighing against suicide, the Court in *Hales v. Petit* declared that the deed cannot be countenanced so that "no evil example be given."[15] The taking of human life invites imitation and self-destruction serves as an "evil example" encouraging emulation by other susceptible members of society.[16] Suicide is "a breach of [the King's] peace" because a suicide is not a private act.[17] Quite to the contrary, it constitutes an offense against society because of potential harm to others. Euthanasia, whether active or passive, diminishes commitment to the preservation of life and compromises respect for life which, in turn, constitutes the fundamental underpinning of the social fabric.

Violence and even passive disregard for the preservation of life produce an indelible mark upon human character—as do compassion, concern and prolongation of life. In a remarkably incisive discussion in the *Nicomachean Ethics*, Aristotle asserts that both virtue and vice must be defined as character traits rather than categorizations of secret acts.[18] A virtuous person is not simply one who performs virtuous acts but one in whom the act flows from an ingrained character trait. Virtue is a habit, spontaneous and unbelabored, someone akin to a spontaneous reflex. The ability to press keys on a piano in the ordered sequence of a concerto does not render the player a pianist. For one to become a musician, the music must become part of the musician's personality and spring effortlessly from his fingers. Habits and skill are acquired. They are the products of practice and reinforcement.

The virtues that we seek to integrate within our personalities are born of virtuous acts repeated in their performance over and over again. Virtue is a disposition developed by repetition of acts that are objectively virtuous. Habits become ingrained as a result of patterned behavior. Failure to respond in a uniform manner, even when the intention is laudable, disrupts the behavior pattern and unsettles character. Examination of pros and cons, advantages and disadvantages, benefits and burdens of care and treatment on a case by case basis means that the therapeutic response is no longer spontaneous. When forthcoming, the decision to preserve life may be virtuous, but it is not the product of a virtuous character. Development of moral character, as Aristotle tells us, depends upon development of ingrained, spontaneous responses.

This should not be confused with the slippery slope argument—not that the slippery slope does not loom as a clear and present danger. The cogency of the Aristotelian position does not lie in the fear that a person lacking a virtuous character will not act in a manner consistent with virtue but in a recognition that an identical act performed by two individuals may be qualitatively different and that development of a virtuous character is integral to man's goal in life.

The development of virtuous character is surely a value society seeks to promote in all of its members. But society has a particular concern with the character development of health care professionals. Persons afflicted by malady or illness have a definite need for assurance that the physician will intuitively do everything possible to preserve life and promote well-being. Such trust cannot be reposed in a physician who is schooled in decision-making calculi that weigh the quality of life to be preserved. In an earlier time in American judicial history courts recognized that such considerations represented a societal interest of a magnitude weighty enough to override patient autonomy. Thus, the physician's paramount objective to preserve life was affirmed in *John F. Kennedy Memorial Hospital v. Heston*[19] and in *United States v. George.*[20] Confidence in the physician lies at the core of the physician-patient relationship and has a positive effect upon the therapeutic process. Conversely, lack of confidence has an adverse effect upon the therapeutic process. A positive relationship is possible only when the patient knows with certainty that the physician will always do his utmost and not abandon his patient as being beyond hope.

It is quite common for this aspect of the physician-patient relationship to be recognized even by persons who do not wish their lives to be prolonged under any and all circumstances. A simple and insignificant anecdote will serve to illustrate this point. Several years ago I delivered a paper at a medical ethics conference in which I advocated a strong vitalist position. A member of the audience, who happened to be a nurse, commented to my wife. "I don't agree with everything your husband said but, if he were a physician, I would certainly want him to be my doctor."

4. Emulation of Divine Love

Moreover, providing care on behalf of a debilitated patient incapable of response or of any meaningful activity represents a unique opportunity for the caregiver precisely because it is, in a fundamental sense, devoid of value to the recipient, at least as value is understood in human terms. In the words "and you shall walk in His ways,"[21] Scripture bids us to emulate G-d's ways to the extent that it is humanly possible to do so. G-d loves man, and this love, or *agape*, is of a unique kind. Divine *agape* is fundamentally different from the *philia* described by Aristotle. Aristotle describes three forms of love or friendship each involving a relationship. Those relationships are rooted in (1) pleasure or delight derived from the object of *philia*; (2) utility or pragmatic benefit derived from the relationship; or (3) a relationship based upon recognition of the virtue, i.e., the worth or intrinsic value, of the object of such *philia.*[22] Divine *agape* can hardly be in the nature of either of the first two forms of *philia*. Divine *agape* cannot be the product of the delight G-d finds in His relationship with men because G-d is incorporeal and not subject to emotions; G-d does not experience pleasure or delight. Divine *agape* cannot be rooted in utility, since, as a completely perfect Being, G-d is lacking in nothing and can derive no benefit to Himself from his relationship with man. Nor can we be so arrogant as to assume that divine love of man is predicated upon man's intrinsic worth, i.e., that G-d loves man because man is intrinsically precious. Any such exalted view of the human condition is negated by Scripture in the declaration "O L-rd what is man that Thou knowest him or the son of man that Thou art mindful of him?"[23] G-d's love of man flows irrepressibly from this essence.

What then is the nature of G-d's love for man? G-d's love can only be *sui generis*, unmotivated and not predicated upon any consideration. It is an act of *caritas*, i.e., of charity in the pristine sense of that term. To understand divine *agape* in even a remotely approximate manner, one must draw an analogy by examining one's love for oneself. One's love of oneself is not based upon pleasure: even a person whose existence is tormented and who experiences life as an unmitigated state of anguish continues to love himself. Similarly, the love one bears toward oneself is not the product of utility, i.e., of benefit that one derives from oneself, since that love endures even when one becomes an unrelieved burden to oneself. And, surely, self-love is not born of a recognition of self-worth. Indeed, the sinner, although fully aware of his deficiencies, is likely to love himself more intensely than the saint. Love of the self is un-caused and, indeed, often underserved. "Love thy neighbor as thyself"[24] constitutes a mandate to love one's fellow in exactly the same manner, i.e., to love him, not for any particular reason, but for no reason. *Agape* must be freely offered without expectation of reciprocation and must be nonjudgmental. Manifestation of that quality of love for one's fellow is a reflection of divine *agape*; it is man walking in the ways of G-d and emulating His love of mankind.

Actions commonly described as acts of charity are generally motivated, at least in part, by one or another of Aristotle's modes of *philia*. To be sure, only the cynical or the naïve act on grounds of utility, i.e., anticipation of reciprocation. But it is entirely noble to perform acts of charity because of a sense of the human worth of the beneficiary or in anticipation of enjoying the unique sense of self-satisfaction that may be derived from the altruistic nature of a charitable act. Paradoxically—or perhaps not so paradoxically—it is precisely our failure to perceive a rational purpose in prolonging the lives of patients whose continued survival seems to be devoid of meaning that enables our acts on their behalf to rise to the level of *agape*. Such an act cannot be based upon love generated by the precious nature of the life that is being preserved because we fail to recognize any intrinsic value in such life. Nor can the act be motivated by the self-satisfaction born of altruistic behavior. Altruism entails acting on behalf of another. However, if the other person derives no benefit from the act, one can hardly derive a glow of satisfaction from having acted on his behalf. One may indeed feel that one has done one's duty, but that feeling is accompanied by a sense of hollowness. And precisely therein lies its purpose. Its purpose lies in the fact that it has no purpose. Of all human acts of charity it most closely approximates the divine because, of all expressions of human love, it most closely represents *agape*. Its value lies in the fact that it has no cause; it is an expression of man's endeavor to become G-d-like and hence godly.

5. A Vehicle for Mitzvah

The sages of the Talmud went beyond recognition of illness as an opportunity accorded to the healthy for expression of *caritas*. They saw in illness an opportunity for the sick to gain merit by virtue of being instruments for expression of loving-kindness. The Gemara, *Nedarim* 39b, states in the name of R. Simeon ben Lakish:

Where is there a biblical allusion to [the *mitzvah* of] visiting the sick? "If these will die in the manner of the death of all men and the visitation of all men be visited upon them, then G-d did not send me" (Numbers 16:29). How is this inferred? Said Rava, "'If these will die in the manner of the death of all men.' [i.e.], they become ill and are confined to bed and people visit them, what will people say? 'G-d did not send me.'"

The term *pekudah* in Scripture and its associated verb forms usually connote "remembering," in the sense of remembering to perform an act or to satisfy a need, e.g., "And G-d remembered Sarah" (*Genesis* 21:1). The term acquires the connotation of "visitation" when associated with the act that is prompted by remembrance. Thus, for example, Genesis 21:1 is rendered by *Targum Onkelos* as "And G-d remembered Sarah" while the verse cited in *Nedarim* 39b is rendered by Onkelos as "the visitation of all men." The conventional understanding of the "visitation" of which the latter verse speaks is the visitation of death to which reference is made earlier in the same verse: "If they will die in the manner of the death of all men." The Gemara, presumably troubled by the obvious redundancy in the verse, interprets the "visitation" to which reference is made as connoting visits paid to the sick patient by family and friends rather than as connoting the visitation of death.

The problem, however, is what is Moses trying to prove? If, as Moses predicts, Korah meets an unnatural death resulting from a supernatural event, that miraculous phenomenon will serve to reinforce Moses' stature as a prophet and as the bearer of divine instruction, contrary to the allegation of Korah. Moses is putting his credentials to the test in the manner of a prophet who proves his prophecy by means of a miracle. Thus, if the announced miracle does not occur, Moses will be exposed as a fraud. Accordingly, the reference to the manner of Korah's impending death is entirely understandable. But how would visits by family and friends prior to his death disprove the claims of Moses? If, for some reason, death can be attributed to a supernatural cause only if it is sudden in nature, Moses could readily have announced that his authority should be regarded as having been confirmed only if Korah dies miraculously and suddenly. The reference to visits by family and friends seems to predicate Moses' claim upon a particular phenomenon that is of no intrinsic relevance.

The Gemara's interpretation of the cited phrase should be understood as reflecting an assertion on the part of Moses to the effect that Korah and his company are totally evil and possess no redeeming merit whatsoever. Their challenge to Moses and to his office is entirely insincere in nature. As the epitome of evil, Korah and his company, declares Moses, lack the merit even passively to provide others with an opportunity for a *mitzvah*. If they die, not only miraculously but suddenly as well, that will be a sign that they possess no redeeming merit, as Moses claims. If they do not die instantaneously, with the result that others are afforded the opportunity to perform kindnesses on their behalf, that, declares Moses, will be proof that he has falsely accused them of being bereft of all redeeming qualities.

This remarkable bit of Talmudic exegesis does not merely uncover a new level of meaning in a biblical verse but serves as a vehicle for the enunciation of an important value: Even when the life of a person on his deathbed seems to be devoid of benefit, meaning or purpose, the patient retains unique human value by virtue of the role he plays in providing an opportunity for love and compassion. Moreover, to be placed in that role is itself a mark of divine favor.

6. Human Life as a *Bonum Per Se*

Finally, difficult as it may be to accept rationally, it must be recognized that, on a different level, human life does represent a purpose in and of itself, i.e., sheer human existence is endowed with moral value. If human life in any of its guises represents a value, that value must logically be either an instrumental good or a *bonum per se*. If human life constitutes only an instrumental good, it follows that life becomes devoid of value when it no longer leads to or promotes that value. When that quality of life has degenerated to the point that it is considered to be devoid of value, there is no compelling reason to distinguish between passive and active euthanasia. If life *per se* does not represent a value, then the taking of life can be wrong only because it extinguishes other goods that are made possible only by the presence of life. When those goods are no longer attainable, the underlying human life can hardly continue to be an instrumental good.

Again, this is not a slippery slope argument. The slippery slope argument seeks to persuade that, although x is morally innocuous, if x is sanctioned it will rapidly lead, through desensitization, inability to make fine and precise moral distinctions, outright malice, or whatever, to y, with y representing something that, at least upon reflection, is clearly unacceptable. The problem with the notion of human life as an instrumental good rather than a *bonum per se* is not that it creates a dynamic in which acceptance of passive euthanasia today improperly leads to condoning active euthanasia tomorrow but that the two are morally indistinguishable. Hence acceptance of one logically entails acceptance of the other. The intuitive repugnance of the conclusion of this moral syllogism should serve to demonstrate not that the reasoning is faulty but that its major premise is faulty.

Moreover, if human life is merely an instrumental good, it becomes necessary to define the nature of the good that constitutes the *telos* of human existence. No doubt that may become the subject of disagreement and may variously be defined as the capacity for rational thought, awareness of personhood, the ability to engage in interpersonal relationships, the capacity to experience pleasure, etc. It rapidly becomes evident that the absence of such a *telos* is not associated only with the terminal, comatose condition or even with the permanent vegetative state but is also absent in some states of insanity and mental deficiency. If that line of reasoning is pursued to its logical conclusion, it results in the assertion that, *mutatis mutandis*, the life of any person not capable of experiencing that *telos* may be snuffed out with moral impunity. Euthanasia would then become morally acceptable in situations not involving terminally ill persons. Applying such criteria, permanently and severely mentally disabled or retarded persons would be candidates for euthanasia. We intuitively recognize that such an argument constitutes a *reductio ad absurdum*. Yet the only way to escape that conclusion is to accept the alternate formulation of the disjunction with which we began, *viz.*, that all human life constitutes a *bonum per se*.

This paper was originally delivered at a conference on "Life and Death after *Cruzan*," sponsored by the National Legal Center for the Medically Dependent and Disabled, in New Orleans, April 1992, and is presented, with additions and revisions, as published in *Issues in Life and Medicine*, vol. 9, no. 2 (fall 1993), pp. 139–149.

Endnotes

1 Genesis 9:5.
2 *Ha-Ketav ve-ha-Kabbalah* (5th ed., 1946), p. 20.
3 *Sanhedrin* 79a.
4 *Loc. cit.*
5 *Sanhedrin* 37a.
6 *Sotah* 22b.
7 *Hilkhot Sotah* 3:20.
8 Numbers 5:11–31.
9 Psalms 118:18.
10 *Berakhot* 10a.
11 Isaiah 38:1.
12 1 Plowden 253, 262, 75 Eng. Rep. 387, 400 (Q.B. 1562).
13 *Be-Mishnah be-Omer u-be-Ma'as* (Bnei Brak, 1967), ed. Aaron Soraski, II, 122.
14 Plato, *Phaedo* 62b–c, reprinted in *Plato I*, 215–217 (Harold North Fowler, trans., 14th ed., 1971) (Loeb Classical Library vol. 36).
15 1 Plowden at 262, 75 Eng. Rep. at 400.
16 *Loc. cit.*
17 *Loc. cit.*
18 Aristotle, *Nicomachean Ethics*, Book II, 1130b (reprinted in *The Basic Works of Aristotle*, pp. 952–53) (Richard McKeon, ed., 25th ed., 1941).
19 279 A.2d 670 (N.J. 1971).
20 239 F. Supp. 752 (D. Conn. 1965).
21 Deuteronomy 28:9.
22 Aristotle, *Nicomachean Ethics*, Book VIII, 1156–57 (reprinted in *The Basic Works of Aristotle*, pp. 1065–12) (Richard McKeon, ed., 25th ed., 1941).
23 Psalms 144:3.
24 Leviticus 19:18.

Bioethical Dilemmas: A Jewish Perspective, vol. 1 (Hoboken, N.J.: Ktav Publishing House, Inc., 1998), ch. 4

Lesson 4

Declaration of Independence, John Trumbull, oil on canvas, 1819. (United States Capitol, Washington, D.C.)

CREATED EQUAL?

EXPLORING A NOT-SO-SELF-EVIDENT TRUTH

Humanity long insisted that mastery over others was a birthright: some were born to dominate, and others to be dominated. In recent history, the Jewish ideals of equality and individuality have been widely adopted so that most people agree that no one is intrinsically inferior or superior. These concepts originate in the Torah's revelation that we are all equally created in G-d's image and that just as G-d cannot be redundant, nor can humans crafted in His image.

TEXT 1

RABBI LORD JONATHAN SACKS, *RADICAL THEN, RADICAL NOW* (LONDON: CONTINUUM, 2003), PP. 65–66

The mythic universe is hierarchical. . . . That, we now know, is the significance of those ancient buildings, the ziggurats, constructed by the Sumerians at the birth of civilization in the Tigris-Euphrates valley. . . . Their architecture was not so much art as cosmology, a theory of the universe given physical shape. The successive tiers of the building represented the rule of the higher powers over the lower. . . . The strong rule the weak, the many dominate the few, the powerful hold sway over the powerless. . . .

In ancient myth and ritual, kings are, or aspire to be, gods. The rest of humanity, in its various gradations, is replaceable. They are worker ants serving the queen, the beasts of burden serving the master. . . . The gradations between ranks and classes were as inevitable as those between animals in the struggle for survival. This was self-evident; this was a law of nature; it was reality.

RABBI LORD JONATHAN SACKS
1948–

Former chief rabbi of the United Kingdom. Rabbi Sacks attended Cambridge University and received his doctorate from King's College, London. A prolific and influential author, his books include *Will We Have Jewish Grandchildren?* and *The Dignity of Difference.* He received the Jerusalem Prize in 1995 for his contributions to enhancing Jewish life in the Diaspora, was knighted and made a life peer in 2005, and became Baron Sacks of Aldridge in 2009.

TEXT 2

G. M. A. GRUBE (TR.), *PLATO*, *REPUBLIC*, BOOK III, 415A
(INDIANAPOLIS/CAMBRIDGE: HACKETT PUBLISHING COMPANY, 1992), P. 91

All of you in the city are brothers . . . but the god who made you mixed some gold into those who are adequately equipped to rule, because they are most valuable. He put silver in those who are auxiliaries and iron and copper in the farmers and other craftsmen. For the most part, you will produce children like yourselves, but, because you are all related, a silver child will occasionally be born from a golden parent, and vice versa.

PLATO
5TH CENTURY BCE

Philosopher. Plato was a student of Socrates and a teacher of Aristotle. His writings explored justice, beauty, and equality and also contained discussions in aesthetics, political philosophy, theology, cosmology, epistemology, and the philosophy of language. Plato founded the Academy in Athens, one of the first institutions of higher learning in the Western world.

Detail from Trajan's Column, Rome, c. CE 113.

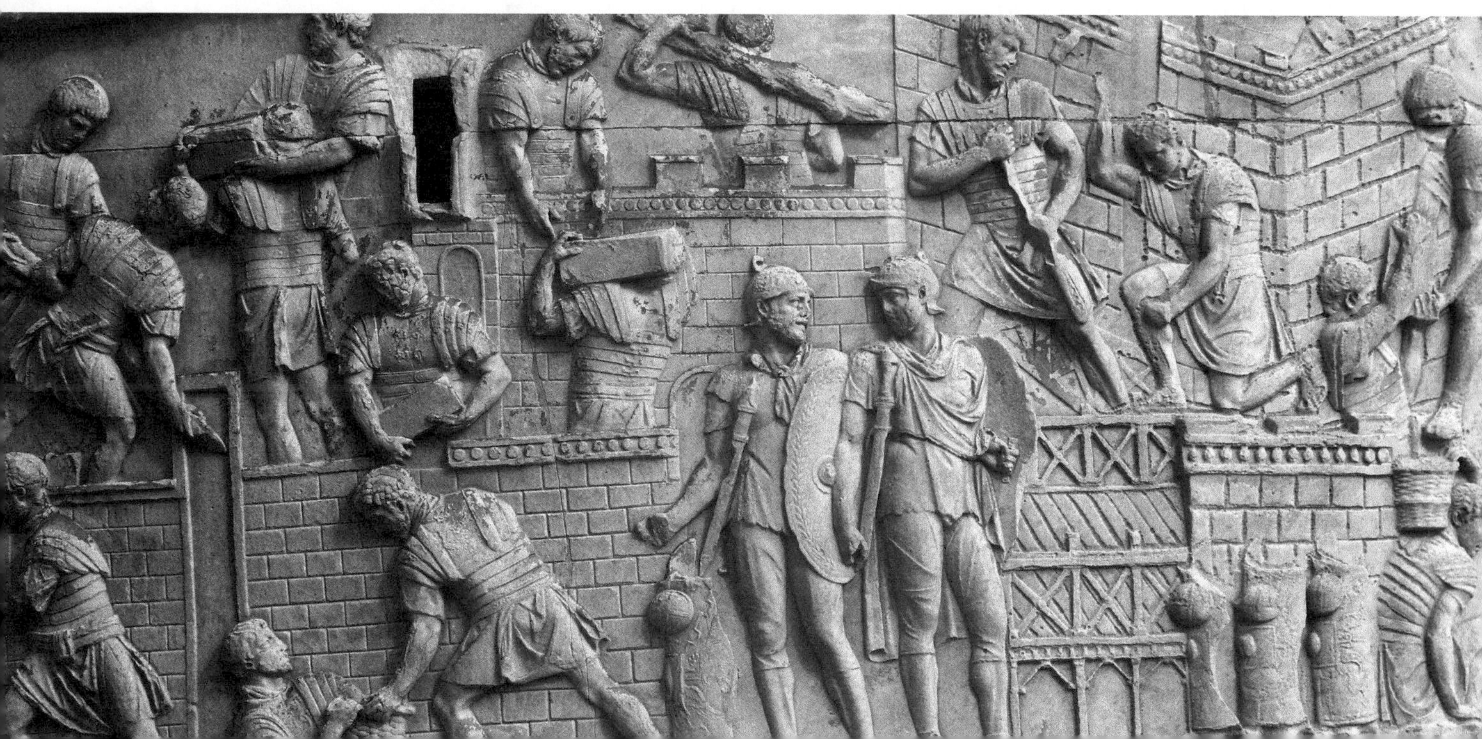

TEXT 3

JOSHUA BERMAN, *CREATED EQUAL: HOW THE BIBLE BROKE WITH ANCIENT POLITICAL THOUGHT* (OXFORD, U.K.: OXFORD UNIVERSITY PRESS, 2008), PP. 26–27, 46

Within the Mesopotamian, Ugaritic, and Egyptian conceptions . . . it is not the common man who is the central focus of the gods, but the king. In Mesopotamia, portents of evil, such as an eclipse or an earthquake, mandated human action to placate the gods, but the action mandated was solely that of the king. Only he recited prayers, offered sacrifices or shaved his head in obeisance. Nothing was required of the people at large. It was not the people the Mesopotamian gods held accountable, but their king. . . .

Religion on a national scale was one from which the common man was generally excluded. Religious laws for the masses are sparse within Hittite legal codes, and are entirely absent from Mesopotamian ones. The common man in these cultures had only a small role to play in the public worship of these deities, which was relegated entirely to the king and the priests.

JOSHUA BERMAN

Joshua Berman received his PhD at Bar-Ilan University and rabbinical ordination from the Israeli Chief Rabbinate. He is currently a Bible professor at Bar-Ilan University. Among his books are *The Temple: Its Symbolism and Meaning Then and Now* and *Created Equal: How the Bible Broke with Ancient Political Thought.*

QUESTION FOR DISCUSSION

What are the implications of viewing humanity in hierarchical terms?

Figure 4.1

Implications of the Social Hierarchy

1	Abuse of the powerless
2	Different laws for different people
3	Sacrificing the individual for the collective
4	Lack of universal education

TEXT 4

EZEKIEL 18:11–12

וְהוּא אֶת כָּל אֵלֶּה לֹא עָשָׂה, כִּי גַם אֶל הֶהָרִים אָכַל וְאֶת אֵשֶׁת רֵעֵהוּ טִמֵּא.
עָנִי וְאֶבְיוֹן הוֹנָה, גְּזֵלוֹת גָּזָל, חֲבֹל לֹא יָשִׁיב, וְאֶל הַגִּלּוּלִים נָשָׂא עֵינָיו.

He did not do any of these good deeds. Rather, he ate of the sacrifices offered at the mountain shrines and defiled his fellow man's wife. He wronged the poor and the needy, committed robberies, did not return collateral, and lifted his eyes to the idols.

Depiction of scales of justice (detail, rightmost panel of triptych). Benjamin Senior Godines, c. 1680. (Jewish Museum London)

TEXT 5

RABBI LORD JONATHAN SACKS, *RADICAL THEN, RADICAL NOW,* PP. 66-67

A sentence was uttered that heralded the greatest paradigm shift in the story of mankind. "So, G-d made man in His own image, in the image of G-d He created him, male and female He created him." This single proposition was an explosive charge at the base of the entire structure of the ancient and medieval world. It took millennia for its potential to be realized. But once stated, the rest was inevitable. From it would flow the great ideas that changed the West—the sanctity of human life, the dignity of the individual, human rights, the sovereignty of justice, the rule of law and the idea of a free society. Nothing could have been more counterintuitive.

That kings, rulers, emperors, pharaohs were the image of G-d—that much the ancient world knew. But that we *all* are—that was revolutionary.

TEXT 6

MISHNAH, SANHEDRIN 4:5

לְפִיכָךְ נִבְרָא אָדָם יְחִידִי, לְלַמֶּדְךָ שֶׁכָּל הַמְאַבֵּד נֶפֶשׁ אַחַת מִיִּשְׂרָאֵל מַעֲלֶה עָלָיו הַכָּתוּב כְּאִילוּ אִבֵּד עוֹלָם מָלֵא, וְכָל הַמְקַיֵּים נֶפֶשׁ אַחַת מִיִּשְׂרָאֵל מַעֲלֶה עָלָיו הַכָּתוּב כְּאִילוּ קִיֵּם עוֹלָם מָלֵא.

וּמִפְּנֵי שְׁלוֹם הַבְּרִיּוֹת, שֶׁלֹּא יֹאמַר אָדָם לַחֲבֵירוֹ אַבָּא גָדוֹל מֵאָבִיךָ.

וְשֶׁלֹּא יְהוּ מִינִין אוֹמְרִים הַרְבֵּה רְשׁוּיוֹת בַּשָּׁמַיִם.

וּלְהַגִּיד גְּדוּלָּתוֹ שֶׁל הַקָּדוֹשׁ בָּרוּךְ הוּא, שֶׁאָדָם טוֹבֵעַ כַּמָּה מַטְבֵּעוֹת בְּחוֹתָם אֶחָד וְכוּלָּן דוֹמִין זֶה לָזֶה, וּמֶלֶךְ מַלְכֵי הַמְּלָכִים הַקָּדוֹשׁ בָּרוּךְ הוּא טָבַע כָּל אָדָם בְּחוֹתָמוֹ שֶׁל אָדָם הָרִאשׁוֹן וְאֵין אֶחָד מֵהֶן דּוֹמֶה לַחֲבֵירוֹ.

לְפִיכָךְ כָּל אֶחָד וְאֶחָד חַיָּב לוֹמַר בִּשְׁבִילִי נִבְרָא הָעוֹלָם.

Initially, only one human being was created:

1. To teach us that one who destroys a single life is considered to have destroyed the entire world, and one who saves a single life is considered to have saved the entire world;

2. To maintain harmony among humanity, that one person would not be able to say to another, "My progenitor is greater than yours";

3. So that heretics should not say that there are many gods [each creating its own line of humanity]; and

4. To communicate the greatness of G-d. For when a person mints many coins from the same mold, all the coins are alike. But G-d mints every person through the mold of the first human, and yet no two people are alike.

Therefore, every person must say, "The world was created for me."

MISHNAH

The first authoritative work of Jewish law that was codified in writing. The Mishnah contains the oral traditions that were passed down from teacher to student; it supplements, clarifies, and systematizes the commandments of the Torah. Due to the continual persecution of the Jewish people, it became increasingly difficult to guarantee that these traditions would not be forgotten. Rabbi Yehudah Hanassi therefore redacted the Mishnah at the end of the 2nd century. It serves as the foundation for the Talmud.

"On Individualism, Socialism, and Chasidism," *by* ***Professor Tali Loewenthal:***

MYJLI.COM/GIFTS

TEXT 7a

DEUTERONOMY 29:9

> אַתֶּם נִצָּבִים הַיּוֹם כֻּלְּכֶם לִפְנֵי ה' אֱלֹקֵיכֶם, רָאשֵׁיכֶם שִׁבְטֵיכֶם, זִקְנֵיכֶם וְשֹׁטְרֵיכֶם, כֹּל אִישׁ יִשְׂרָאֵל.

All of you are standing today before your G-d; the leaders of your tribes, your elders and your officers—every Jewish person.

Rabbi Simon Jacobson *discusses the balance of the individual and community in Jewish thought:*

MYJLI.COM/GIFTS

TEXT 7b

MIDRASH, *TANCHUMA*, NITSAVIM 2

> אַף עַל פִּי שֶׁמָּנִיתִי לָכֶם רָאשִׁים, זְקֵנִים, וְשׁוֹטְרִים, כּוּלְּכֶם שָׁוִין לְפָנַי, שֶׁנֶּאֱמַר, "כֹּל אִישׁ יִשְׂרָאֵל".

Even though I appointed leaders, elders, and officers over you, you are all equal in My eyes. As the verse says, "every Jewish person."

MIDRASH TANCHUMA

A Midrashic work bearing the name of Rabbi Tanchuma, a 4th-century Talmudic sage quoted often in this work. Midrash is the designation of a particular genre of rabbinic literature usually forming a running commentary on specific books of the Bible. *Midrash Tanchuma* provides textual exegeses, expounds upon the biblical narrative, and develops and illustrates moral principles. *Tanchuma* is unique in that many of its sections commence with a halachic discussion, which subsequently leads into nonhalachic teachings.

TEXT 8

TALMUD, PESACHIM 25B

הַהוּא דְאָתָא לְקַמֵיהּ דְרָבָא, אָמַר לֵיהּ: מָרֵי דוּרַאי אָמַר לִי: "זִיל קַטְלֵיהּ לִפְלָנְיָא וְאִי לָא קָטְלִינָא לָךְ".

אָמַר לֵיהּ: "לִיקְטְלוּךְ וְלֹא תִּיקְטוֹל. מַאי חָזִית דִדְמָא דִידָךְ סוּמָק טְפֵי, דִילְמָא דְמָא דְהַהוּא גַבְרָא סוּמָק טְפֵי?"

A man once came before Rava and said, "The ruler of my village instructed me to kill someone, and if I refuse, he will kill me."

Rava replied, "Allow yourself to be killed, and don't kill the other. Why do you see your blood as redder than his blood? Perhaps his blood is redder than yours?"

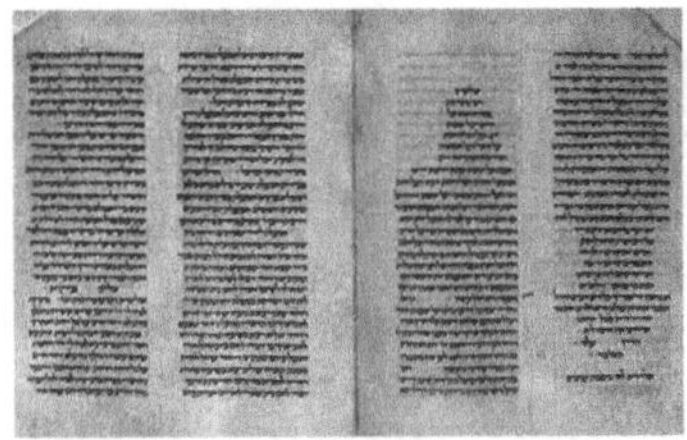

BABYLONIAN TALMUD

A literary work of monumental proportions that draws upon the legal, spiritual, intellectual, ethical, and historical traditions of Judaism. The 37 tractates of the Babylonian Talmud contain the teachings of the Jewish sages from the period after the destruction of the 2nd Temple through the 5th century CE. It has served as the primary vehicle for the transmission of the Oral Law and the education of Jews over the centuries; it is the entry point for all subsequent legal, ethical, and theological Jewish scholarship.

TEXT 9a

SIFRA, KEDOSHIM, *PARSHAH* 2, 4:12

"וְאָהַבְתָּ לְרֵעֲךָ כָּמוֹךָ" (וַיִקְרָא יט, יח), רַבִּי עֲקִיבָא אוֹמֵר, זֶה כְּלַל גָדוֹל בַּתּוֹרָה.

בֶּן עֲזַאי אוֹמֵר, "זֶה סֵפֶר תּוֹלְדוֹת אָדָם" (בְּרֵאשִׁית ה, א), זֶה כְּלַל גָדוֹל מִזֶה.

"You shall love your fellow like yourself" (LEVITICUS, 19:18). Rabbi Akiva said, "This is a great principle in the Torah."

Ben Azai said, "The following verse conveys an even greater principle: 'This is the written account of the descendants of Adam; [when G-d created Adam, in the likeness of G-d He created him]' (GENESIS 5:1)."

***SIFRA* (TORAT KOHANIM)**

An ancient rabbinic exegesis on the Book of Leviticus. The subject matter of this work is predominately Temple-era-related laws inasmuch as much of the Book of Leviticus focuses on the Temple service. According to Maimonides, the compiler and editor of this work was the Talmudic sage Rav (175–247 CE). Others attribute it to an earlier redactor. The work is quoted often in the Talmud.

TEXT 9b

RABBI AVRAHAM BEN DAVID, AD LOC.

שֶׁאִלּוּ מִן הַפָּסוּק הָרִאשׁוֹן לֹא שָׁמַעְנוּ אֶלָּא כָּמוֹךָ. הֲרֵי שֶׁנִּתְבַּזָּה הוּא, אוֹ נִתְקַלֵּל הוּא, וְנִגְזַל, וְנֶחְבָּל, יִתְבַּזֶּה חֲבֵרוֹ עִמּוֹ, וְיִתְקַלֵּל עִמּוֹ, וְיֵחָבֵל עִמּוֹ. לְכָךְ נֶאֱמַר, "בִּדְמוּת אֱלֹקִים עָשָׂה אוֹתוֹ" (בְּרֵאשִׁית ה, א). אֶת מִי אַתָּה מְבַזֶּה, וְאֶת מִי אַתָּה מְקַלֵּל? דְמוּת דְיוֹקָנוֹ שֶׁל מָקוֹם. זֶה הַכְּלַל גָּדוֹל מִן הָרִאשׁוֹן.

From the first verse, we only learn to love another "like yourself." Thus, a person who had been shamed, cursed, victimized by theft, or beaten might think that it is permissible to allow a friend to be similarly shamed, cursed, or beaten. Therefore, the Torah says, "In the likeness of G-d He created him"—as if to say: Who are you shaming? Who are you cursing? The image of G-d! Thus, this verse is a greater principle than the first.

RABBI AVRAHAM BEN DAVID (RAAVAD III), C. 1125–1198

Mystic and author. Rabbi Avraham served as rabbi of Posquieres (today Vauvert) in Provence. He is most famous for his critical notes on Rambam's *Mishneh Torah;* he also wrote commentaries on the Talmud, *Sifra,* and Rif and authored *Baalei Hanefesh,* a compilation of laws relating to Jewish family law. Raavad was wealthy and served as a patron for the charity institutions in Posquieres.

TEXT 10

LEVITICUS 19:15

> לֹא תַעֲשׂוּ עָוֶל בַּמִּשְׁפָּט, לֹא תִשָּׂא פְנֵי דָל, וְלֹא תֶהְדַּר פְּנֵי גָדוֹל. בְּצֶדֶק תִּשְׁפֹּט עֲמִיתֶךָ.

Do not pervert justice: Do not show partiality to the poor or favoritism to the great. Judge your neighbor fairly.

Professor Ari Goldman *discusses Jewish contributions to the field of journalism:*

MYJLI.COM/GIFTS

TEXT 11

JERUSALEM TALMUD, TERUMOT 8:4

> סִיעוֹת בְּנֵי אָדָם שֶׁהָיוּ מְהַלְּכִין בַּדֶּרֶךְ, פָּגְעוּ לָהֶן גוֹיִם וְאָמְרוּ: תְּנוּ לָנוּ אֶחָד מִכֶּם וְנַהֲרוֹג אוֹתוֹ, וְאִם לַאו, הֲרֵי אָנוּ הוֹרְגִים אֶת כּוּלְּכֶם - אֲפִילוּ כּוּלָּן נֶהֱרָגִים לֹא יִמְסְרוּ נֶפֶשׁ אַחַת מִיִּשְׂרָאֵל.

If a traveling group is confronted by non-Jews who say, “Give us one of your number so that we can kill him, and if not, we will kill all of you”—even if they are all going to be killed, they should not hand over a single soul.

JERUSALEM TALMUD

A commentary to the Mishnah, compiled during the 4th and 5th centuries. The Jerusalem Talmud predates its Babylonian counterpart by 100 years and is written in both Hebrew and Aramaic. While the Babylonian Talmud is the most authoritative source for Jewish law, the Jerusalem Talmud remains an invaluable source for the spiritual, intellectual, ethical, historical, and legal traditions of Judaism.

TEXT 12

TALMUD, BAVA BATRA 21A

בְּרַם זָכוּר אוֹתוֹ הָאִישׁ לַטוֹב וִיהוֹשֻׁעַ בֶּן גַמְלָא שְׁמוֹ, שֶׁאִלְמָלֵא הוּא נִשְׁתַּכַּח תּוֹרָה מִיִשְׂרָאֵל.

שֶׁבַּתְּחִלָּה, מִי שֶׁיֵשׁ לוֹ אָב - מְלַמְדוֹ תּוֹרָה, מִי שֶׁאֵין לוֹ אָב - לֹא הָיָה לָמֵד תּוֹרָה . . . עַד שֶׁבָּא יְהוֹשֻׁעַ בֶּן גַמְלָא וְתִיקֵן, שֶׁיְהוּ מוֹשִׁיבִין מְלַמְדֵי תִּינוֹקוֹת בְּכָל מְדִינָה וּמְדִינָה וּבְכָל עִיר וָעִיר. וּמַכְנִיסִין אוֹתָן כְּבֶן שֵׁשׁ, כְּבֶן שֶׁבַע.

Rabbi Lord Jonathan Sacks *addresses the U.K. House of Lords on education:*

MYJLI.COM/GIFTS

Yehoshua ben Gamla is remembered favorably. Because if not for him, the Torah would have been forgotten.

Initially, fathers would teach their children Torah, but orphans had no one to teach them. . . . This continued until Yehoshua ben Gamla instituted that teachers be installed in every province and town. Children were admitted into school at the age of six or seven.

Jewish Children with their teacher in Samarkand. Photo by Sergei Mikhailovich Prokudin-Gorskii, Russia, c. 1905–1915. (Library of Congress, Washington, D.C.)

TEXT 13

CECIL ROTH, *THE JEWISH CONTRIBUTION TO CIVILIZATION* (NEW YORK: HARPER & BROTHERS PUBLISHERS, 1940), P. 43

Education was considered a religious duty. Illiteracy was almost unknown among the Jews and even the illiterate had the profoundest respect for learning. A universal system of education had existed in Palestine since the first or second century BCE, and Josephus had explicitly avowed, "Our principal care of all is this: to educate our children well." That early ideal was never lost sight of. Hence in the Ghetto period there existed, in the smallest Jewish community, an education system of a breadth and universality of which the modern State in Europe or America has even now barely equaled and certainly not surpassed.

CECIL ROTH
1899–1970

British Jewish historian. Dr. Roth was a professor of Jewish Studies at Oxford University and later served as visiting professor at Bar-Ilan University in Israel and at the City University of New York. A prolific author, he wrote more than 600 historical works on Jewish topics, such as the Dead Sea Scrolls, and Jewish art. Roth served as editor of the *Encyclopedia Judaica* from 1965 until his passing.

JOSEPHUS
C. 37–100

Jewish historian. Born Yosef ben Matityahu Hakohen, he changed his name to Titus Flavius Josephus upon becoming a Roman citizen. His two principal works, *The Jewish War* and *Antiquities of the Jews,* are considered primary sources in documenting Jewish history during the Second Temple period. Despite surrendering his garrison to the Romans during the great revolt and later accepting Roman patronage, Josephus viewed himself as a faithful Jew.

TEXT 14

EPHRAIM KANARFOGEL, *JEWISH EDUCATION AND SOCIETY IN THE HIGH MIDDLE AGES* (DETROIT, MI.: WAYNE STATE UNIVERSITY PRESS, 2008), P. 16

Christian scholars were aware of the heightened commitment of Jewish parents to the education of their children and of the spiritual motivation behind that commitment.

A student of Peter Abelard writes, "If the Christians educate their sons, they do so not for G-d, but for gain in order that the one brother, if he be a clerk, may help his father and mother, and his other brothers. They say that a clerk will have no heir and whatever he has will be ours and the other brothers'. . . . But the Jews, out of zeal for G-d and love of the law, put as many sons as they have to letters, that each may understand G-d's law. . . . A Jew, however poor, if he had ten sons would put them all to letters, not for gain, as the Christians do, but for the understanding of G-d's law, and not only his sons but his daughters."

EPHRAIM KANARFOGEL

Historian. Rabbi Kanarfogel is a professor and dean at Yeshiva University and one of the foremost scholars of medieval Jewish history and rabbinic literature. He has authored 4 books and edited another. He has also published more than 50 articles and reviews.

PETER ABELARD
1079–1142

Philosopher, theologian, and poet. During his early academic pursuits, Abelard wandered throughout France, eventually settling in Paris. After studying at the cathedral school of Notre-Dame de Paris, Abelard established his own school in Melun, a nearby suburb.

The intellectual life of medieval Jews, as seen through Hebrew illuminated manuscripts and decorated printed books, by ***Professor Ephraim Kanarfogel:***

MYJLI.COM/GIFTS

TEXT 15

YECHIEL J. M. LEITER, *JOHN LOCKE'S POLITICAL PHILOSOPHY AND THE HEBREW BIBLE* (CAMBRIDGE, NEW YORK: CAMBRIDGE UNIVERSITY PRESS, 2018), PP. 177–183

Locke begins his Second Treatise discussion on the state of nature by declaring that humans are naturally in a state "of equality, wherein all the power and jurisdiction is reciprocal, no one having more than another." . . .

What sort of equality is Locke advancing? Is it an equality that rests on a theological or completely secular substructure? . . .

Equality for Locke is indeed inseparable from theology. . . . [Locke] explains why equality is the natural state of humankind: "For men being all the workmanship of one Omnipotent and infinitely wise Maker; all servants of the one Sovereign Master, sent into the world by his order . . . and being furnished with like faculties, sharing all in the community of nature, there cannot be supposed any such subordination among us, that may authorize us to destroy one another, as if we were made for one another's uses, as the inferior ranks of creatures are for ours." . . .

Locke's choice to establish his theory of innate human equality on the Hebrew Bible's account of creation is a telling elective move insofar as he did not include

YECHIEL J. M. LEITER

Philosopher. Dr. Leiter holds a PhD in political philosophy. He taught political theory at the Law School of Kiryat Ono Academic College and is a resident scholar at Jerusalem's Herzl Institute. Leiter, who is also a rabbi, wrote two books on political theory and numerous essays on Israeli politics.

any Christian Scripture. . . . In it, he found a human equality that is innate in its divine ordination, and hence fundamentally unconditional and unalterable.

Stamps by Mishmeres Khoylim (Watch of the Sick) in Vilna, Yiddish inscription reads "Mishmeres Khoylim gives the poor man a doctor at home, ice, medicine, and clinics for help". (YIVO Institute for Jewish Research, New York)

TEXT 16

TALMUD, SOTAH 14A

מַה הוּא מַלְבִּישׁ עֲרוּמִּים, דִכְתִיב: "וַיַעַשׂ ה' אֱלֹקִים לְאָדָם וּלְאִשְׁתּוֹ כָּתְנוֹת עוֹר וַיַלְבִּישֵׁם" (בְּרֵאשִׁית ג, כא), אַף אַתָּה הַלְבֵּשׁ עֲרוּמִּים. הַקָדוֹשׁ בָּרוּךְ הוּא בִּיקֵר חוֹלִים, דִכְתִיב: "וַיֵרָא אֵלָיו ה' בְּאֵלוֹנֵי מַמְרֵא" (בְּרֵאשִׁית יח, א), אַף אַתָּה בַּקֵר חוֹלִים. הַקָדוֹשׁ בָּרוּךְ הוּא נִיחֵם אֲבֵלִים, דִכְתִיב: "וַיְהִי אַחֲרֵי מוֹת אַבְרָהָם וַיְבָרֶךְ אֱלֹקִים אֶת יִצְחָק בְּנוֹ" (בְּרֵאשִׁית כה, יא), אַף אַתָּה נַחֵם אֲבֵלִים. הַקָדוֹשׁ בָּרוּךְ הוּא קָבַר מֵתִים, דִכְתִיב: "וַיִקְבֹּר אוֹתוֹ בַגַיא" (דְבָרִים לד, ו), אַף אַתָּה קְבוֹר מֵתִים.

As G-d clothes the naked—as it is written, "And G-d made garments of skin for Adam and his wife, and He clothed them" (GENESIS 3:21)—so should you dress the naked. As G-d visited the ill—as it is written, "And G-d appeared to Abraham in the planes of Mamre" (GENESIS 18:1)—so should you visit the ill. As G-d comforted the mourners—as it is written, "And it was after the passing of Abraham, and G-d blessed his son Isaac" (GENESIS 25:11)—so should you comfort the mourners. As G-d buried the dead—as it is written, "And G-d buried Moses in the valley" (DEUTERONOMY 34:6)—so should you bury the dead.

KEY POINTS

1 Modern society regards equality as a bedrock value. The ancients rejected this concept, truly believing that some people were born to rule and others were born to be ruled.

2 Discriminatory ideas lead to discriminatory practices. For the ancients, this translated into abuse of the lower classes, inequality before the law, dismissal of individual rights, and mass illiteracy.

3 The Torah teaches that every person was created in the divine image. This translates into two teachings: (a) we are all equal, and (b) no one is redundant.

4 As a consequence of this teaching, Jewish law (a) prohibits abuse and mandates (b) equality before the law, (c) protection of individual rights, and (d) education for all.

5 A number of eighteenth-century philosophers who taught that all people are created equal were influenced by the Torah.

6 That we are all created in the divine image means that we are all equally created for a purpose. We must teach ourselves and those around us to embrace our G-d-given individuality and equality in the context of our responsibilities.

Appendix

TEXT 17

PETER GARNSEY, *LEGAL PRIVILEGE IN THE ROMAN EMPIRE: STUDIES IN ANCIENT SOCIETY* (LONDON: ROUTLEDGE, 1976), PP. 153–154

The "dual-penalty system" . . . recognized the distinction between "legal" and "non-legal" penalties. In practice, each group of penalties was aligned with a broad social category, such that members of the upper classes, or *honestiores*, suffered only penalties drawn from the first group, and members of the lower classes, only penalties from the second group. "Deportation" and "relegation," two forms of exile, were standard penalties in the first group. The former deprived the condemned of citizenship but not freedom, and the latter of neither. Execution, which was rare for the *honestiores*, was by decapitation. . . . The most serious "lower class penalty" is called by the jurists *summum supplicium* ("the highest punishment"). The term stood for aggravated forms of the death penalty including exposure to wild animals, crucifixion, and death by fire. Next, condemnation to hard labor in the mines was for life, and the condemned was reduced to a status akin to slavery. Condemnation to live and fight as a gladiator was just as degrading and carried a higher risk of death. . . . Corporal punishment

PETER GARNSEY

Historian. Garnsey is an emeritus professor of the history of classical antiquities at Cambridge University. His research interests include the history of political theory, intellectual history, social and economic history, and physical anthropology.

was also reserved for *humiliores*. Torture was, by tradition, only applied to slaves. . . . As for the treatment of accused men before trial, *honestiores* could generally avoid imprisonment.

TEXT 18

JAMES GEORGE FRAZER, *ILLUSTRATED GOLDEN BOUGH: A STUDY OF MAGIC AND RELIGION* (NEW YORK: SIMON & SCHUSTER, 1996), PP. 150–151

The Athenians regularly maintained a number of degraded and useless beings at the public expense, and when calamity such as plague, drought, or famine befell the city, they sacrificed two of these outcast scapegoats . . . by being stoned to death.

JAMES GEORGE FRAZER
1854–1941

Anthropologist. Frazer taught at Cambridge University and was influential in the modern studies of mythology and comparative religion. He wrote many books, including *The Golden Bough*, which documents similarities between magical and religious beliefs around the world.

Figure 4.2

All Others

Receive every person with a pleasant countenance. (*Ethics of the Fathers* 1:15)	וֶהֱוֵי מְקַבֵּל אֶת כָּל הָאָדָם בְּסֵבֶר פָּנִים יָפוֹת. (אָבוֹת א, טו)
Receive every person with joy. (ibid., 3:12)	וֶהֱוֵי מְקַבֵּל אֶת כָּל הָאָדָם בְּשִׂמְחָה. (אָבוֹת ג, יב)
Who is wise? The one who learns from every person. (ibid., 4:1)	אֵיזֶהוּ חָכָם? הַלּוֹמֵד מִכָּל אָדָם. (אָבוֹת ד, א)
Do not scorn any person. (ibid., 4:3)	אַל תְּהִי בָז לְכָל אָדָם. (אָבוֹת ד, ג)
Be humble before every person. (ibid., 4:10)	וֶהֱוֵי שְׁפַל רוּחַ בִּפְנֵי כָל אָדָם. (אָבוֹת ד, י)
Be first to greet every person. (ibid., 4:15)	הֱוֵי מַקְדִּים בִּשְׁלוֹם כָּל אָדָם. (אָבוֹת ד, טו)

TEXT 19

MAIMONIDES, *MISHNEH TORAH,* LAWS OF THE SANHEDRIN 2:5

מַלְכֵי בֵּית דָוִד - אַף עַל פִּי שֶׁאֵין מוֹשִׁיבִין אוֹתָם בְּסַנְהֶדְרִין, יוֹשְׁבִין וְדָנִים הֵם אֶת הָעָם, וְדָנִים אוֹתָם אִם יֵשׁ עֲלֵיהֶן דִּין.

Although the kings of the House of David may not be included in the Sanhedrin, they may sit in judgment over the people. Conversely, they may be called to judgment if a person has a complaint against them.

RABBI MOSHE BEN MAIMON (MAIMONIDES, RAMBAM), 1135–1204

Halachist, philosopher, author, and physician. Maimonides was born in Córdoba, Spain. After the conquest of Córdoba by the Almohads, he fled Spain and eventually settled in Cairo, Egypt. There, he became the leader of the Jewish community and served as court physician to the vizier of Egypt. He is most noted for authoring the *Mishneh Torah,* an encyclopedic arrangement of Jewish law, and for his philosophical work, *Guide for the Perplexed*. His rulings on Jewish law are integral to the formation of halachic consensus.

TEXT 20

CECIL ROTH, *THE JEWISH CONTRIBUTION TO CIVILIZATION*, P. 14

Prophet after prophet dared to admonish the ruler for his breach of the fundamental laws, for his callousness to human misery, for his oppression to the poor. It is remarkable that in almost all cases the prophet's reproof was heard with forbearance, as though to acknowledge his right to criticize and the essential justice of his claim.

A remarkable phrase occurs in the description of the king's prerogatives in the Pentateuch (DEUTERONOMY 27:20) which sums up the Hebraic idea of the monarchy: "that his heart be not lifted up *above his brethren*."

Additional Readings

DID HUMAN RIGHTS BEGIN WITH TORAH?

BY JOSHUA BERMAN

Question:

My son came home from school with papers from a unit on the origins of democracy and human rights. Everything is traced to thinkers such as John Locke, and then a big jump back to the Stoics and Athens. Where do we Jews fit into this picture?

Response:

The Torah is the birthplace of modern ideas of equality. In fact, in its time, the Torah was a revolutionary book of political thought.

Throughout the ancient world, the truth was self-evident: all men are not created equal. You were what you were born: a king, a noble, or a serf. An orderly society was one in which people knew their place. As Aristotle put it in (supposedly) democratic Athens, justice meant that "equals should be treated as equals and unequals as unequals."

It's fascinating to see how the stories of the Torah, and even more so its laws, systematically reworked those of ancient norms and institutions, creating a society that discouraged hierarchy and stratification and empowered and ennobled the citizenry.

Take the Torah's economic laws, for example. Elsewhere, land was owned by the king and by the temples, while the common folk worked as serfs or as slaves. But in the Torah, G-d—who officially owns the land—gives it over to the Israelites. Every common Israelite is a land owner (Leviticus 25), which means that every Israelite has a source of income—history's first example of universal private ownership of land by the citizens.

Or take the issue of debt relief. In other cultures, a king would cancel debts in his first year of reign, precisely when he needed a boost of political capital, at once endearing him to the masses, and at the same time weakening the rich lenders, the group most in position to challenge him. Debt cancellation of this sort is actually the original Greek meaning of our modern day English words amnesty and philanthropy. The Greek historian Plutarch writes that when the Spartan ruler Agis sought to impose debt relief, the measure was considered by his detractors as nothing more than a Robin-Hood scheme: "By offering to the poor the property of the rich, and by distribution of land and remission of debts, he [bought] a large bodyguard for himself, not many citizens for Sparta."

Agis was simply following the standard practice of rulers in antiquity. Against that backdrop, consider the debt-relief program prescribed by Torah: in the Torah, debt-cancellation is enacted automatically every seven years. No longer the political tool of a new monarch, debt relief in the Bible becomes the legislated right of the common citizen (Deuteronomy 15).

The Torah revolutionized taxation as well. Elsewhere, taxes, or tithes, were levied to support the palace and the temples. But the Torah introduces a new type of tax; a tax that productive farmers pay to support the less-well-off: history's first redistributive tax for a social purpose (Deuteronomy 14).

But perhaps nothing was as radical as the Bible's notion of political office. A bit of constitutional history: think of the British parliamentary system. There's a House of Lords and a House of Commons. The thinking was to divide legislative power so that the two houses could balance each other. But what is

JOSHUA BERMAN

Joshua Berman received his rabbinical ordination from Israel's Chief Rabbinate and is a Bible professor at Bar-Ilan University. Among his books are *The Temple: Its Symbolism and Meaning Then and Now* and *Created Equal: How the Bible Broke with Ancient Political Thought.*

shocking to American sensitivities is that the British understood that the best way to achieve this balance was by taking advantage of existing class distinctions, and actually enshrining them, by dividing political power along those very same lines.

The history of mixed governments, where several bodies share power, is very old. But throughout history the concept was always the same: identify the competing classes within society and assign each a little bit of the power. Only with the American Founding Fathers do we eventually find a new notion of political office, in which a political office exists without reference to class, and which any citizen is eligible to hold.

This revolutionary notion of political office has only one precursor: the Torah. Any citizen can be chosen to be a judge (Deuteronomy 16). In fact, the Torah doesn't speak about the process of choosing judges, other than that the people (the collective "you") must choose them from among themselves. That is even more significant when one considers that the monarch was beneath the law. The "elders" and "judges" we meet throughout the Bible—and later in the Mishnah—formed a veritable parliament for the people, of the people. In practice, many came from common homes and supported themselves with menial labor and crafts.

As for the monarch, the Torah specifies that the people will have a king over them, only if they initiate the idea (Deuteronomy 17:14; cf. 1 Samuel 8). Until David was chosen as king, any citizen could have been chosen (Deuteronomy 17). Even afterwards, the hereditary rights were predicated upon the king finding favor in the eyes of G-d and the eyes of the people. This is the halachah today as well: the future Davidic king will be deemed legitimate only if he is able to rally the people around him (Maimonides, Laws of Kings 11:4–5).

Moreover, the Bible does not specify anybody to choose the king. Again, as with the judges, it simply assigns this task to the collective "you" of the whole of Israel; the citizenry as a whole is to be represented in the choice of its leaders. G-d must also give his approval of the candidate, via the prophet. Conceptually, however, the choice belonged to the people (as we see in the story of Samuel anointing Saul).

The egalitarian revolution is also seen with regard to the Bible's view of technologies of communication. We understand how critical computer literacy is to leveling the playing field of knowledge and power and are thankful that we live in a culture that seeks to encourage it. And we understand why the world's darkest dictatorships do little to encourage such literacy: To educate the masses in computer literacy is to empower them.

The Torah entered the world a few years before the internet, but it took advantage in an extraordinary way of an equally potent technology of communication: the alphabet. Elsewhere, writing systems, such as hieroglyphics in Egypt, were extremely cumbersome, and took years to master. But the scribes that did were guaranteed a good life, because of the special skills they possessed. In fact, an ancient Egyptian poem describes a father's urgings to his son that he attend scribal school, and how it will guarantee him a place in the upper class. "You'll love scribal school more than your own mother," the father promises.

The Torah, however, was written using the alphabet—which anyone can learn—and is the first text in the ancient world to suggest that it be copied and disseminated to the masses (Exodus 24 and Deuteronomy 31). The Torah was unafraid of the Israelites achieving literacy, because it sought to create an ennobled and empowered citizenry. For more on the revolution of the alphabet, see "The Twitter Revolution."

There can be no question that the obligation to instruct children in the commandments and teachings of the Torah (Deuteronomy 6:7) was greatly facilitated by the fact that the Torah was written in an easily learned script. The Bible was the first document ever written for public consumption in an alphabetic script.

Perhaps nowhere did the Torah revolutionize the standing of the common person, as it did with regard to the standing of women. In the narrative literature of the ancient Near East, we find that women fill only two roles: they either satisfy men's desires, or they tempt them. It is in the Torah that we first encounter women like Sarah, Rebecca, Miriam and Yocheved who are noted for their industriousness, insight, courage, and spiritual acuity. For the first time in the history of western literature women are people too.

But what about slavery? It is true that the Torah does use the term *eved ivri*, but this is mistakenly translated as "Hebrew slave." The word *eved* in the Bible can be used to describe the service of a highly placed minister to his king, or even of Moses' service to the Almighty. The relationship laid out by the Torah called *eved ivri*, is a method of helping the indebted work their way out of insolvency under favorable terms, that allow them to get back on their feet again—without a permanent blemish to their credit rating. Concerning the non-Jewish slave, see "Torah, Slavery and the Jews."

It is true that only the sons of Aaron could become *kohanim*. Yet, here, too, we can see how the Torah revolutionized what it meant to be a "priest." Priesthood in the ancient Near East brought with it privileges that rendered priests an empowered elite. In Torah, however, priests are neither an economic nor political class. They had no special rights before the law or political power.

The Torah worked to make sure that priests served the people, and not the other way around. Elsewhere, priests were real-estate magnates who controlled all the state property (see Genesis 48). In the Torah, the *kohanim* are expressly forbidden to hold income producing lands. Elsewhere, the laws of the cult were strictly guarded, and commoners were forbidden from entering the central shrine. The Torah publicizes all the laws of the Temple, and common people play a vital and constant role in the Temple rituals. Elsewhere, priests are depicted as beyond reproach. The Torah underscores the humanity and fallibility of the priests. Virtually the only stories we possess about the *kohanim* are the account of how Aaron built the golden calf (Exodus 32) and how his sons, Nadab and Abihu, overstepped their bounds in the Tabernacle (Leviticus 10)—not exactly stories meant to glorify.

It should come as no surprise then, that the Bible in its entirety knows no word for "noble," and no word for "class," and stands without precedent as the birthplace of egalitarian thought.

THE INFLUENCE OF THE HEBREW COMMONWEALTH UPON THE ORIGIN OF REPUBLICAN GOVERNMENT IN THE UNITED STATES

BY OSCAR SOLOMON STRAUS

It is remarkable, that of the many historians who have written so ably and minutely of the history of the United States, none should have observed in their writings the relationship between our republic and the commonwealth of the Hebrews, especially in the light of the earliest constitutions of several of the New England colonies expressly framed upon the model of the Mosaic code as a guide, and of the frequent references thereto made by the ministers in their political sermons, who constantly drew their civil creed from the history of those times, and held up this ancient form of government as a model inspired under the guidance of the Most High. . . .

A volume would not contain all the politico-theological discourses delivered during the decade prior to the restoration of peace, wherein the Hebrew Commonwealth was held up as a model, and its history as a guide for the American people in their mighty struggle for the blessings of civil and religious liberty. I have purposely only quoted such of these discourses as were delivered by ministers who were eminent not only in the pulpit, but were equally distinguished as scholars, as patriots, and as legislators.

Thus far the Hebrew Commonwealth has been referred to as the model and guide adopted in the sermons and discourses of our patriotic divines; we shall now trace it in the halls of legislation, and in the writings and political pamphlets published during the period prior to the adoption of the Constitution. We must not lose sight of the fact that neither the Declaration of Independence nor the success of our armies in the struggle decided for us our form of government, or secured for posterity the blessings of civil and religious liberty, the former only served to make the latter possible. These were the victories of the statesmen, heroes and the patriots of the pen. The machinery of government under the articles of confederation was so defective, weak, and ineffectual that men, wise men, true and loyal Americans, aye, many in the army, by reason of the inability of the government to pay the half-starved soldiers, demanded a government that would revive from prostration the public credit and faith of the nation, that would provide for the payment of interest on the public debt; they felt the need of a government with a strong arm, an elective monarchy. "Now, just as day was dawning and independence about to be secured, every thing seems to tumble in chaos about them, threatening a state of things worse than their former condition as colonists."[1]

A paper embodying the views of the army of Washington while stationed about Newburg was drawn up and presented to their commander-in-chief by Colonel Nicola, an old army officer, held in high esteem by Washington. This, after describing the perilous state of feeling in the army and the dangerous aspect of affairs, and showing the necessity, now that peace was assured, of settling at once on a form of government which should be a strong one, took up the several forms of government in the world, and summed up by declaring that a republican government was the most unstable and insecure, and a constitutional monarchy like that of England, the strongest and safest, and, in short, offered to make Washington dictator. It concluded by saying: "Owing to the prejudices of the people it might not at first be prudent to assume the title of Royalty, but if all other things were adjusted, we believe strong arguments might be produced for admitting the title of King." Like Gideon, the righteous judge of the Hebrew Commonwealth, whom the people of Israel offered to make king in their unbounded gratitude, and in admiration of his signal service in

OSCAR SOLOMON STRAUS, 1850–1926

Politician. Straus was United States secretary of commerce and labor under President Theodore Roosevelt from 1906–1909. He was the first Jewish United States cabinet secretary, and also served as the United States minister to the Ottoman Empire.

delivering them from the hands of their most powerful enemies, Washington declined the crown.

This monarchical-party spirit was so strong, that it survived even after the adoption of the Constitution until the election of Jefferson as President, who refers to it in his inaugural address.[2] No one arraigned the monarchical tendencies with a more vigorous and fearless pen; no one contributed more in keeping alive the fires of liberty during those times that tried men's souls, than Thomas Paine, that much maligned and abused man, who has been accused of every crime that malice could invent. This man, the friend of Franklin, through whose patronage he came to America, the editor of the *Pennsylvania Magazine*, the Secretary of the Committee of Foreign Affairs of the Continental Congress, beloved and esteemed by Washington, by whom he was invited, when in distressed circumstances, to share the hospitalities of his home, to whom James Monroe, in 1794, then Minister to Great Britain, wrote, while Paine was confined in the Luxemburg as prisoner, by the order of Robespierre, for espousing the cause of liberty in France, as follows: "You are considered by them (the people of the United States) as not only having rendered important services in our own revolution, but as being on a more extensive scale the friend of human rights, and a distinguished and able advocate in favor of public liberty. To the welfare of Thomas Paine the Americans are not, nor can they be, indifferent." Washington says of the author of "Common Sense," in a letter to Joseph Reed, dated January 31, 1776: "A few more of such flaming arguments as were exhibited at Falmouth and Norfolk, added to the sound doctrine and unanswerable reason contained in the pamphlet 'Common Sense,' will not leave numbers at a loss to decide on the propriety of separation." "This book" ("Common Sense"), says Dr. Rush, "burst forth from the press with an effect that has been rarely produced by types and paper in any age or country." The former part of this remarkable production is devoted to the subject of "Monarchy and Hereditary Succession." The argument is drawn entirely from the Hebrew Commonwealth. "Monarchy is ranked in Scripture," says he, "as one of the sins of the Jews, for which a curse in reserve is denounced against them." "All anti-monarchical parts of Scripture, have been very smoothly glossed over in monarchical governments, but they undoubtedly merit the attention of countries which have their governments yet to form." And then he recites the history of the entire "transaction," to the introduction of Saul as King. "But where, say some," are his words, "is the king of America? I'll tell you, friend: he reigns above, and doth not make havoc of mankind like the royal brute of Britain. Yet that we may not appear to be defective even in earthly honors, let a day be set apart for proclaiming the charter; let it be brought forth placed on the divine law, the word of G-d; let a crown be placed thereon, by which the world may know that, so far as we approve of monarchy, in America the law is king."

He narrates the conduct of that truly great judge of Israel, who was summoned by the voice of the people from the wheat field to assume the chief magistracy of the nation, and to deliver his people from their strongest and most powerful foes, the Midianites. These are his words, in the second chapter of "Common Sense": "The Jews, elated with success, and attributing it to the generalship of Gideon, proposed making him king, saying: 'Rule thou over us, thou and thy son and thy son's son.' Here was temptation in its fullest extent; but Gideon, in the piety of his soul, replied: 'I will not rule over you, neither shall my son rule over you; the L-rd shall rule over you.' Gideon doth not decline the honor, but denieth the right to give it." Paine then continues the scriptural narrative concerning the people demanding the king, about one hundred years after this period, under Samuel, and quoting in full Samuel's admonitions, concludes in these words: "These portions of the Scripture are direct and positive; they admit of no equivocal construction. That the Almighty hath here entered his protest against monarchical government is true, or the Scriptures are false."

Unfortunately, we have in most instances only skeleton reports of proceedings and debates of the Federal and State conventions on the adoption of the Constitution. Doubtless the model of the ancient commonwealth, its history and lessons, were frequently employed by the distinguished representatives; the meagreness of the records leaves this to conjecture only. In the Legislatures of the various States before whom the Constitution came for adoption, the delegates again and again referred to this original model of popular government. In New York, for instance, Robert R. Livingston, the Chancellor of the State, refers to it;[3] so also John Lansing,[4] who, in his speech urging its adoption, says: "Sir, the instances from the history of the Jewish Theocracy evince that there are certain situations in communities which will unavoidably lead to results similar to those we experience. The Israelites were unsuccessful in war; they were sometimes defeated by their enemies. Instead of reflecting that these calamities were occasioned by their sins, they sought relief in the appointment of a king, in imitation of their neighbors." So also the Hon. Mr. John Smith,[5] who quotes in full the admonition of Samuel to the children of Israel, describing the manner in which a king would rule over them. In short, again and again, in and out of our halls of legislation, was the history of the Hebrew Commonwealth referred to, narrated, rehearsed, and analogies drawn therefrom by the advocates of a republican form of government in answer to those who favored monarchy, so that the admonitions of Samuel were as familiar to the people of America as the words of the L-rd's Prayer.

In the light of these facts it is not at all surprising that the committee, which was appointed on the same day the Declaration of Independence was adopted, consisting of Dr. Franklin, Mr. Adams, and Mr. Jefferson, to prepare a device for a seal for the United States, should, as they did, have proposed as such device, Pharaoh sitting in an open chariot, a crown on his head and a sword in his hand, passing through the dividing waters of the Red Sea in pursuit of the Israelites; with rays from a pillar of fire beaming on Moses, who is represented as standing on the shore extending his hand over the sea, causes it to overwhelm Pharaoh; and underneath, the motto: "Rebellion to tyrants is obedience to G-d."[6]

Dr. David Tappan, who, after the declaration of peace, was chosen professor at Harvard College, in the course of his lectures on the "Jewish Antiquities," says that the demand of the children of Israel to Samuel, to set a king over them, was exceedingly displeasing to Samuel, and when he referred the matter to G-d, the Most High declared that by this act they had rejected him; that he should not reign over them. "From hence some writers have inferred that monarchy is in its very nature criminal; that it impiously invades the prerogative of the Supreme Ruler, as well as the equal rights of man." "This inference," says the learned professor, "was plausibly enforced on the American people, in the beginning of the year 1776, by a very popular but desultory writer (doubtless meaning Thomas Paine), and this sentiment, with others equally well timed, operated, with the swiftness and force of the electric fluid, in preparing the country for a formal separation from the British monarch."

Many more authorities might be adduced upon the same subject. Whether we conclude or not that the Republic of the United States is the direct heir of the Hebrew Commonwealth, we cannot fail to admit that the trials, sufferings, and fortitude of the children of Israel during their long and weary wanderings from the land of their oppressors until the organization of popular government on the banks of the Jordan, have served in no inconsiderable degree as a glorious example and inspiring incentive to the American people in their heroic struggle for the blessings of civil and religious liberty, and that the prophetic warning of the last Judge of Israel, followed by the corroborating revelations of history, furnish in themselves the argument that battered down the absurd doctrine of "Divine Right of Kings," and its enslaving corollaries, "Unlimited Submission" and "Non-Resistance." No one but He who rules the destiny of nations in all ages could have ordained that the bright sun of Canaan should rise again after ages with refulgent splendor over the vast continent of America, and that the pure and unselfish spirit of Moses, Joshua, and Samuel should live again in a Franklin, a Washington, and an Adams. May we, the people of America, who have learned so much by the example of this ancient commonwealth in its rise to glory and freedom, also profit by the lessons of its decline. The history of all nations, whether ancient or modern, teaches us that there is no government, however perfect, which is not subject to corruption and abuse of its functions, and that it is the highest duty of every citizen in a democratic government to guard against delegating political power to any men but those who will administer that power as a public trust.

Let those narrow-minded men who would corrupt the grand charter of our liberties by sectarian amendments, read the record of their country's birth, and from them learn that civil and religious liberty in spirit are inseparable, and when they strike down the one they destroy the other. Freedom of person, freedom of conscience, and honest government, constitute the creed of our political faith, and they alone can secure peace, liberty, and safety.

Endnotes

[1] See article in *Harper's Magazine,* Oct., 1883, by J. T. Headley.
[2] Jefferson writes as follows in the introduction to his "Anas": "The contests of that day were contests of principle between the advocates of republican and those of kingly government." See also letter of James Monroe (Dec., 1816) to Andrew Jackson, giving his recollections of the monarchical tendencies which were shown by certain leaders of the Federal party, both before and after the adoption of the Constitution. He says: "Many of the circumstances on which my opinion is founded, took place in debate and in society, and therefore find no place in any public document. I am satisfied, however, that sufficient proof exists, founded on facts and opinions of distinguished individuals, which became public, to justify that which I had formed. . . ."
[3] Elliot's Debates, Vol II., page 210.
[4] Elliot's Debates, Vol II., page 218.
[5] Elliot's Debates, Vol II., pages 225 and 226.
[6] A copy of the report recommending the above advice is preserved among the papers of the Continental Congress in the State Department in Washington.

Excerpted from *The Origin of Republican Form of Government in the United States of America* (New York: Putnam, 1887), ch. VII

THE JEWISH CONTRIBUTION TO CIVILIZATION
THE REVIVAL OF LEARNING

BY CECIL ROTH

The Renaissance, when it crossed the Alps from Italy to Germany, took on a different complexion. The serious, introspective Germanic spirit took into consideration various questions which the light-hearted Italians had preferred not to raise, or the answers to which they had taken for granted. The spirit of inquiry, which had been fostered by a re-examination of medieval science, was now applied to medieval religion. Literary criticism, developed in order to cope with the texts of classical literature, was applied to that of the Latin Bible. The new-found passion for going back to the sources was applied to the Catholic tradition, and the same spirit which had questioned authority in philosophy began to question it in matters of faith. The Renaissance, in fact, developed in its northern form into the Reformation. This in turn had its repercussions south of the Alps in the Catholic Reaction, or Counter-Reformation. In the end, the religious life of Europe, whether it titularly retained the old faith or embraced the new form, was revolutionized.

The Jews' part in bringing about the Reformation is frequently exaggerated, and generally misunderstood. The Reformation, like all Christian reform movements before and after, implied a return to the Scriptures. All agitators for reform necessarily went to the Bible for support, and occasionally approximated biblical practice in one matter or the other. It was hence natural that one of the commonest terms of ecclesiastical vituperation in the Middle Ages was "Judaizer"—an epithet which recurs in the controversial works of the period with wearisome frequency.

But in fact it was seldom justified. The Jew, as such, had no interest in the dispute, one way or the other. There was little for him to choose, theologically speaking, between the Reformed and Catholic forms of Christianity. Nor was there any material reason why he should prefer one to the other. It was true that Martin Luther, at the outset of his career, had referred to the Church's atrocious treatment of the Jews as an additional argument against it. Yet later he reversed his opinion, and inveighed against the Jews with a virulence which surpassed the worst precedent that the Middle Ages could provide. For many years to come, the treatment of the Jews by Catholic and Protestant Europe was much the same; and, if the latter subsequently changed its policy, this was due to economics and expediency rather than to abstract, disinterested toleration.

It is thus misleading to speak of a direct Jewish influence upon the Reformation.[1] Yet the influence of Jewish scholarship, and hence of individual Jewish scholars, was far from negligible. As has been pointed out, the Reformation was based upon the rejection of Catholic tradition in favor of the authority of the Bible and the removal from the latter of the glosses by means of which (as the Reformers claimed) the Church of the Middle Ages had attempted to maintain its ascendancy over religious thought. But the Bible was available to the Western World only in its official Catholic version, the Vulgate; it was the Jews alone who possessed the Hebrew original and the key to its interpretation. Hence, just as Italian savants applied to Greek scholars for guidance in their researches into Plato, so German theologians applied to Jewish Rabbis for assistance in understanding the Hebrew Scriptures. It was only a coincidence, perhaps, that the intellectual clash in Germany began with an attempt on the part of the Dominicans to suppress

CECIL ROTH, 1899–1970

British Jewish historian. Dr. Roth was a professor of Jewish Studies at Oxford University and later served as visiting professor at Bar-Ilan University in Israel, and at the City University of New York. A prolific author, he wrote more than 600 historical works on Jewish topics, such as the Dead Sea Scrolls, and Jewish art. Roth served as editor of the *Encyclopedia Judaica* from 1965 until his passing.

the Talmud, which was doughtily championed by Johannes von Reuchlin; yet it was symptomatic of the trend of events. All the great leaders of reform—Luther, Zwingli, Melanchthon, Tyndale, Servetus, and so on—studied Hebrew. Many of them, too, had Jewish scholars to teach them. Reuchlin, for example, had been instructed by Jacob Loans (physician to the Emperor Frederick III) in Germany and by Obadiah Sforno in Italy; these two savants have been reckoned, for that reason, among the fathers of the Protestant Reformation.

The newly aroused interest did not end with the Hebrew text of the Bible. In order to understand the Scriptures, it was necessary to have recourse to rabbinical literature, so as to discover what was the Jewish tradition on the subject. From this period dates the real beginning of Christian-Hebrew scholarship, the establishment of effective chairs of Hebrew at the principal European universities and the emergence of a class of Christian Hebraists of real ability, whose contributions to Jewish scholarship have sometimes been of the utmost value.

The recourse to Jewish tradition was fruitful and left a permanent mark. The writings of the great medieval Franco-Jewish biblical commentators, Solomon ben Isaac of Troyes (Rashi) and David Kimchi of Narbonne, were of the highest importance; for it was upon them that the new translations of the Bible, the foundation of the Reformation, depended. Luther, indeed, relied principally upon Nicholas de Lyra, the fourteenth-century Franciscan exegete, said to have been a Jew by birth. His critics indeed sneered at him on that account. Had Lyra not lyred, they said, Luther could never have danced. But Lyra himself depended to an overwhelming extent on the writings of Rashi, whose interpretations in many instances he simply adapted, giving them a Christian tinge. Subsequently, Lyra's writings were furnished with an important supplement (likewise used by Luther) by Paul de Santa Maria, Bishop of Burgos, who had formerly been Rabbi Solomon Levi and naturally derived to a great extent from Jewish sources. Kimchi's commentary was used in a large degree by successive generations of Christian exegetes, particularly in the preparation of the English "Authorized Version" of 1611. To such an extent was this so, that, it has been aptly said, though no Jews were tolerated in England at the time when this magnificent achievement was being produced, Rabbi David Kimchi was present at Westminster in spirit. Hence, just as Jewish collaborators assisted in the labor of translation of secular and scientific texts into Latin, which marked the beginning of the revival of learning, so the Hebraic spirit, Jewish learning, and individual Jewish scholars participated to a marked extent in its latest phase—the biblical research and reexamination of doctrine which accompanied the revival of religion.

Endnote

1 An exception is to be made only as regards the Marranos, or crypto-Jews of Spain and Portugal. Compulsorily converted to Catholicism, they could not be expected to appreciate its spirituality; yet in many cases they entirely lacked Jewish knowledge and loyalties. They were hence a particularly favorable soil for the Reform doctrine, and played an important part in its propagation in Flanders. Thus Marc Perez, the Calvinist leader at Antwerp in the middle of the sixteenth century, was of Jewish extraction, as were many others.

The Jewish Contribution to Civilization (New York, London: Harper & Brothers Publishers, 1940), pp. 71–75

Lesson 5

DROPPING OUT AND TUNING IN

HOW SHABBAT CHANGED THE WORLD AND TRANSFORMS OUR LIVES

Sabbath-Ruhe auf der Gasse (Sabbath Rest on the Alley), Moritz Daniel Oppenheim, oil on canvas, Germany, 1866. (The Jewish Museum, New York)

Originally, those who labored did so endlessly. The Torah introduced the concept of a day off, mandating all members of Jewish society to pause from work for a full day each week to focus on life's purpose, worship, and family. The ancient world ridiculed the Shabbat, but humanity has since recognized its tremendous benefits. The Jewish call to schedule time to focus on what is truly important is more critical now than ever.

TEXT 1

TALMUD, SHABBAT 10B

אָמַר לוֹ הַקָדוֹשׁ בָּרוּךְ הוּא לְמֹשֶׁה: מַתָּנָה טוֹבָה יֵשׁ לִי בְּבֵית גְנָזַי וְשַׁבָּת שְׁמָהּ וַאֲנִי מְבַקֵשׁ לִיתְּנָהּ לְיִשְׂרָאֵל, לֵךְ וְהוֹדִיעֵם.

G-d said to Moses, "I have a precious gift in My storehouse of hidden treasures. Shabbat is its name, and I desire to give it to the Jewish people; go and inform them."

BABYLONIAN TALMUD

A literary work of monumental proportions that draws upon the legal, spiritual, intellectual, ethical, and historical traditions of Judaism. The 37 tractates of the Babylonian Talmud contain the teachings of the Jewish sages from the period after the destruction of the 2nd Temple through the 5th century CE. It has served as the primary vehicle for the transmission of the Oral Law and the education of Jews over the centuries; it is the entry point for all subsequent legal, ethical, and theological Jewish scholarship.

Israëlieten houden Sabbat (The Children of Israel keep the Sabbath), Christoffel van Sichem (II), letterpress printing on paper, Amsterdam, c. 1645. (Rijksmuseum, Amsterdam)

QUESTION FOR DISCUSSION

Would you say that Shabbat is a gift in *your* life? In what way?

Please share if you are comfortable doing so.

TEXT 2

EXODUS 31:13

אֶת שַׁבְּתֹתַי תִּשְׁמֹרוּ, כִּי אוֹת הִוא בֵּינִי וּבֵינֵיכֶם לְדֹרֹתֵיכֶם לָדַעַת כִּי אֲנִי ה' מְקַדִּשְׁכֶם.

You shall guard My *Shabbatot* [Sabbaths], for it is a sign between Me and you throughout the ages so that you may know that it is I, G-d, Who sanctifies you.

Chief Rabbi Israel Meir Lau *discusses Shabbat observance in modern Israel:*

MYJLI.COM/GIFTS

TEXT 3

LOUIS H. FELDMAN, *JEW AND GENTILE IN THE ANCIENT WORLD* (PRINCETON, N.J.: PRINCETON UNIVERSITY PRESS, 1996), PP. 165–166

Seneca . . . derides the observance of the Sabbath as inexpedient because the Jews thus lose one-seventh of their lives in idleness and often, indeed, suffer loss through failure to act in times of urgency. The charge that the Jews are lazy (TACITUS, HISTORIES 5.4.3; JUVENAL 14.105–6) may have originated in this idleness on the seventh day. . . . Indeed Philo (DE SPECIALIBUS LEGIBUS 2.15.60) seems to be answering such a charge when he says, "On this day [the Sabbath] we are commanded to abstain from all work, not because the law inculcates slackness; on the contrary, it always inures men to endure hardship and incites them to labor."

LOUIS H. FELDMAN
1926–2017

Professor of classics and antiquities. Dr. Feldman's works include *Jew and Gentile in the Ancient World* and *Judaism and Hellenism Reconsidered.*

SENECA
C. 4 BCE–65 CE

Roman philosopher, statesman, orator, and tragedian. Seneca was Rome's leading intellectual figure in the mid-1st century CE.

PUBLIUS CORNELIUS TACITUS
C. 56–117

Senator and historian of the Roman Empire. His two major works are *The Annals* and *The Histories.*

JUVENAL
C. 1ST-2ND CENTURIES CE

Roman satirical poet, best known for his vitriolic writings on Roman society and its mores.

PHILO OF ALEXANDRIA
C. 15 BCE–50 CE

Jewish Hellenist philosopher. Philo attempted to synthesize Jewish thought with Greek philosophy.

TEXT 4

MIDRASH, *BEREISHIT RABAH* 39:8

בְּשָׁעָה שֶׁהָיָה אַבְרָהָם מְהַלֵּךְ בַּאֲרַם נַהֲרַיִם וּבַאֲרַם נָחוֹר, רָאָה אוֹתָן אוֹכְלִים וְשׁוֹתִים וּפוֹחֲזִים, אָמַר הַלְוַאי לֹא יְהֵא לִי חֵלֶק בָּאָרֶץ הַזֹּאת. וְכֵיוָן שֶׁהִגִּיעַ לְסֻלָּמָהּ שֶׁל צוֹר, רָאָה אוֹתָן עֲסוּקִין בְּנִכּוּשׁ בִּשְׁעַת הַנִּכּוּשׁ, בְּעִדּוּר בִּשְׁעַת הָעִדּוּר, אָמַר הַלְוַאי יְהֵא חֶלְקִי בָּאָרֶץ הַזֹּאת. אָמַר לוֹ הַקָּדוֹשׁ בָּרוּךְ הוּא (בְּרֵאשִׁית יב, ז): "לְזַרְעֲךָ אֶתֵּן אֶת הָאָרֶץ הַזֹּאת".

When Abraham was traveling through Aram Naharaim and Aram Nachor, he saw the inhabitants eating and drinking and reveling. "May I have no portion in this land," he exclaimed. But when he reached the cliffs of Tyre, he saw them busying themselves with weeding during the season for weeding, and hoeing during the season for hoeing. "If only my portion could be in this land," he exclaimed. Said G-d to him, "To your children, I shall give this land" (GENESIS 12:7).

BEREISHIT RABAH

An early rabbinic commentary on the Book of Genesis. This Midrash bears the name of Rabbi Oshiya Rabah (Rabbi Oshiya "the Great"), whose teaching opens this work. This Midrash provides textual exegeses and stories, expounds upon the biblical narrative, and develops and illustrates moral principles. Produced by the sages of the Talmud in the Land of Israel, its use of Aramaic closely resembles that of the Jerusalem Talmud. It was first printed in Constantinople in 1512 together with 4 other Midrashic works on the other 4 books of the Pentateuch.

TEXT 5

GENESIS 2:2–3

וַיְכַל אֱלֹקִים בַּיּוֹם הַשְּׁבִיעִי מְלַאכְתּוֹ אֲשֶׁר עָשָׂה . . . וַיְבָרֶךְ אֱלֹקִים אֶת יוֹם הַשְּׁבִיעִי וַיְקַדֵּשׁ אֹתוֹ, כִּי בוֹ שָׁבַת מִכָּל מְלַאכְתּוֹ אֲשֶׁר בָּרָא אֱלֹקִים לַעֲשׂוֹת.

On the seventh day, G-d completed His work that He had done. . . . And G-d blessed the seventh day and He sanctified it; for on it, He rested from all His work, which G-d created to make.

Every person experiences Shabbat differently. Hear from a panel of women on their unique experiences and relationships with this holy day:

MYJLI.COM/GIFTS

The Creation, from the *Sarajevo Haggadah*, Spain, 14th century. (National Museum of Bosnia and Herzegovina, Sarajevo)

TEXT 6

THE REBBE, RABBI MENACHEM MENDEL SCHNEERSON,
IGROT KODESH 27, P. 377, GLOSS

תַּכְלִית וּשְׁלֵימוּת הַטוֹב הוּא שֶׁהָאָדָם יַגִּיעַ . . . לְדַרְגַּת דוֹמֶה לְבוֹרְאוֹ . . . וְלָכֵן רָצָה הַקָּדוֹשׁ בָּרוּךְ הוּא שֶׁהָאָדָם יַשִּׂיג אֶת עִנְיָנָיו לֹא מִן הַמּוּכָן, כִּי אִם עַל יְדֵי עֲשִׂיָּה וַעֲבוֹדָה, בִּכְדֵי שֶׁיִּהְיֶה [לֹא רַק בִּשְׁלֵימוּתוֹ שֶׁל "מְקַבֵּל", שְׁלֵימוּת שֶׁל נִבְרָא, אֶלָּא גַם] "מַשְׁפִּיעַ" (מְהַוֶּוה), דוֹמֶה לְבוֹרֵא. (וְעַד שֶׁעַל יְדֵי זֶה יֵיעָשֶׂה (כִּלְשׁוֹן חֲכָמֵינוּ זִכְרוֹנָם לִבְרָכָה שַׁבָּת קיט, ב) "שׁוּתָּף לְהַקָּדוֹשׁ בָּרוּךְ הוּא בְּמַעֲשֵׂה בְּרֵאשִׁית", בְּכָל הַבְּרִיאָה).

The truest and ultimate definition of goodness is for a person to achieve . . . a state of being similar to the Creator. . . . This is why G-d wants people to meet their needs through toil and effort. G-d desires that we become more than recipient creatures; G-d desires that we become givers, akin to the Creator. Thereby, we become partners with G-d in all of creation.

RABBI MENACHEM MENDEL SCHNEERSON 1902–1994

The towering Jewish leader of the 20th century, known as "the Lubavitcher Rebbe," or simply as "the Rebbe." Born in southern Ukraine, the Rebbe escaped Nazi-occupied Europe, arriving in the U.S. in June 1941. The Rebbe inspired and guided the revival of traditional Judaism after the European devastation, impacting virtually every Jewish community the world over. The Rebbe often emphasized that the performance of just one additional good deed could usher in the era of Mashiach. The Rebbe's scholarly talks and writings have been printed in more than 200 volumes.

TEXT 7

RABBI LORD JONATHAN SACKS, *A LETTER IN THE SCROLL* (NEW YORK: FREE PRESS, 2009), P. 84

The concept of a covenantal bond between G-d and man is revolutionary and has no parallel in any other system of thought. . . . Only in Judaism do we encounter the proposition that, despite their utter disparity, G-d and man come together as "partners in the work of creation." I know of no other vision that confers on mankind so great a dignity and responsibility.

RABBI LORD JONATHAN SACKS
1948–

Former chief rabbi of the United Kingdom. Rabbi Sacks attended Cambridge University and received his doctorate from King's College, London. A prolific and influential author, his books include *Will We Have Jewish Grandchildren?* and *The Dignity of Difference.* He received the Jerusalem Prize in 1995 for his contributions to enhancing Jewish life in the Diaspora, was knighted and made a life peer in 2005, and became Baron Sacks of Aldridge in 2009.

Jewish Craftsmen and Tradesmen, illustration for *The Statute of Kalisz,* Arthur Szyk, Paris, 1927.

Exercise 5.1

In the left column, list some of the tasks that you performed in the past week out of mere necessity. In the right column, list tasks that you feel are truly important, in which you would have been—or were indeed—wise to have invested more time and effort this past week.

URGENT What I Did Out of Necessity	**IMPORTANT** Activities That Are Truly Important to Me

Exercise 5.2

The Ten Commandments appear twice in the Torah, once in the book of Exodus and once in the book of Deuteronomy. Underline the phrases of the Fourth Commandment—the commandment to observe Shabbat, found below—as it appears in Deuteronomy (the column on the right), which differ from, or add to, the text in Exodus.

A halachic crash course on the laws of Shabbat:

MYJLI.COM/GIFTS

EXODUS 20:8–11

זָכוֹר אֶת יוֹם הַשַּׁבָּת לְקַדְשׁוֹ.

שֵׁשֶׁת יָמִים תַּעֲבֹד וְעָשִׂיתָ כָּל מְלַאכְתֶּךָ.

וְיוֹם הַשְּׁבִיעִי שַׁבָּת לַה' אֱלֹקֶיךָ, לֹא תַעֲשֶׂה
כָל מְלָאכָה אַתָּה וּבִנְךָ וּבִתֶּךָ עַבְדְּךָ וַאֲמָתְךָ . . .

כִּי שֵׁשֶׁת יָמִים עָשָׂה ה' אֶת הַשָּׁמַיִם וְאֶת הָאָרֶץ אֶת הַיָּם וְאֶת כָּל
אֲשֶׁר בָּם וַיָּנַח בַּיּוֹם הַשְּׁבִיעִי, עַל כֵּן בֵּרַךְ ה' אֶת יוֹם הַשַּׁבָּת וַיְקַדְּשֵׁהוּ.

Remember the Shabbat day to sanctify it.

Six days you shall labor and perform all your work.

But the seventh day is a Shabbat to G-d, your G-d. You shall perform no work, neither you, your son, your daughter, nor your male or female servant. . . .

Because for six days, G-d made the heaven, the earth, the sea, and all that is in them, but He rested on Shabbat. G-d therefore blessed the day of Shabbat and made it holy.

DEUTERONOMY 5:12–15

שָׁמוֹר אֶת יוֹם הַשַּׁבָּת לְקַדְּשׁוֹ כַּאֲשֶׁר צִוְּךָ ה' אֱלֹקֶיךָ.

שֵׁשֶׁת יָמִים תַּעֲבֹד וְעָשִׂיתָ כָּל מְלַאכְתֶּךָ.

וְיוֹם הַשְּׁבִיעִי שַׁבָּת לַה' אֱלֹקֶיךָ, לֹא תַעֲשֶׂה
כָל מְלָאכָה אַתָּה וּבִנְךָ וּבִתֶּךָ וְעַבְדְּךָ וַאֲמָתֶךָ . . .

וְזָכַרְתָּ כִּי עֶבֶד הָיִיתָ בְּאֶרֶץ מִצְרַיִם וַיֹּצִאֲךָ ה' אֱלֹקֶיךָ מִשָּׁם בְּיָד
חֲזָקָה וּבִזְרֹעַ נְטוּיָה, עַל כֵּן צִוְּךָ ה' אֱלֹקֶיךָ לַעֲשׂוֹת אֶת יוֹם הַשַּׁבָּת.

Guard the Shabbat day to sanctify it, as G-d, your G-d, commanded you.

Six days you shall labor and perform all your work.

But the seventh day is a Shabbat to G-d, your G-d. You shall perform no work, neither you, your son, your daughter, nor your male or female servant. . . .

You shall remember that you were a slave in the land of Egypt and that G-d, your G-d, took you out from there with a strong hand and with an outstretched arm; therefore, G-d, your G-d, commanded you to observe the day of Shabbat.

Figure 5.1

Shabbat Food for Thought

G-D RESTED ON THE SEVENTH DAY OF CREATION	G-D REDEEMED OUR NATION FROM EGYPTIAN BONDAGE
G-d created the universe.	G-d engages with the universe. G-d suspended nature to liberate the Jewish people.
What purpose was the world created for?	What is my role as a Jew?

TEXT 8

KIDDUSH FOR FRIDAY EVENING

> בָּרוּךְ אַתָּה . . . אֲשֶׁר קִדְּשָׁנוּ בְּמִצְוֹתָיו וְרָצָה בָנוּ, וְשַׁבַּת קָדְשׁוֹ בְּאַהֲבָה וּבְרָצוֹן הִנְחִילָנוּ, זִכָּרוֹן לְמַעֲשֵׂה בְרֵאשִׁית. תְּחִלָּה לְמִקְרָאֵי קֹדֶשׁ, זֵכֶר לִיצִיאַת מִצְרָיִם . . .

Blessed are You . . . Who has sanctified us with His commandments and desired us, and He has given us, in love and goodwill, His holy Shabbat as an inheritance, in remembrance of the work of Creation. It is the first of the holy festivals, commemorating the Exodus from Egypt. . . .

***Tevi Troy** recounts his experiences of observing Shabbat while working in the White House:*

MYJLI.COM/GIFTS

TEXT 9

THE REBBE, RABBI MENACHEM MENDEL SCHNEERSON,
SICHOT KODESH 5734:1, PP. 329–331

> אֶחָד הָעִנְיָנִים שֶׁבָּהֶם תָּלוּי קִיּוּם שֶׁל עַם בִּכְלַל וְעַם בְּנֵי יִשְׂרָאֵל בִּמְיוּחָד - שֶׁלְּדַאֲבוֹנֵנוּ הוּזְנַח לְגַמְרֵי - הֲרֵי זֶה קִיּוּם הַמִּשְׁפָּחָה . . .
>
> מָצִינוּ בְּנוֹגֵעַ לְמִנְיַן בְּנֵי יִשְׂרָאֵל, שֶׁנּוֹסַף עַל הַזְכָּרַת הַמִּסְפָּר שֶׁל כָּל בְּנֵי יִשְׂרָאֵל - "שֵׁשׁ מֵאוֹת אֶלֶף וּשְׁלֹשֶׁת אֲלָפִים וַחֲמֵשׁ מֵאוֹת וַחֲמִשִּׁים (במדבר א, מו)", מַדְגִּישָׁה וְחוֹזֶרֶת זֹאת בְּכָל שֵׁבֶט בִּפְנֵי עַצְמוֹ, שֶׁאוֹפֶן הַמִּנְיָן הָיָה "לְמִשְׁפְּחוֹתָם לְבֵית אֲבוֹתָם", הַיְינוּ, שֶׁמָּנוּ אוֹתָם בְּתוֹר מִשְׁפָּחָה . . .
>
> וּבְכֵן: הַסִּיבָּה לְכָל הַ"קְשָׁיִים" שֶׁיֶּשְׁנָם בֵּין אָבוֹת וּבָנִים (כְּכָל הַשֵּׁמוֹת הַ"יָּפִים" אוֹ "אֵינָם יָפִים" . . . שֶׁנִּיתְּנוּ עַל זֶה בִּשְׂפַת הַמְּדִינָה) הִיא - בִּגְלַל שֶׁגַּם כַּאֲשֶׁר נָתְנוּ חִינּוּךְ טוֹב, חָסְרָה הַהַדְגָּשָׁה שֶׁ. . . נַעֲשֵׂית עַל פִּי הֲלָכָה מְצִיאוּת חֲדָשָׁה - מְצִיאוּת שֶׁל מִשְׁפָּחָה, שֶׁאָז נִיתּוֹסַף אֵצֶל הָאָב

חֲשִׁיבוּת גְדוֹלָה בְּיוֹתֵר מִכְּמוֹ שֶׁהָיָה בְּתוֹר מְצִיאוּת בִּפְנֵי עַצְמוֹ מִבְּנֵי בֵּיתוֹ, וְעַל דֶּרֶךְ זֶה בְּנוֹגֵעַ לְהָאֵם, וּבְנוֹגֵעַ לְיַחַס שֶׁל הַבֵּן וּבַת לַאֲבִיהֶם וְאִמָּם . . .

אֶחָד הָעֵצוֹת בָּזֶה - שֶׁגַּם בְּלַאו הָכִי הֲרֵי זֶה דָּבָר גָּדוֹל, שֶׁבְּיוֹם הַשַּׁבָּת קוֹדֶשׁ יִהְיוּ כּוּלָּם בְּיַחַד:

בְּדֶרֶךְ כְּלַל, הִנֵּה מִצַּד הַנְהָגַת הָעוֹלָם, יֵשׁ עִנְיָנִים שֶׁמְּבַלְבְּלִים לַאַחְדוּת שֶׁל בְּנֵי הַמִּשְׁפָּחָה, שֶׁכֵּן, הָעִנְיָנִים שֶׁבָּהֶם עוֹסֵק הָאָב, אֵינָם אוֹתָם עִנְיָנִים שֶׁבָּהֶם עֲסוּקָה הָאֵם, אוֹ הַבֵּן וְהַבַּת - כְּפִי שֶׁהַמַּצָּב הוּא בְּדֶרֶךְ הַטֶּבַע . . .

וְלָכֵן, יֵשׁ לְהִשְׁתַּדֵּל שֶׁהָחֵל מֵעֶרֶב שַׁבָּת לִפְנוֹת עֶרֶב, וְעַל אַחַת כַּמָּה וְכַמָּה בְּלֵיל שַׁבָּת, שֶׁאָז עֲרוּכִים סְעוּדָה הָרְאוּיָה לִשְׁמָהּ, סְעוּדַת שַׁבָּת - יִתְאַסְּפוּ בְּיַחַד כּוּלָּם, הָאָב וְהָאֵם עִם הַבָּנִים וְהַבָּנוֹת, בְּאוֹתוֹ חֶדֶר וְעַל אוֹתוֹ שׁוּלְחָן, וְיִשְׁתַּדְּלוּ שֶׁהַדִּיבּוּר בֵּינֵיהֶם יִהְיֶה בְּאוֹפֶן הַמַּתְאִים וְשַׁיָּךְ לְעִנְיַן הַשַּׁבָּת.

וְכַאֲשֶׁר יִתְנַהֲגוּ כַּךְ בְּיוֹם הַשַּׁבָּת, שֶׁאָז אֵין עִנְיָנִים מַפְרִידִים שֶׁל "עוּבְדִין דְחוֹל", כַּךְ שֶׁנָּקֵל יוֹתֵר שֶׁיִּהְיֶה צֵירוּף וְחִיבּוּר וּדְבֵיקוּת כָּל בְּנֵי הַמִּשְׁפָּחָה בְּיַחַד בְּתוֹר מְצִיאוּת אַחַת - אֲזַי תִּהְיֶה "מִשְׁפָּחָה בְּרִיאָה" בְּיוֹם הַשַּׁבָּת, וְעַל יְדֵי זֶה תִּהְיֶה "מִשְׁפָּחָה בְּרִיאָה" גַּם בְּמֶשֶׁךְ כָּל יְמֵי הַשָּׁבוּעַ שֶׁלְּאַחֲרֵי זֶה, כִּי הָעִנְיָנִים הַמְצַרְפִים וּמְחַבְּרִים כּוּלָּם יַחַד (בְּיוֹם הַשַּׁבָּת, וּבִפְרַט בִּסְעוּדַת שַׁבָּת), יַכְרִיעוּ וְיִתְגַּבְּרוּ עַל הַחִילּוּקִים שֶׁיֶּשְׁנָם בֵּין הָאָב וְהַבֵּן וְהָאֵם לְבַת ("כְּאִמָּה כְּבִתָּהּ") בְּנוֹגֵעַ לְהִתְעַסְקוּתָם הַפְּרָטִית, וְעַד שֶׁגַּם הַפְּרָטִים עַצְמָם יִצְטָרְפוּ כּוּלָּם יַחַד בְּאוֹפֶן שֶׁכָּל פְּרַט מַשְׁלִים וּמוֹסִיף אֶת הַפְּרַט הַשֵּׁנִי.

וְכֵיוָן שֶׁאֵין עִנְיָן שֶׁנַּעֲשֶׂה מֵעַצְמוֹ, וְעַל אַחַת כַּמָּה וְכַמָּה כְּשֶׁיֶּשְׁנוֹ הֶרְגֵּל שֶׁל כַּמָּה שָׁנִים לְהִתְנַהֵג בְּדֶרֶךְ שֶׁל הֶעְדֵּר שִׂימַת-לֵב לְגַמְרֵי לְעִנְיַן הַמִּשְׁפָּחָה - הִנֵּה עַל כָּל פָּנִים מִכַּאן וּלְהַבָּא צָרִיךְ לָדַעַת שֶׁזֶּהוּ עִנְיָן שֶׁדּוֹרֵשׁ שִׂימַת-לֵב, יְגִיעָה וְהִשְׁתַּדְּלוּת פַּעַם אַחַר פַּעַם, וְאָז יֶשְׁנָהּ הַהַבְטָחָה שֶׁכַּאֲשֶׁר "יָגַעְתָּ" אֲזַי בְּוַדַּאי "וּמָצָאתָ".

A critical component of any nation's existence, especially the existence of the Jewish nation, but one that has unfortunately been neglected, is the preservation of the family unit. . . .

The importance of family is illustrated by the method in which G-d counted the Jewish nation. In addition to the census of the entire nation, the Torah emphasizes for each tribe that its members were counted, "according to their families" (NUMBERS 1:2), meaning, they were counted as family *units*. . . .

Practically speaking, many of the difficulties that arise between parents and children, even when children are provided a proper education, have been caused by the underemphasis of the importance of the family as a *unit*. In a cohesive family, each individual attains more significance as a member of the family unit than he or she had on their own. . . .

One way to address this issue—which is an important practice in any case—is for the family to spend Shabbat *together*.

There are many factors that can undermine family unity since, naturally, the father, mother, son, and daughter are each occupied in different matters. . . .

We must therefore endeavor that, starting from Friday evening and certainly on Friday night when the Shabbat meal is held, the entire family—father, mother, sons, and daughters—should *gather*, in the same room, at the same table, and *converse*—understandably, on topics that are appropriate for Shabbat.

On Shabbat, when weekday affairs, so conducive to separation and discord, are absent, it is easier for the family members to fuse together as a single entity. And when the family unit will be healthy on Shabbat, the family will be "healthy" also throughout the week. The unifying factors present on Shabbat (and particularly during the meal) will prevail over all their differences, thereby ensuring that each of their individual paths complete and complement the paths of the others.

Nothing happens on its own, especially considering that for numerous years the significance of the family unit has been habitually overlooked. But it is time to acknowledge that this is an area that requires focus, energy, and repeated effort. And the Torah promises us that if you make an effort, you will succeed.

Saturday afternoon, Moritz Daniel Oppenheim, oil on canvas, Germany, 1866. (The Israel Museum, Jerusalem)

QUESTION FOR DISCUSSION

Which topics of conversation would you suggest in order to achieve the desired effect described by the Rebbe?

TEXT 10a

RABBI YAAKOV BEN ASHER, *ARBAAH TURIM*, *ORACH CHAYIM* 590:1

אִיתָא בְּמִדְרָשׁ: אָמְרָה תּוֹרָה לִפְנֵי הַקָּדוֹשׁ בָּרוּךְ הוּא: רִיבּוֹנוֹ שֶׁל עוֹלָם, כְּשֶׁיִּכָּנְסוּ יִשְׂרָאֵל לָאָרֶץ, זֶה רָץ לְכַּרְמוֹ וְזֶה רָץ לְשָׂדֵהוּ, וַאֲנִי מַה תְּהֵא עָלַי? אָמַר לָהּ: יֵשׁ לִי זוּג שֶׁאֲנִי מְזַוֵּוג לָךְ וְשַׁבָּת שְׁמוֹ, שֶׁהֵם בְּטֵלִים מִמְּלַאכְתָּם וִיְכוֹלִים לַעֲסוֹק בָּךְ.

It is taught in the Midrash: The Torah said to G-d, "When the Jewish people enter the Land of Israel and run to their vineyards and fields, what will become of me?" G-d replied, "I have a match that I can pair you with. Its name is Shabbat; on this day, they will not work and will be able to engage with you."

RABBI YAAKOV BEN ASHER (*TUR*, BAAL HATURIM), C. 1269–1343

Halachic authority and codifier. Rabbi Yaakov was born in Germany and moved to Toledo, Spain, with his father, the noted halachist Rabbi Asher, to escape persecution. He wrote *Arbaah Turim ("Tur")*, an ingeniously organized and highly influential code of Jewish law. He is considered one of the greatest authorities on halachah.

TEXT 10b

RABBI SHNE'UR ZALMAN OF LIADI, *TANYA, KUNTRES ACHARON* 9

בִּהְיוֹת מוּדַעַת זֹאת לְיוֹדְעֵי חָכְמָה נִסְתֶּרֶת, בְּכָל הַמִּצְוֹת יֵשׁ פְּנִימִיּוּת וְחִיצוֹנִיּוּת, וְחִיצוֹנִית מֵהַשַּׁבָּת הוּא שְׁבִיתָה מֵעֲשִׂיָּה גַשְׁמִיִּית כְּמוֹ שֶׁשָּׁבַת ה' מֵעֲשׂוֹת שָׁמַיִם וָאָרֶץ גַשְׁמִיִּים. וּפְנִימִית הַשַּׁבָּת הִיא הַכַּוָּנָה בִּתְפִלַּת הַשַּׁבָּת וּבְתַלְמוּד תּוֹרָה לְדָבְקָה בַּה' אֶחָד כְּמוֹ שֶׁכָּתוּב שַׁבָּת לַה' אֱלֹקֶיךָ.

As is known to the initiates in the mystical wisdom [of kabbalah], in every mitzvah there is an internal and external aspect. The external aspect of Shabbat is the cessation of physical activity, just as G-d ceased making the physical heaven and earth. The internal dimension of Shabbat is one's intention in the Shabbat prayers and during one's Torah study to cleave to the One G d, as it is written, "It is Shabbat to G-d, your G-d" (EXODUS 20:10).

RABBI SHNE'UR ZALMAN OF LIADI (ALTER REBBE), 1745–1812

Chasidic rebbe, halachic authority, and founder of the Chabad movement. The Alter Rebbe was born in Liozna, Belarus, and was among the principal students of the Magid of Mezeritch. His numerous works include the *Tanya*, an early classic containing the fundamentals of Chabad Chasidism, and *Shulchan Aruch HaRav*, an expanded and reworked code of Jewish law.

TEXT 11

AMIDAH OF SHABBAT MINCHAH PRAYERS

יוֹם מְנוּחָה וּקְדֻשָּׁה לְעַמְּךָ נָתָתָּ.

A day of rest and holiness, You have given Your people.

Figure 5.2

Major areas of focus during Shabbat

1 Thinking about the Creator and His ongoing interaction in our lives

2 Contemplating our purpose as His creations, collectively and individually, as well as our purpose as Jews

3 Spending quality time together and strengthening the family unit

4 Devoting time to Torah study, prayer, and similar spiritual pursuits

TEXT 12

JONATHAN SARNA, *AMERICAN JUDAISM* (NEW HAVEN: YALE UNIVERSITY PRESS, 2004), PP. 162–164

Numerous jobs in the clothing trade, the cigar trade, and even on farms and in peddling made working on the Jewish Sabbath a condition of employment. With the six-day work week commonplace and Sunday closing laws strictly enforced, unsympathetic employers decreed that "if you don't come in on Saturday, don't bother coming in on Monday." . . .

A heartrending Yiddish prayer (*techinah*) written in America for women to recite privately when they lit their Sabbath candles, and printed in a widely distributed women's prayer book . . . [expresses the sentiment of the times]. Speaking in the first person to G-d, the prayer laments that in "this diaspora land" where the "burden of making a living is so great," resting on Sabbath and holidays had become impossible, and it pleads for divine compassion. "Grant a bountiful living to all Jewish children," it entreats, "that they should not . . . have to desecrate your holy day."

JONATHAN D. SARNA
1955–

Historian. Dr. Sarna is the Joseph H. & Belle R. Braun Professor of American Jewish History and chair of the Hornstein Jewish Professional Leadership Program at Brandeis University, the chief historian of the National Museum of American Jewish History in Philadelphia, and a member of JLI's Academic Advisory Board. Sarna has written, edited, or coedited more than 30 books. He is best known for his book *American Judaism: A History*, winner of the Jewish Book Council's "Jewish Book of the Year Award" in 2004. Dr. Sarna served as the chief course consultant for JLI's *To Be A Jew in the Free World.*

TEXT 13

PHILIP SOPHER, "WHERE THE FIVE-DAY WORKWEEK CAME FROM," *THE ATLANTIC*, AUGUST 21, 2014

In 1908, a New England mill became the first American factory to institute the five-day week. It did so to accommodate Jewish workers, whose observance of a Saturday sabbath forced them to make up their work on Sundays, offending some in the Christian majority. The mill granted these Jewish workers a two-day weekend, and other factories followed this example.

TEXT 14

"RANDI ZUCKERBERG 'LIKES' UNPLUGGING FOR SHABBAT," YNETNEWS.COM, SEPTEMBER 4, 2016

Randi Zuckerberg, an entrepreneur, radio host and sister to Facebook co-founder Mark Zuckerberg, discussed and encouraged "unplugging" from electronic devices on Shabbat while at the One-to-One forum in New York this past June.

Zuckerberg, who currently has over 1.75 million Facebook followers, worked at the social media giant until 2011, when she founded Zuckerberg Media, a social media firm. Though she works in digital media, she still advocates taking a regular break and unplugging. . . .

RANDI ZUCKERBERG
1982–

A native of New York, Randi Zuckerberg graduated from Harvard University with a degree in psychology. Her brother Mark founded Facebook in 2004, and Randi joined as one of its first employees, serving as director of marketing and a spokesperson for the company. Randi later founded Zuckerberg Media and, among other pursuits, serves as editor in chief of Dot Complicated, a digital lifestyle website.

Addressing the forum, Zuckerberg discussed the concept of unplugging from the perpetual connection to one's telephone.

She said, "I find that it's so important in my own life. Any big entrepreneur, any CEO you talk to—they're not coming up with the world-changing ideas by being constantly plugged in and constantly on text message, distracted, getting emails. You can only come up with those amazing world-changing ideas by giving yourself the time and space distraction-free to be creative. . . .

"I talk about unplugging a lot, and people are like, 'Wow, that's such a new concept—so exciting,' and I'm like, 'Well, it's not actually that new. This is like a multi-thousand-year-old concept of Shabbat and unplugging and taking time.'"

***Dr. Lisa Aiken** discusses Shabbat and technology overdependence:*

MYJLI.COM/GIFTS

Exercise 5.3

1 Which aspects of Shabbat described in this lesson are already a part of my life, and which can I add?

2 How can I benefit specifically from integrating more of Shabbat into my Friday–Saturday routine?

3 What factors might have impeded me from doing so until now?

4 What can I do to overcome these obstacles?

5 How might I be able to share the gift of Shabbat and its messages with others?

A guided meditation to ease you into Shabbat's calming sphere, led by ***Rabbi Shais Taub****:*

MYJLI.COM/GIFTS

KEY POINTS

1 Toil is a Jewish value. G-d created the world in a manner that allows for and requires human input; He created humanity with the ability to develop and fully utilize the Creation. Through our efforts to positively impact the world, humankind partners with G-d in the creation of the universe.

2 Shabbat demonstrates the value of making time to focus on the "important" things in life, by tuning out of matters that we otherwise treat as "urgent."

3 Shabbat reminds us that G-d created the universe and continues to engage with the universe. These ideas give us perspective on who we are and what our purpose is.

4 On Shabbat, we direct our toil toward important pursuits, such as exploring our identity and purpose, deepening our relationships with our families, and concentrating on prayer and Torah study.

5 The challenges that arise between parents and children can be mitigated by utilizing the Shabbat meals to communicate and strengthen the cohesiveness of the family unit.

6 Shabbat is G-d's gift to the Jews. In addition to its many other benefits, it is a sign of the relationship between G-d and the Jewish people. But the central premise of reserving time for what's really important in life is of universal relevance to all of humanity.

Appendices

TEXT 15

MIDRASH, *EICHAH RABAH* 3:5

כְּתִיב (תְּהִלִּים סט, יג): "יָשִׂיחוּ בִי יֹשְׁבֵי שָׁעַר", אֵלוּ אֻמּוֹת הָעוֹלָם, שֶׁהֵן יוֹשְׁבִין בְּבָתֵּי תַּרְטִיאוֹת וּבְבָתֵּי קַרְקְסִיאוֹת. "וּנְגִינוֹת שׁוֹתֵי שֵׁכָר", מֵאַחַר שֶׁהֵן יוֹשְׁבִין וְאוֹכְלִין וְשׁוֹתִין וּמִשְׁתַּכְּרִין, הֵן יוֹשְׁבִין וּמְשִׂיחִין בִּי וּמַלְעִיגִים בִּי וְאוֹמְרִים בְּגִין דְלָא נִצְרוֹךְ לְחָרוּבָא כִּיהוּדָאֵי, וְהֵן אוֹמְרִים אֵלוּ לָאֵלוּ, כַּמָּה שָׁנִים אַתְּ בָּעֵי מִחֵי, וְהֵן אוֹמְרִים כַּחֲלוּקָא דִיהוּדָאֵי דְשַׁבַּתָּא . . .

וּמַכְנִיסִים אֶת הַמּוּמוֹס לַתֵּיאַטְרוֹן שֶׁלָּהֶם וְרֹאשׁוֹ גָלוּחַ, וְהֵן אוֹמְרִים אֵלוּ לָאֵלוּ עַל מָה רֹאשׁוֹ שֶׁל זֶה מְגֻלָּח, וְהוּא אוֹמֵר הַיְהוּדִים הַלָּלוּ שׁוֹמְרֵי שַׁבָּתוֹת הֵן, וְכָל מַה שֶּׁהֵם יְגֵיעִין כָּל יְמוֹת הַשַּׁבָּת אוֹכְלִים בַּשַּׁבָּת, וְאֵין לָהֶם עֵצִים לְבַשֵּׁל בָּהֶם, וְהֵם שׁוֹבְרִים מִטּוֹתֵיהֶם וּמְבַשְּׁלִים בָּהֶן, וְהֵם יְשֵׁנִין בָּאָרֶץ וּמִתְעַפְּרִים בֶּעָפָר וְסָכִין בְּשֶׁמֶן, לְפִיכָךְ הַשֶּׁמֶן בְּיֹקֶר.

It says (PSALMS 69:13), "They that sit in the gate talk of me"—this refers to the nations of the world who sit in theaters and circuses. The verse continues, "And I am the song of the drunkards"—this refers to their custom where, after eating, drinking, and becoming intoxicated, they sit and talk of me, scoffing, "Let's take care not to [overspend and] be compelled to eat carobs like the Jews [who spend their money on delights for Shabbat]."

They ask one another, "How long do you wish to live?" To which they reply, "As long as the Jew's Shabbat shirt." [Unlike their own garments, the Jew's Shabbat shirt

EICHAH RABAH

A Midrashic text on the Book of Lamentations, produced by the sages of the Talmud in the Land of Israel. Its language closely resembles that of the Jerusalem Talmud. It was first printed in Pesaro, Italy, in 1519, together with 4 other midrashic works on the other 4 *megilot*.

would last for long because it was only worn one day a week.] . . .

They bring a clown with a shaven head into the theater and ask one another, "Why is his head shaven?" To which they reply, "The Jews observe the Shabbat, and whatever they earn during the week they eat on Shabbat. Having nothing left for the week and having no wood to cook with, they break their beds and use them as fuel. Consequently, they sleep on the ground [and their hair falls out as a result. In addition,] they get covered with dust, and so they anoint their hair with oil. This drives up the price of oil!"

TEXT 16

EVIATAR ZERUBAVEL, *THE SEVEN DAY CIRCLE: THE HISTORY AND MEANING OF THE WEEK* (CHICAGO: UNIVERSITY OF CHICAGO PRESS, 1989), P. 11

A continuous seven-day cycle that runs throughout history paying no attention whatsoever to the moon and its phases is a distinctively Jewish invention. Moreover, the dissociation of the seven-day week from nature has been one of the most significant contributions of Judaism to civilization . . . essentially increasing the distance between human beings and nature. The continuous week was therefore one of the most significant breakthroughs in human beings' attempts to break away from being prisoners of nature and create a social world of their own.

EVIATAR ZERUBAVEL
1948–

Sociologist. Zerubavel is a professor of sociology at Rutgers University. He specializes in the sociology of cognition and everyday life, including topics such as time, boundaries, and categorization.

TEXT 17

JONATHAN SARNA, *AMERICAN JUDAISM* (NEW HAVEN: YALE UNIVERSITY PRESS, 2004), P. 163

The wealthy Orthodox builder and communal leader Harry Fischel (1865–1948), for example, looked back on his "early struggles" over Sabbath observance as the defining "spiritual conflict" of his life. He recounted its climactic scene in words that suggest that his experience was as rare as it was life-changing. After weeks of searching for work as a new immigrant, Fischel recalled that he found the job of his dreams in an architecture firm. He worked happily for five days and then requested to take Saturday off at no pay so he could observe the Sabbath. His request was firmly denied, and he was ordered to come into work or lose his job. "It seemed," he recounted, "as though G-d had decided to give him another test of his devotion to his religious principles and his ability to withstand temptation." After a sleepless night, he resolved to compromise: "He would not give up his position, but before going to work he would attend services in the synagogue." The very existence of early-morning Sabbath services for those who needed to work is, of course, deeply revealing. His worship complete, Fischel prepared to go to his office, but the sight of other Jews observing the Sabbath and the shock that he knew his parents would experience "could they but know the step he contemplated" gave him a pause: "Suddenly, although the day was in mid-August and the heat was stifling, he trembled as with the ague. A chill went through every fibre of his being, as though he were confronted with the biting winds of January. At the same time a strange sensation attacked his heart and he was unable to move. It seemed as though he were paralyzed and he would have fallen, had not his body been supported by a friendly wall. When with difficulty he recovered himself, his decision had been reached." Thanks to this "mysterious manifestation of the Divine Power," he felt able to resist what he described as "the greatest temptation he had ever known." In the clarity of the moment, "he knew that neither then nor later would it ever be possible for him to desecrate the Sabbath."

Fischel lost his job but subsequently prospered—good fortune that he credited to his lifelong "principle" of Sabbath-observance.

Additional Readings

THE JEWISH SABBATH MOVEMENT IN THE EARLY TWENTIETH CENTURY

BY BENJAMIN KLINE HUNNICUTT

During the first three decades of the twentieth century and especially the 1920s, Jewish groups and individuals paid an increasing amount of attention to questions of the Sabbath, how it should be observed and what its larger place was in American culture. The Sabbath also became an important cause for a number of Jews, combining religious purpose with social reform goals. The Sabbath had a practical social dimension since it directly involved the reduction of the work week and as such coincided with labor's demands for the five-day week. Spokesmen for the Sabbath movement supported labor's shorter-hour cause, reasoning that modern industrial developments made jobs harder, more stressful, specialized and unrewarding, and as such increased the practical need for more time off. But concerns about workers' health, safety, and social well-being were joined in the Sabbath movement by larger, more idealistic, and religious motives. Individuals and groups saw in the idea of the Sabbath some profound truths that transcended the workaday world and opened up a new kind of human reform and a new field for "genuine" progress. They came to believe that the Sabbath, as a special time set aside for real human needs and apart from material concerns, provided the model and rationale for the "progressive shortening of the hours of labor"—a labor clause that began to outrun practical reform goals with the beginning of the five-day week. They also saw values contained by the Sabbath that countered modern materialism, "spurious progress," mass, cheap culture, and the philistinism of the "gospel of consumption." Hence these people represented the twentieth century's Sabbatarianism as combining a very real improvement of the worker's life (a shorter work week), a general criticism of a culture and economy sunk in materialism, without a transcendent vision, and a new direction for a qualitatively different type of progress.

One of the main difficulties that Jews faced in America during the nineteenth and early twentieth centuries was the loss of Saturday as the historical Sabbath. By law and custom, Americans worked six days a week and, if possible, took Sunday off. Paradoxically, the reason why most Americans worked the six-day week was due in part to a social reform which was sparked by religious concerns, the nineteenth-century Christian Sabbatarian movement. This movement, in the 1820s and 1830s, had a strong social reform motive and a stronger result, although it was heavily sentimental and designed for the most part for religious purposes. But even though Jews and Christians alike shared its social benefits, Jews were denied its religious possibilities. Any deviation from the six-day-Sunday-off pattern was difficult, almost impossible unless one worked the full seven days (even though this was exceptional since blue laws augmented the Sabbatarian's reform). Although the Jewish concern for keeping the Sabbath was as keen as the Christian, Jews were practically prohibited this religious freedom and forced by society and their jobs to observe Sunday as what amounted to a national religious holiday.[1]

Throughout the nineteenth and early twentieth centuries, Jews faced this problem but never resolved it. The problem also caused a rift among Jews between the Orthodox and Reform leadership. Orthodox

BENJAMIN KLINE HUNNICUTT

Professor of leisure studies at the University of Iowa. Hunnicutt focuses his research on our society's relationship with work and leisure time. He has published three books on the subject, most recently, *Free Time: The Forgotten American Dream* (2013).

spokesmen were afraid that the Sabbath as a unique part of their religion was dying out—being observed more in the breach than in the keeping. Often they would predict that the Sabbath was doomed because of the constraints of the American culture. They saw in the death of the Sabbath one more force that would speed up the assimilation and even the conversion of the Jewish people. For example, Rabbi Israel Herbert Levinthal argued that "if we see Jewish life crumbling before our very eyes in America it is mainly due to the fact that we have lost our Sabbath."[2] That this view was widely held was demonstrated by a joint statement issued by the Union of Orthodox Rabbis of the United States and Canada, the Rabbinical Assembly of America, the Union of Orthodox Jewish Congregations of America, and the United Synagogue of America: ". . . this violation of the Sabbath, if continued indefinitely, must inevitably lead to the gradual disintegration of our people."[3] For the Orthodox and a number of Conservatives, the preservation of the Sabbath was a precondition to the preservation of American Judaism. The Sabbath also contained ideals and values central to their religion. It was the special, holy time for ritual matters, for community, for family, for tradition, and for the individual and his G-d, set aside from the busy, materialistic and profane world. A strict observance of that day preserved the forms and institutions of Judaism to be sure, but it also contained central truths that were timeless.

The importance of the Sabbath cannot be overstated. Since prominent Jews were later to graft the traditional ideas associated with the Sabbath onto the larger social reform cause of the "progressive shortening of the hours of labor," some insight into how the Sabbath was viewed during this period is useful. A fine, poetic example may be found in Ben Eliezer's book, *Letters of a Jewish Father to his Son*. In the chapter, "Princess Sabbath," Ben Eliezer stated that "the Sabbath is probably the greatest cultural contribution that the Jews have made to the world," even surpassing "the gift of the idea of the unity of G-d." The Sabbath has acted both as "a national unifying and cementing influence" for Jews as well as a "universal humanizing factor." Its place in the tradition was assured in talmudic literature with such passages as: "The Sabbath outweighs the whole of the Torah and he who observes it properly has all his sins forgiven." Ben Eliezer, as did many Jews, believed that the observance of the Sabbath put man into contact with his real needs and his true nature, and put the material world into perspective.

> *What does . . . give the Sabbath its sacred significance is the fact that during its 24 hours, there is an abandoning of all material interests, followed by complete retirement into a self-contained spiritual world, free from earthly cares and worries. . . . For it is only in such an environment, free from the thoughts of daily affairs, that the highest religious and ethical sentiments can come uppermost to mind. . . . By cultivating such an atmosphere . . . [modern Jews] would also grow in knowledge possessed by their forefathers . . . that our souls are capable of deriving more lasting pleasure from other joys which raise man beyond the level of mere animal enjoyment, drawing him nearer to the source of the great unknown from which he emanates.*[4]

The Sabbath was, in fact, the goal of work and material concerns: the time "longed for . . . with the same fervor as a prince awaiting his bride." Labor and "the thought of labor" were important chiefly because they led to the Sabbath and to "its self-contained spiritual world." In this Jews and Christians agreed. The Sabbath was a kind of "eschaton" in this world, a taste of that eternal Sabbath described by St. Augustine at the end of his *Confessions*.

On the other hand, during the last half of the nineteenth and first quarter of the twentieth century, many progressive rabbis, in an attempt to "modernize" Judaism, held Sunday services and argued that all American congregations should permit Sunday observances. The rabbinical conference at Pittsburgh in 1885 unanimously agreed that:

> *Whereas we recognize the importance of maintaining the historical Sabbath as a bond with our great past and a symbol of the unity of Israel the world over; and,*
> *Whereas, on the other hand, it cannot be denied that there is a very large number of Jews who, owing to economic and industrial conditions, are*

> *not able to attend services on our sacred day of rest; be it:*
> *Resolved, that in the judgment of this conference there is nothing in the spirit of Judaism to prevent the holding of divine services on Sunday, or any other day of the week, where the necessity of such services is felt.*[5]

This resolution was reaffirmed in 1902, 1905, 1906 and afterwards, periodically until the 1920s in the Committee on "Weekday Services," by the Central Conference of American Rabbis. The Central Conference also watered down the Orthodox notion of how the Sabbath should be kept, agreeing that activities like tramrides, work at necessary jobs, shaving, and secular amusements were permissible given the realities of the American environment.[6]

In addition, the more radical leadership pressed for the total transfer of the Sabbath to Sunday immediately following the Pittsburgh Conference. The center for this movement seems to have been the *Jewish Tidings*, a publication out of Rochester, New York, which espoused the cause.[7] This notion remained viable in Reform Judaism until 1902 when in New Orleans, after a long and heated debate, the Central Conference committed itself to a struggle for the Saturday Sabbath. The Conference resolved that it was "in favor of maintaining the historical Sabbath as a fundamental institution of Judaism and exerting every effort to enforce its observance."[8]

Despite their disagreement, Orthodox and Reform groups joined together in the struggle for the Saturday Sabbath as it developed from 1903 to 1920. The two most important groups engaged in this movement were the Central Conference of American Rabbis and the Orthodox Jewish Sabbath Alliance. On the one hand, the Central Conference did not vigorously pursue its 1902 commitment. It continued to promote Sunday services (rearranging rituals accordingly) and to interpret Sabbath laws in a more "liberal" manner and seems to have held little hope that Saturday observance and traditional rules could be revived in America. But the Sabbath Alliance took the initiative in the movement and was much more active, fully committing itself to the ideal of the traditional Sabbath.[9]

Nevertheless, during this early period, both groups used the same two techniques. Both endorsed the broader social reform of one day's rest out of seven (a cause supported originally by the Federal Council of Churches of Christ in 1908 and afterwards), but argued that industry and business should make special accommodations for their Jewish workers by allowing them to take Saturday instead of Sunday off. In contrast to the Central Conference's passive endorsement of the scheme (it never got far beyond Conference resolutions), the Sabbath Alliance actively promoted the staggered work week in New York, Boston, Philadelphia, and other major cities where Jews were employed by specific industries in large numbers. Both groups also joined together in opposition to Sunday blue laws. Again the Sabbath Alliance was more active, launching what the *New York Times* called a national "campaign" against these laws. Hence Jewish Sabbatarianism faced two fronts at first: the rearranging of the work week to allow for free Saturdays and the defeating of blue laws to open up Sunday work. Both were necessary if the Sabbath was to be observed on Saturday in a country where the six-day week was standard.[10]

This original and narrowly focused struggle seemed doomed from the start. The Alliance had little success in promoting the staggered work week since industrial managers were unwilling or unable to administer the production and personnel problems that would have resulted from a reduced and changed work force for two days a week. Progressive businessmen, who supported the six-day work week, were not willing to extend its potential religious benefit to Jews by altering the work force and thereby the very means of production. Even Jewish employers, the target for most of the Sabbatarians' efforts, were not ready to disrupt their businesses for this cause. In addition, some members of the Sabbath Alliance conceded that even in the best of circumstances, the staggered work week could be instituted only by special industries in large cities and would not solve the Sabbath problem for the majority of Jews.[11]

Consequently, during these early years, the Central Conference of the Sabbath Alliance devoted most of their efforts against enforcement of the nineteenth-century blue laws and the passing of new ones. But again, in this effort they faced great difficulty. Beginning around 1918 the L-rd's Day Alliance, the Central Sabbath Crusade Committee, the International Reform Bureau, and several other Christian organizations were promoting a new and militant campaign for the strict observance of Sunday. The original social gospel concern with the six-day week as a constructive labor reform had by this time deteriorated into a new and repressive drive to eliminate by local and state ordinances and even federal laws all sorts of Sunday activities including movies, newspaper publications, sports, voluntary recreation pursuits, as well as most commerce and all manufacturing. As with Prohibition and immigrant restriction the dark side of modern reform was exhibited by the wave of blue laws passed in the 1920s. In many cases the campaign for strict Sunday observance had anti-Semitic overtones. For example, blue laws in Boston and New York were often enforced selectively against Jews. In addition, leaders of the L-rd's Day Alliance such as H. L. Bowlby attacked the Jewish Sabbath Alliance, charging that its efforts were motivated by the desire to give Jews an unfair business advantage on Sunday or else were a front for the movie trade, which, according to Bowlby, was dominated by Jewish interests. The result of the new campaign for strict Sunday observance was a vigorous enforcement of existing blue laws and the passing of numerous new laws by city councils and state legislatures.[12]

In this situation supporters of the Jewish Sabbath could do little except fight a rearguard action. Nevertheless, beginning in 1920, the Jewish Sabbath Alliance began its national "campaign" against blue laws. Its major argument was that such legislation "forced Jews to observe a Christian holiday" and as such violated the Constitutional provision for the separation of church and state. Acting on this assumption, the Sabbath Alliance promoted the introduction of the Dickstein Bill in the New York legislature in 1920, a bill that would have allowed Jews to operate commercial concerns on Sunday (a law similar to statutes in New Jersey and Oklahoma). But because of the rising tide of public sentiment about Sunday reform, this bill was defeated in March, 1921. Several other such bills were introduced in state legislatures in the 1920s, including one proposed by Bernard Downing, senator from New York City, that would have prohibited on Saturday all activities prohibited on Sunday. Downing supported his bill by declaring, "if this bill becomes law, it will give 1,600,000 Jews . . . no further justification for saying that legislation designed to compel them to observe our Sunday laws involves discrimination, placing them at an economic disadvantage, . . . and a little more rest and leisure will do us no harm." But these bills had little chance in state legislatures that were passing new blue laws in record numbers.[13]

Moreover, in their fight against blue laws, the Jewish organizations had little help from the courts, although the Sabbath Alliance at first considered them to be a major hope for redress. By the 1920s, the Supreme Court of the United States had twice accepted the constitutionality of Sunday laws, with *Hennington v. Georgia* (163, U.S. 299, 1896) and *Pettit v. Minnesota* (177, U.S. 164, 1900), even though never ruling on the First Amendment issue of separation of church and state involved. However, lower courts were laying the foundations for the secular interpretation of these laws, ruling in over fifteen instances that the police power of localities permitted enforcement of Sunday laws, and that they were civil, not religious in purpose, since they permitted everyone to have one day of rest in the week, essential for public order, rest, recreation, health, and welfare. The New Jersey court, for example, held in *Kislingbury v. Treasurer of Plainfield* (160A. 654, 10 NJ misc. 798) that the New Jersey law exempting Jews and others who observed Saturday from prosecution under the state's Sunday closing ordinance was unconstitutional in its exemption and that the First Amendment did not speak on the issue of Sunday laws.[14]

Hence in their first attempts to free American Jews to observe the traditional Sabbath, the Sabbath Alliance and Central Conference seemed blocked by the nature and requirements of industry, the wave of Christian Sunday reform, legislatures more interested in passing Sunday blue laws than exempting people from them, and courts not willing to apply the First Amendment to this issue. It was only when the Sabbath Alliance began to concentrate on larger labor reform matters that it was able to make headway in its first, primarily religious cause. In the five-day week its members found what seemed to be a natural vehicle for both their concern for the Sabbath and their hopes for more general social justice achievements. Again in support of the five-day week, the Orthodox Sabbath Alliance led the way. It is interesting to note that other more liberal groups were slow to recognize the coincidence of this labor reform and the religious cause. Historians have always supposed that the liberal, reform groups such as the Central Conference were those who advocated this program of social reform, but in the struggle for the Sabbath/five-day week, it was Orthodox Jewry which demonstrated its own brand of social consciousness.

As early as 1910, Rabbi Bernard Drachman, president of the Sabbath Alliance, told that group that the problem of the Sabbath was so interwoven with American conditions that the issue could be resolved only if both Saturday and Sunday were observed as days of rest by "Christians and Jews alike." As the efforts to exempt Jews from Saturday work failed and the attempts to open up Sunday work proved fruitless and generated hard feelings among Christian Sabbatarians, more people came to appreciate the wisdom of Drachman's original vision. Beginning in 1919, the Sabbath Alliance supported local unions in New York, Boston, Philadelphia, and other cities which were launching their campaigns for the five-and-a-half-day week, a campaign that worked directly toward the institution of Saturday holidays.[15]

It is hard to judge religion's influence on this new labor cause. But since the unions that first pressed for the five-day week were composed mostly of Jews, the desire to revive Saturday observance was very prevalent in Jewish groups, and national Jewish organizations as well as local congregations endorsed the five-day week, a prima facie case has been made that religion was a motive of union members in this cause. But union leaders did not stress the five-day week's religious benefit. In fact, they seldom mentioned it. Instead, they represented their unions with economic and social arguments that were applicable to all workers.There is no way of telling whether economic and social consideration of the desire for the traditional Sabbath was more important for the Jewish union members who were beginning to demand and strike for the five-day week. But since the religious and the economic/social purposes coincided in a practical fashion, and the union's economic/social arguments were endorsed by religious groups and even given a theological dimension, the question of union members' motives may be left unanswered for the purpose of this essay.[16]

The first national union to propose the five-day week was the Amalgamated Clothing Workers Union of America, which passed resolutions for this goal in their biennial conventions, beginning in 1920. Led by Sidney Hillman, this national union worked with local unions, especially in New York, during the decade to incorporate 40-hour clauses in trade agreements, or a clause that committed manufacturers to institute this reform "as soon as possible." But for several local Jewish unions, progress through trade agreements and resolutions was too slow. Strikes were called by the needle trade, the New York City clothing workers, and the Patterson, New Jersey silk workers and several other local unions between 1920 and 1924, which included demands for either the five-and-a-half-day or five-day week. These early strikes were settled for the most part by compromise, the workers agreeing to give up the hours' benefit for higher wages. But beginning in 1924, a series of major successful strikes were called by 50,000 New York City Ladies' Garment Workers' Union members (the largest strike in the nation that year), 40,000 clothing workers in New York City in 1926, 5,000 fur workers in New York and 3,000 in Boston (both in 1926) and all members of the New York and Philadelphia Cloth Hat and Cap Workers' Union in 1927, as well as other smaller unions in children's dresses, bathrobes, and kimonos. In these strikes, the 40-hour/five-day week was a major issue. When coupled with demands for higher wages, the issue dominated. For example, observers of the 17-week strike of the New York furriers concluded that "the main difficulty [prolonging the strike] seems to have been what points the union should barter away in order to gain the forty-hour week." These strikes were successful, so much so that by 1927 the Bureau of Labor Statistics concluded that the five-day work week was "practically the rule in trade agreements in the clothing industry."[17]

Together with the painters' and plasterers' unions, other building trades such as plumbers and carpenters, and printing and publishing unions, these unions in the clothing industry with large, Jewish memberships initiated the five-day week movement. That their efforts were productive was demonstrated by the fact that before the war, less than twenty manufacturing establishments nationally had adopted the five-day week. Nearly all of these were managed and staffed by Jews. But during the 1920s, over 240 manufacturers adopted this plan. By 1929, approximately 400,000 to 500,000 employees were working on a five-day pay basis. The 1920s was truly the decade of the beginning of the five-day work week.[18]

Between 1920 and 1925, the American Federation of Labor had its hands full mopping up "pockets of long hour resistance." Even though the eight-hour day/six-day week had become the norm by the 1920s, enough unions were still struggling to catch up with this standard to occupy the AFL's attention. Although it had endorsed the Amalgamated Clothing Worker's five-day week drive in 1920, it was not until 1926 that the AFL was ready to turn its full attention to this cause as the next logical step in the century-long process of shorter hours. The AFL supported the five-day week as one of its primary goals. But enough options were before it—the six- or seven-hour day and the five-and-a-half-day week—that it chose to commit itself to the larger cause of "the progressive shortening of the hours of labor" during the 1926 Convention.[19]

Jewish organizations actively supported these labor developments. In February, 1924, the convention of Orthodox Rabbis of New York, New Jersey and Connecticut met in New York City and endorsed the five-day week. This convention's efforts to "further the establishment of the five-day-week system" was an outgrowth of the Sabbath Alliance and the local congregations' original support of clothing, fur, and needle trade unions and the joint efforts of several Jewish groups to combat blue laws. A new note of optimism and conciliation was present at the convention. Several speakers (among them Drachman) noted that since opposition of blue laws was failing and bringing "protests from Christians," the five-day week offered a compromise. The convention concluded "so, to please both Jews and Christians, the plan for two days of rest each week was adopted."[20]

The idea gained ground rapidly among Jews and others. In 1925, the Sabbath Alliance formed an interdenominational committee to promote the cause, composed of such men as Drachman, Carlyle B. Haynes, Cyrus Adler, and N. Taylor Phillips. Spokesmen for this group agreed that "this great public reform . . . will . . . tend to remove the greatest causes of friction and religious intolerances existing in America today." Also, in 1925, representatives of several rabbinic bodies (Orthodox, Reform, and Conservative) met in New York to "further the five-day week in American industry." They launched what they called "a vigorous campaign in publications, lobbying, and promotion." Included in these efforts as leaders were M. Z. Margolies, Chaim Block and A. B. Burak of the Union of Orthodox Rabbis, Samuel Schulman and Nathan Stern of the Central Conference of American Rabbis, and "lay organizations" such as the Union of Orthodox Jewish Congregations of America, the Sabbath Alliance, and Young Israel. In addition, beginning in 1924, the United Synagogue of America planned a series of conferences between employers and labor unions "with a view to the establishing of a five-day week in as many industries as possible." By 1927, the Union of Orthodox Jewish Congregations, the Central Conference of American Rabbis, the Rabbinic Assembly, the United Synagogue, and the Union of Orthodox Rabbis of the United States and Canada had endorsed this cause as a general labor reform and in several instances actually encouraged the efforts of local unions, such as the needles trade and the Ladies' Garment Workers'. However, it was the Orthodox groups that took the active leadership role while the Reform group, such as the Central Conference, acted mostly as a cheering section.[21]

The primary concern of all the groups and individuals was, of course, the revitalization of the Sabbath observance on Saturday. The five-day week cause and its successes turned the original pessimism of Reform Jews into a new enthusiasm and proved to be a justification for the Orthodox leadership's holding onto the cause. But Jewish Sabbatarianism was altered and expanded by the five-day week issue. The issue led naturally to larger concerns: broad scale labor reforms and general questions about economic development and cultural progress. The five-day week served the practical cause of Jewish Sabbatarianism to be sure; but Jewish Sabbatarianism, as expanded by the issue, served in turn to justify the broader labor reform of the "progressive shortening of the hours of labor" and to inform the cultural, social, and economic debate about the decreasing importance of work and the increasing importance of free time.

Rabbi Israel Herbert Levinthal expressed the logical broadening of the argument for the Sabbath in this way:

> *I can see but one way to save the Sabbath for the Jew, and that is through the establishment of the five-day week. . . . I would favor the five-day week even if I were not interested in the preservation of the Jewish Sabbath. I would favor it because it would add health and strength to the American people. It would promote the home and home life, giving the father an added opportunity to become more intimately acquainted with . . . his children.*[22]

In a like manner, other prominent Jews who supported the five-day week agreed with the social and economic arguments of union leaders. During the struggle for the ten-hour day, the eight-hour day, and the six-day week, unions relied on fairly simple, common sense arguments. They had stressed safety factors, health benefits, moral considerations, and increased production in their defense of the earlier advances. But with the beginning of the 40-hour/five-day week drive and the commitment to "the progressive shortening of the hours of labor" these earlier, generally acceptable goals were less applicable. It was not clear at all that Saturdays off improved production, was necessary for rest, or made the work place safer. Union leaders found that they had to discover new arguments to justify this new reform.

To do this men such as William Green, president of the American Federation of Labor, Matthew Woll, vice-president of the AFL, A. O. Whorton, president of the International Association of Machinists, and Sidney Hillman, founder and president of the Amalgamated Clothing Workers of America turned their attention to the larger economy. They suggested that shorter hours were essential in order to deal with chronic unemployment and with general overproduction—new problems of the new era. These union leaders, and others, especially in the New York garment industry, firmly believed that with increasing mechanization, the economy was beginning to be overbuilt and the demand for goods such as textiles was being saturated. As production "outran the rate of natural consumption," general overproduction and chronic, acute unemployment would soon follow. In order to deal with these two new developments, they stressed two solutions—higher wages and shorter hours. Higher wages would allow workers to buy the necessities of life and as such increase the consumption of certain types of traditional products. Shorter hours, on the other hand, would create more jobs and would act to increase wages.[23] But they would also limit production that was beginning to outstrip demand. As A. O. Wharton put it:

> *Increased production accentuates the problem of overproduction or underconsumption. Increased wages and reduced hours go hand in hand with increased production. . . . Economic balance can be maintained only if . . . wages advance and leisure hours increase. If some sort of balance is not maintained, we are headed straight for disaster.*[24]

Unions were perhaps the first major group in American history to suggest that economic growth had a limit, a limit being reached in the 1920s and as such made the limiting of production necessary to stabilize the new, mature economy.

Bernard Drachman echoed the arguments of the union officials. He pointed out "the only cure for overproduction is limitation of production" since "it is perfectly possible under modern methods of production, that commodities can be produced in quantities greater than can be consumed. . . ." He also suggested that as a result, technological unemployment, especially in the garment industry was increasing and would continue to increase as technology outran the "rate of natural consumption. . . . The machines invented in recent years . . . with uncanny, almost demoniacal super ability . . . accomplish . . . tasks formerly requiring the labor of thousands and for the . . . displaced multitudes no opportunities of employment present themselves." Drachman saw shorter hours as a way to improve the workers' bargaining position for higher wages (by making labor scarce and hence more valuable) and also to deal with unemployment caused by overproduction. Shorter hours would distribute fairly the available work which was diminishing and would limit production to "reasonable levels." He concluded that he supported "the idea of the shorter work week, not only on economic grounds, but also on social, cultural, and spiritual grounds." This reform would stabilize the economy and help deal with unemployment. But it would also provide a new kind of freedom from material concerns and a new opportunity for human achievements by the masses.[25]

Union leaders also stressed the fact that work had lost its ethical and human dimensions and was becoming increasingly hard and "dehumanizing." As such, it had increased the importance of leisure. Formerly, they believed, work had been a place for creativity, community, craftsmanship, the way for social mobility, and the vehicle for self expression, personal fulfillment, and individualism. But modern means of production had changed all that, creating jobs that were specialized, repetitive, boring and routine as well as establishing a permanent industrial labor force. As William Green put it,

> *there must be a progressive reduction of the hours of labor, so that men and women may have time to rebuild their exhausted physical energies. This is more than ever important in the highly specialized process of modern industry, where speed and monotony tax physical existence to the utmost.*

He saw the AFL policy as a "complement of labor's long struggle to prevent work from becoming deadening toil." Sidney Hillman agreed that the "speed and strain of American industry was always greater."[26]

Green, Woll, and Hillman also defended the "leisured proletariat" by criticizing the "devitalized nature of modern work" and by renewing their support of traditional values that had been lost in modern occupations. Green, for example, insisted in order that " . . . our social and human values may not be merged with the machines until, they too, become mechanical, shorter hours [were] essential because they safeguard our human nature" and "lay the foundation for the higher development of spiritual and intellectual powers." He predicted "a dawn of a new era, leisure for all" and "a revolution in living" because of reduced hours. He saw leisure as a new opportunity for craftsmanship, creativity, community development, for fellowship, the "finer things in life" such as "music, art, literature, and travel," as a way "to worker's education" and "increased knowledge of technological principles," and for "recreation and recuperation . . . necessary to sustain vigor." For Green, gradually increasing leisure could redeem traditional values that had been lost at work, as well as open up new democratic vistas for the masses.[27]

Matthew Woll, like other union leaders, criticized work in new forms and looked to leisure to compensate workers for human values that they had lost. But he also criticized that fact that "unfortunately, our industrial life is dominated by the materialistic spirit of production, of work and more work, giving little attention to the development of the human body, the human mind, or the spirit of life. . . . All the finer qualities of life are entirely ignored." The dehumanized nature of modern jobs was complicated by the "materialistic spirit" of the business community. For Woll, increasing leisure was both a "restraining influence" limiting production to basic needs as well as a hedge against the material values of the "New Era."[28]

Jews active in the Sabbath movement agreed with the idea that work was becoming less rewarding and meaningful and that leisure offered the opportunity to recover some of the old values that work once had. Felix Cohen, for example, offered a parable of the modern economy that was able to provide the necessities of life and still supported work as a prime virtue.

> *Adam's children inherited the [curse of work] and soon learned to make a virtue of necessity. Idleness came to be regarded as a sin rather than a source of love, art, inspiration, and wisdom.*

Offered a chance by "G-d's messenger" or by the machine to slip the bonds of toil, men chose instead to "sing new hymns in praise of the sweetness of chains" and hold onto work because "they had so long praised each other . . . for industriousness. . . . The message of the machine is that we shall work without end."

According to Cohen, much of that work was useless. It no longer had the firm, external sanction of necessity. Work was being channeled in absurd directions: the production of useless or shoddy articles, advertising and a new industry, war. If useless work were abolished, then the work week could be reduced to "thirty hours immediately" and a "general working week of ten hours is then a fairly immediate possibility," given the rate of increased productivity. For Cohen, work's new forms—specialization, mechanization, and impersonal organization—destroyed the old nineteenth-century ideals about work's value, such as creativity, craftsmanship, self-fulfillment. In this he agreed with the union leaders. But he also suggested that work's purpose—its product—had been undercut by the machine. Much of modern work was useless, was without a firm purpose because there was "no natural" use for its product. Consequently work had been made a demigod—a thing worshipped for its own sake. It mattered little if its products were useless. One consumed them out of respect for this supreme virtue, like it or not.[29]

Sabbatarians, such as Cohen, extended the union leaders' arguments and engaged in the larger economic debates about overproduction with a new breed of economic businessmen. In contrast to the union and some pessimistic businessmen who were stressing limited production, most businessmen and economists were entering, practically and ideologically, a new age of mass consumption. They did not accept the argument that human needs for industrial products were finite or set by some nineteenth-century idea of human nature. Instead they took a new view of economic growth. They promoted what Edward Cowdrick called the "new economic gospel of consumption." In their view, the best way to deal with unemployment and overproduction was not to limit production by reducing working hours, but by stimulating demand. For many businessmen, if supply exceeded demand, then the reasonable response was to increase and insure consumption of those goods in oversupply through new domestic and foreign markets, advertising and even higher wages. They were sure that Americans would naturally (or be convinced to) buy those things produced by industry which they had never needed before and consume goods and services, not in response to some set of economic motives, but according to a standard of living that constantly improved. They concluded that human needs were social and plastic, capable of being molded to fit the needs of a growing economy by the hard work of marketing experts, advertisers and business leaders.[30]

Businessmen's new interest in consumption had been well documented as well as their optimism that demand could be stimulated. Herbert Hoover's Committee on Recent Economic Changes, however, presented one of the first and finest examples of this documentation. The Committee pointed out that "economists have long declared that consumption, the satisfaction of wants, would expand with little evidence of satiation, if we could so adjust our economic processes as to make dormant demands effective." But businessmen had proven this assumption in the 1920s. This "almost insatiable appetite for goods and services, this abounding production of all things which almost any man could want, which is so striking a characteristic of the period covered by the survey" eliminated suspicion that the demand could be saturated and markets limited. The Committee found that

> *people . . . have become steadily less concerned about the primary needs—food, clothing, shelter. . . . The slogan of the "full dinner pail" is obsolete. . . . Our wants have ranged more widely and we now demand a broad list of goods and services which come under the category of optional purchases.*

It is in the area of "optional purchases" that the Committee saw the best hope for economic advance. Criticizing the pessimists' ideas about "remote saturation points" the Committee observed that

> *the survey has proved conclusively what was long held to be theoretically true, that our wants are*

> *almost insatiable, that one want satisfied makes way for another. The conclusion is that economically we have a boundless field before us; that there are new wants that will make way endlessly for newer wants as fast as they are satisfied. . . . As long as the appetite for goods and services is practically insatiable, as it appears to be, and as long as productivity can be consistently increased, it seems that we can go on with increasing activity.*[31]

Union leaders did not meet this argument head on. But some Jewish supporters of the five-day week did. For example, Abba Hillel Silver, later president of the Central Conference of American Rabbis, saw in the Sabbath movement a direct counter argument—one that justified the "progressive shortening of the hours of labor" and opposed what he called the "philistine" gospel of consumption. He began by describing the Sabbath as representing "the day of rest, the consecrated covenant between G-d and man." As such it was "much more than mere relaxation from labor. It is a sign and symbol of man's higher destiny."[32] The five-day week could help solve the economic problem of overproduction and unemployment to be sure. But the progressive shortening of the hours of labor could open up a new field of human progress. Increased leisure could provide a time for culture, for learning, for individual creativity and freedom, for the appreciation of life and creation, for spiritual exercise, and for essential rituals, those things which Ben Eliezer ascribed to the Sabbath as the "universal humanizing factor." Silver suggested "we must say to ourselves . . . so far shall I go in my pursuit of the things of life and no further. Beyond that I am a free man, a child of G-d. Beyond that I have a soul and I must give to it time, energy, and interest." He saw in the gospel of consumption a new way in which "our population has been victimized." Just when the opportunity for real human development had been opened through technology and increased free time, it had been closed again by businessmen intent on selling the "golden fleece" of useless luxuries and "excessive wealth." For Silver, human needs for industrial products could still be defined—they were not infinite. Increased productivity and job specialization had created two potential avenues of progress, one spurious and one genuine. If Americans chose to pursue "success" defined in terms of the piling up of useless luxuries, they would turn their backs on the more human form of progress offered by reduced working hours. For Silver, the Sabbath was the pattern for a new form of progress, being cut in the American economy by shorter hours and increased leisure for human, non-material needs.[33]

The job preparing individuals for "worthy use of leisure" was great. But Silver saw the new wealth of free time as a force revitalizing the church, the family, and the school. As people who were able to spend more of their time and energy in these more human institutions, they would naturally learn how to use their time to develop their higher potentials and humane interests.

Moreover, according to Silver, it was no longer possible to assume that all work was valuable because of its extrinsic results. The relationship between work and the necessities of life was becoming increasingly tenuous. Businessmen and economists ignored this problem. Instead, they had begun to understand work and increased wealth as indeterminant values, relative to no set of given, basic or higher standards. Yet, they continued to support and value these things. As such, work, increased production and consumption were redefined as ends in themselves, values to be used to judge other economic and social needs. Losing extrinsic justification, these things took on intrinsic values during the decade. For Silver, these ideas were a corruption of that which was truly valuable in itself—that which Ben Eliezer describes as "the highest religious and ethical sentiments." For him, the Sabbath was the only true "telos" in its "self-contained spiritual world," the model for a qualitatively new kind of progress through increased leisure. Businessmen and economists had entered the realm of philosophy and theology in their "gospel of consumption," promoting the old virtue of work and economic growth by new, virtually existential arguments. Silver believed that work and increased productivity were still instrumental in that they could meet rational needs and then lead to real virtues through shorter hours of work—to human activities that were really worth doing for their own sakes.[34]

The Jewish Sabbath movement, beginning as a narrowly focused attempt to allow Jewish workers to have free Saturdays and to work on Sunday, broadened in two stages. Failing in the first limited attempt, the movement flourished in the second stage as a supportive part of the general labor movement for the five-day week. Finding practical success in this reform, individuals in the Sabbath movement then went on to engage in even larger economic and social debates about modern progress and work, using the Sabbath model as a philosophical base. Certainly many Jews were content with the five-day week's practical accomplishments. It did, after all, satisfy their original purpose and constitute a significant social reform. But others such as Drachman, Cohen, and Silver went on to support the "progressive shortening of the hours of labor," reasoning that as human needs for industry's products were met, increased technology and productivity should free the worker from his job for other, "higher" pursuits. They understood the economy as beginning to offer two avenues for progress—increased wealth and luxuries or increased leisure. Rejecting the first option as a philistine "chasing after the phantom of insatiable desires," they supported the second as the way to authentic progress, humanistic rather than materialistic, individualistic rather than collective. They saw in the Sabbath the "symbol of man's higher destiny" and in increased leisure the practical opportunity to broaden and spread the Sabbath's values and truths.

Endnotes

1 David Philipson, *The Reform Movement in Judaism* (New York: Macmillian, 1931), pp. 195–214, 373; *Historical Statistics of the United States from Colonial Times to the Present* (Washington, D.C.: Government Printing Office, 1975), pp. 155, 172; Robert Moats Miller, *American Protestantism and Social Issues* 1919–1939, p. 172.

2 *New York Times*, January 10, 1925, p. 15:2.

3 *New York Times*, September 17, 1926, p. 9:2.

4 Ben Eliezer [pseudonym], *Letters of a Jewish Father to His Son* (London: J. Murray, 1928), pp. 214, 216–217.

5 Philipson, *op. cit.*, p. 375.

6 *Yearbook of the Central Conference of American Rabbis*, XV (1905), 60, 61, 72–74; XVI (1906), 87–113; XXIV (1914), 84–91.

7 Stuart E. Rosenberg, "The Jewish Tidings and the Sunday Services Question," *Publications of the American Jewish Historical Society*, XLII (June, 1952), 371–385.

8 *Yearbook of CCAR*, XIII (1902), 77, 102–122.

9 *Ibid.*, XVI (1906), 87–113; Frank T. DeVyver, "The Five-Day Week," *Current History*, XXXIII (November, 1930), 223–227.

10 John A. Hutchinson, *We Are Not Divided: A Critical and Historical Study of the Churches of Christ in America* (New York: Round Table Press, 1941), p. 104; *New York Times*, May 31, 1909, p. 16:1; December 1, 1920, p. 36:1.

11 *New York Times*, February 7, 1924, p. 20:4.

12 *New York Times*, December 11, 1920, p. 3:8; July 12, 1921, p. 27:2; June 13, 1922, p. 20:3; May 27, 1927, p. 16:2; January 7, 1921, p. 18:3; March 14, 1923, p. 3:5; January 21, 1925, p. 1:4; January 31, 1925, p, 17:1; January 21, p. 5:3; March 7, 1921, p. 28:2; April 3, 1921, p. 14:4; June 27, 1921, p. 15:3; January 17, 1921, p. 28:2; March 5, 1924, p. 17:3.

13 *New York Times*, February 9, 1921, p. 3:2; March 24, 1921, p. 3:2; March 24, p. 36:3; March 11, 1924, p. 21:8; *American Jewish Year Book*, XXVI (1924), 24–26.

14 *New York Times*, June 16, 1924, p. 16:3; John J. McGrath, *Church and State in American Law* (Milwaukee: Bruce Publishing Co., 1962), Code Virginia 1930 and 4570, *Broad-Grace Arcade Corporation v. Bright,* 48 F. 2d 348, affirmed 52 S. Ct. 137, 284 U.S. 588, 76 L. Ed. 507; Ky. St and 1321—*Stand Amusement Co. v. Commonwealth,* 43 S.W. 2d 321, 241 Ky. 48; Code Pub. Loc. Laws 1930, art. 4 and 6 (18); Const. art. 11A.—Ness v. Ennis, 160 A. 8, 162 Md. 529; *Komen v. City of St. Louis,* 289 S.W. 838, 316 Mo. 9; *New York Times,* October 12, 1924, Section VIII, p. 11:3, *State v. Dean,* 184 N.W. 275, 149 Minn. 410; *Pirkey Bros. v. Commonwealth* 114 S.E. 764, 134 Va. 713, 29, A.L.R. 1290.

15 DeVyver, *loc. cit.*, p. 223.

16 Marion C. Cahill, *Shorter Hours: A Study of the Movement Since the Civil War* (New York: Columbia University Press, 1932), p. 253; National Industrial Conference Board, *The Five-Day Week in Manufacturing Industries* (New York: National Industrial Conference Board, 1929), p. 28; *American Jewish Year Book*, XXVI (1924), 24.

17 Matthew Josephson, *Sidney Hillman: Statesman of American Labor* (New York: Doubleday, 1952), pp. 177–180; *Monthly Labor Review*, XVI (August, 1923), 503; XVIII (June, 1924), 1366–1368; XXIII (December, 1926), 1153; XX (June, 1925), 1390–1391; Bureau of Labor Statistics *Bulletin #439* (June, 1924), 373, 374, 573–575; *Bulletin #435*, 20–21.

18 National Industrial Conference Board, *op. cit.* pp. 15–24. *Monthly Labor Review*, XXIII (December, 1926), 1153–1169; John P. Frey, "Labor's Movement for a Five-Day Week," *Current History Magazine*, XXV (December, 1926), 369–373.

19 Chester M. Wright, "Epoch-Weakening Decisions in the Great American Federation of Labor Convention at Detroit," *American Labor World*, (1926), 22–24; American Federation of Labor (AFL), *Report of the Proceedings of the 46th Annual Convention* (Washington, D.C.: AFL, 1926); see especially the Report of the Committee on the Shorter Workday, pp. 195–207; Sidney Hillman, "Attitude of Organized Labor Toward the Shorter Work Week," *Monthly Labor Review*, XXIII (December, 1926), 1167–1168.

20 *New York Times*, February 7, 1924, p. 20:4.

21 *New York Times*, May 10, 1926, 21:4; January 14, 1925, 5:3; September 17, 1926, p. 9:2; *Yearbook of CCAR*, XXIV (1924), 51; *American Jewish Yearbook*," (1925), 26–28.

22 *New York Times*, January 10, 1925, p. 15:2.

23 William Green, "The Five Day Week," *American Federationist*, XXXIII (November, 1926), 1299, 1300; for Green and Woll's

attitudes see also American Federation of Labor, *op. cit.*, pp. 195–207; for Hillman's view see "Attitude of Organized Labor Toward the Shorter Work Week," *Monthly Labor Review*, XXIII (December, 1926), 1167–1168; William Green, "Leisure for Labor," *Magazine of Business*, LVI (August, 1929), 136–137; James M. Lynch, "Shorter Working Day Urged as Alleviation for Depression Cycles," *American Labor World* (November, 1926), 28, 29.

24 James L. Wright, "Is the Machine Replacing Men?" *Nation's Business* (September, 1927), 79.

25 Bernard Drachman, *Looking at America* (New York: Books for Libraries Press, 1934), pp. 97–102.

26 William Green, "Leisure for Labor," *loc. cit.*, pp. 136–137; William Green, *The Five-Day Week: Inevitable* (New York: American Federation of Labor, 1932), pp. 1–6; Wright, "Is the Machine Replacing Man?" *loc. cit.*, p. 79.

27 Green, "Leisure for Labor," *loc. cit.*, pp. 136–137; Green, "The Five-Day Week," *loc. cit.*, pp. 567–574.

28 Matthew Woll, "Labor and the New Leisure," *Recreation*, XXVII (1933), 418; Matthew Woll, "Leisure and Labor," *Playground*, XIX (1925), 322.

29 Felix Cohen, "The Blessing of Unemployment," The American Scholar, II (1933), 203–214.

30 Report of the 15th Annual Meeting of the Chamber of Commerce, "Prosperity and Production," *Nation's Business*, XV (May 20, 1927), 40, 41; William Foster and Waddill Catchings, "What is Business Without a Buyer?" *Nation's Business*, XIV (June, 1926), 27; William Craig, "Digest of the Business Press," *Nation's Business*, XIV (June, 1926), 14; Glen Buck, "This American Ascendancy," *Nation's Business*, XV (March, 1927), 15; "Business Views in Review," *Nation's Business*, XV (July, 1927), 117; (August, 1927), 95; Edward Cowdrick, "The New Economic Gospel of Consumption," *Industrial Management*, LXXIV (October, 1927), 208; Irvin S. Paull, "When is Industry's Job Complete?" *Nation's Business*, XV (December, 1927), 28, 29; James L. Wright, "Is the Machine Replacing Man?" *Nation's Business*, XV (September, 1927), 78–80, for views about increased consumption by James Maloney and Secretary of Labor David, who argued that "the luxuries of yesterday become the necessities of today"; Merle Thorpe, "The Amazing Decade," *Nation's Business*, XVI (September, 1928), 9; J. H. Collins, "Producer Goes Exploring for the Consumer," *Saturday Evening Post*, CXCV (April 7, 1923), 8; T. C. Sheehan, "Must We Limit Production?" *Magazine for Business*, LIII (February, 1928), 150–152.

31 *Report of the President's Committee on Recent Economic Changes, Recent Economic Changes* (New York: National Bureau of Economic Research, 1929), pp. xv, xviii, 52, 59, 80, 81, 574–578.

32 Abba Hillel Silver, "Leisure and the Church," *Playground*, XX (January, 1927), 539.

33 Abba Hillel Silver, *Religion in a Changing World* (New York: Richard R. Smith, Inc., 1930), pp. 63, 77, 143–146, 184–187, 190–194.

34 Samuel Strauss, "Things Are in the Saddle," *Atlantic Monthly* (November, 1924), 577–588; idem, *American Opportunity* (Boston: 1935), pp. 182–193.

Benjamin Kline Hunnicutt, "The Jewish Sabbath Movement in the Early Twentieth Century," *American Jewish History* 69:2 (Dec. 1979), pp. 196–225

THE SHABBAT EXPERIMENT: LIMITING OR LIBERATING?

BY LISA SUGARMAN

So consider this (and I mean really take a minute and think this through): No emails. No telephones (yes, that includes cells). No TV. No iPods or laptops. No driving. No radio. No electronics whatsoever. Period. For 24 hours. Imagine giving up everything with an on/off switch. Could you do it? And why would you want to? Would it restrict or release you?

Well, a few months ago in this column I opened my big mouth and admitted to the entire town of Marblehead that every once in awhile I fantasize about chucking all the devices and gadgets in my life just so I could remember what real life feels like. Not permanently, just sort of a reboot for the soul.

Ever since I put it out there it's been on my mind. I wanted to make it happen but the timing never seemed to be right. Plus, I'd be lying if I said I wasn't a little intimidated by the thought of giving everything up. It sounded great in theory but when you think about the actual ramifications it ends up looking like a pretty outrageous idea, especially considering how most of us live our lives day to day. We're constantly either refreshing, updating, or checking something and if we're not doing that we're chauffeuring someone somewhere or making a call or using a gadget that's supposed to make the quality of our life better.

But does it?

So when the email came in from my daughter's Hebrew school, Chabad, a few weeks ago inviting people to take The Shabbat Challenge I knew someone was sending me a sign that this was my shot. So I took it.

For anyone who doesn't know what's involved in "keeping Shabbat," it means that every week, from sundown on Friday to sundown on Saturday, Jews all over the world unplug. Fifty-two weeks a year. And for those 24 hours, they stay unplugged. They eat, they rest, they reflect, many pray, they spend time with family and friends, and they recover physically and spiritually from their week.

Chabad picked the weekend in late January and they spelled out the rules: driving, not okay; board games, okay; power, not okay; walking, okay (it's a long list). So for one, full day my family would flip the master breaker and go completely dark. And we decided that if we were going to do it we were going to go all in, which for a Reformed family who practices the most liberal form of Judaism that was WAY in. The fact that it was temporary definitely took the edge off. But it was still intimidating no matter how you looked at it.

So we picked which lights would stay on for the full 24 hours; we unscrewed the light bulb in the fridge so it didn't go on when we opened the door; we cooked everything before sundown on Friday night; we unplugged every device; we picked out all our board games and books. And then it came.

And it was painless.

Without really even noticing, Shabbat settled in and the vibe of our whole house shifted. It was a quietude that was defined by the fact that we knew it would last, even for only a day. All the pressure was gone. The anticipation of rushing or fussing or preparing had disappeared. Once we committed to the challenge everything was surprisingly easy. And it became shockingly obvious that we all carry around a very misplaced sense of urgency. When there's actually very little that we can't do without.

My brother-in-law gave me the best analogy right before sunset. He said, "There's a beauty created in the quietude of the Sabbath that's difficult to describe or capture otherwise. You need to focus on that quietude rather than on the things you might otherwise be doing." Then he put it in terms that I could really understand. He said that my sister-in-law made some

LISA SUGARMAN

Lisa Sugarman writes the nationally syndicated opinion column "It Is What It Is" and is the author of *How to Raise Perfectly Imperfect Kids and Be OK with It—Real Tips & Strategies for Parents of Today's Gen Z Kids*, *Untying Parent Anxiety: 18 Myths That Have You in Knots—And How to Get Free*, and *LIFE: It Is What It Is*.

amazing salsa the other night and also some homemade tortilla chips with a hint of lime. He said he noticed the hint of lime when he ate the chips without the salsa but then forgot all about it once he started dipping into the fiery salsa. After the salsa was gone he said he started eating the chips dry again and realized how much he liked that subtle hint of lime that was invisible in the context of the salsa. He said the same thing goes for the Sabbath. Enjoy removing the noise to find the quietude that's always there waiting to be revealed.

Ok, so we may have bent the rules a little and taught our girls how to play Texas Hold'em to pass the time (gambling can't exactly be promoted on Shabbat, but it's a game and games are ok). But since flexibility is the real root of Reformed Judaism we cut ourselves some slack. We also stayed in our pajamas until 4 in the afternoon, getting dressed only to walk down to Preston Beach to see the sunset. And by that point, even the sound of the cars on the road seemed a little intrusive because we were used to such a comfortable quiet. It was a little surreal, at least for me, feeling so far away from home even though I was right there. Probably because everything felt so different.

In the end, the 24 hours flew by and we all ended up with much more than we bargained for. It gave us a clarity and peace that would be tough to duplicate any other way. And it changed each one of us somehow, too. My girls said they were shocked at how fast the time went by and how "not boring" the experience was. And my husband, who would sleep with an earpiece in if he could, said he felt amazingly liberated to shut everything down and just walk away. And for him that's big.

Now this doesn't mean we're going all in and making this a weekly thing, but it definitely gave us all something to think about. It showed us that there's a place we can always go to get away—far away, like a staycation for the spirit. And those are in right now, aren't they? So it's ironic: after all that, the real challenge was letting the Sabbath go. Who knew?

March 11, 2010 http://lisasugarman.com/the-shabbat-experiment-limiting-or-liberating/

THE WORLD OF THE SHTETL

BY ELIE WIESEL

On Shabbat, if poverty did not vanish altogether, it was attenuated. One can never speak enough of what Shabbat was like in the shtetl—and what it did for its inhabitants. The Shabbat helped people endure the other six days of the week, often gray and dark, heavy with sorrow and anxiety. Hence the waiting for Shabbat, which actually began much earlier. Thursday evening or early Friday morning, the housewife would already be busy preparing the hallah, gefilte fish, and cholent, the traditional elements of a Shabbat meal in the shtetl. The white tablecloth, the white shirt: everything had to be ready, and everything was the housewife's responsibility. One easily forgets that we owe the gift of Shabbat to the queen of the home, *Shabbat malka*, the Shabbat queen. We couldn't wait for her arrival.

In the stores, business was conducted with haste. Sellers and customers were equally in a hurry to go home. Men would go to the ritual bath, the *mikvah*, then dress and prepare to be worthy of welcoming the Shabbat, already on the horizon. The first to spot her would be the beadle, the shammash: he would go around stores and homes shouting "*Yidden, greit zicht tzu Shabbes!*"—Jews, ready yourselves for the Sabbath! Or a variation on the same theme: "*Yidden, s'is bald Shabbes oif der velt!*"—Jews, it's almost Sabbath in the world! At home, one did not need these reminders: the mother, mine too, lit the candles honoring Shabbat, one for each member of the family, and blessed them silently, with gestures of grace and tenderness. Suddenly, her face would be illuminated by a light coming from another world, from another time, a light at once frail and eternal. And her beauty was multiplied sevenfold, so that even now as I am writing these words, the tears well up in my throat.

In the shul also, everything seemed different. More luminous, the candelabras. More serene, the faces. More melodious, the prayers. The Talmud is right: on Shabbat, one gains an added soul, the *neshama yeteira*.

Then, at the end of the service, many worshipers began running toward the visitors in shul. If there were none the shammash would yell aloud, "Are there strangers here?" It was forbidden, absolutely forbidden, to allow anyone to be without an invitation to partake with some family in a Shabbat meal. Frequently people would fight over a visitor. It was an honor to invite him or her to their table. I myself can hardly remember a Shabbat without an honored guest in our home.

Whenever my maternal grandfather, Reb Dodye, was with us, we would feel doubly honored. And I was three times as happy. I have sworn never to forget him, nor his return from the Shabbat-eve office. He would stop on the threshold, kiss the mezuzah, and, his face burning with delight, start the Wizsnitzer "*Sholem aleikhem malakhei ha'shareit*"—Be blessed, angels in the service of peace. And it was as if peace now reigned over heaven and earth, a peace that brought together men and women of all nations, of all ages, a dream of which Shabbat remains the uplifting and inspiring symbol.

The end of Shabbat was signaled by mother and grandmother. Shortly before the Havdalah ceremony, which separates light from darkness and the sacred from the profane, the Shabbat from the weekdays, both women, like all mothers, would recite the special prayer attributed to the great Rebbe Levi-Yitzhak of Berditchev: "*Gott fun Avrohom, Yitzhok un Yankev . . .*" G-d of Abraham, Isaac, and Jacob, extend your protection over Thy children and ours . . . When the prayer ends, the Havdalah begins.

ELIE WIESEL, 1928–2016

Writer, professor, and political activist. Wiesel was born in Sighet, Romania, and was deported by the Nazis to Auschwitz when he was 15. He wrote more than 40 books of fiction and nonfiction, including the acclaimed memoir *Night*, which has been published in more than 30 languages. In 1986, Wiesel won the Nobel Prize for Peace. He has received numerous awards, including the Presidential Medal of Freedom and the U.S. Congressional Gold Medal.

Whereupon another song takes hold of my memory: "*Bobeshi, zog nokh nit G-d fun Avrohom . . .*" It's a little child pleading with his grandmother not to recite her prayer, not yet, let her wait a bit longer, the sun hasn't set yet in the west, let Shabbat last a while longer . . . The little child loves the Shabbat and refuses to leave it behind—to be left behind.

Which, of course, recalls an old Hasid or rebbe who, during the mystical Third Meal, is doing in his way what the grandmother could have done in hers. He sings a song: "*Ven ich volt ge'hat koi'ekh,*" if I had the strength, "*volt ich in di gassen gelofen,*" I would run through the streets, "*un ich volt geshre'in hoikh,*" and I would yell with all my might, "*Shabess, heiliger shabess,*" Holy, holy Sabbath . . . And legend has it that as long as he sang, the Shabbat would remain with him and his followers. So he sang and sang. . . .

Wise Men and Their Tales: Portraits of Biblical, Talmudic, and Hasidic Masters (New York: Schocken Books, 2003), pp. 328–330

Lesson 6

Children holding signs bearing a proud Jewish message at a Lag Ba'Omer parade in Brooklyn, NY, May 1970.

TIME TO IMPROVE

THE JEWISH CONCEPT OF PROGRESS

Ancient societies were staunchly anti-progress, considering human history locked in endless cycles. The Torah insisted otherwise: we can, must, and will change the world for the better; war will eventually cease; and justice and kindness will ultimately prevail—provided that this goal is harmoniously married to ethical monotheism. It charged the Jews with sharing this vision with humanity, and today's world is more open and eager than ever to hear our empowering message.

TEXT 1

THOMAS CAHILL, *THE GIFTS OF THE JEWS* (NEW YORK: NAN A. TALESE, 1998), P. 5

All evidence points to there having been, in the earliest religious thought, a vision of the cosmos that was profoundly cyclical. The assumptions that early man made about the world were, in all their essentials, little different from the assumptions that later and more sophisticated societies, like Greece and India, would make in a more elaborate manner. As Henri-Charles Puech says of Greek thought in his seminal *Man and Time*: "No event is unique, nothing is enacted but once . . . ; every event has been enacted, is enacted, and will be enacted perpetually; the same individuals have appeared, appear, and will appear at every turn of the circle."

The Jews were the first people to break out of this circle, to find a new way of thinking and experiencing, a new way of understanding and feeling the world, so much so that it may be said with some justice that theirs is the only new idea that human beings have ever had. But their worldview has become so much a part of us that at this point it might as well have been written into our cells as a genetic code.

THOMAS CAHILL
1940–

American scholar and writer. Born in New York City to Irish-American parents, Cahill has a pontifical degree in philosophy and an MFA in film and dramatic literature from Columbia University. Cahill has taught at Queens College, Fordham University, and Seton Hall University. He is best known for *The Hinges of History* series, in which he recounts formative moments in Western civilization.

HENRI-CHARLES PUECH, 1902–1986

French historian. Puech authored a three-volume work titled *Histoire des Religions (The History of Religions)*, published in 1970.

Rabbi DovBer Pinson *elaborates on cyclical and linear time:*

MYJLI.COM/GIFTS

TEXT 2

RABBI LORD JONATHAN SACKS, *RADICAL THEN, RADICAL NOW* (LONDON: CONTINUUM, 2003), PP. 99–101

There is acceptance in Judaism. We call this *tzidduk hadin*, coming to terms with suffering and loss, saying that "all that G-d does is for the best." But Jewish law asks us to accept only that which cannot be changed, and there is no evil in the future that cannot be changed.

The significance of this is fundamental. The great literary genre of ancient Greece was tragedy, and tragedy is born in the idea that there is a fate (*moira*) that is inexorable. Man struggles against it and is always doomed to failure. Tragedy in the Greek sense is a concept that simply cannot be translated into biblical Hebrew. Not only is there no such word, there cannot be, for in Judaism, there is no fate that is inevitable. . . .

Ours is an age of Eastern and New Age mysticisms and therapies of various kinds. Mysticism is a way of accepting the world by rising above it. Therapy is a way of accepting myself as I am. Both are ways of reconciling ourselves to a world we believe we cannot change, and both, from a Jewish point of view, are inadequate accounts of what it means to be human. Acceptance of what is, is a failure to hear the call of what ought to be.

RABBI LORD JONATHAN SACKS
1948–

Former chief rabbi of the United Kingdom. Rabbi Sacks attended Cambridge University and received his doctorate from King's College, London. A prolific and influential author, his books include *Will We Have Jewish Grandchildren?* and *The Dignity of Difference*. He received the Jerusalem Prize in 1995 for his contributions to enhancing Jewish life in the Diaspora, was knighted and made a life peer in 2005, and became Baron Sacks of Aldridge in 2009.

TEXT 3a

ISAIAH 2:2,4

וְהָיָה בְּאַחֲרִית הַיָּמִים . . . וְכִתְּתוּ חַרְבוֹתָם לְאִתִּים וַחֲנִיתוֹתֵיהֶם לְמַזְמֵרוֹת,
לֹא יִשָּׂא גוֹי אֶל גּוֹי חֶרֶב וְלֹא יִלְמְדוּ עוֹד מִלְחָמָה.

It shall come to pass in the end of days that . . . they shall beat their swords into plowshares and their spears into pruning hooks; nation shall not lift sword against nation, neither shall they learn war anymore.

Rabbi Simon Jacobson *discusses the Jewish gift of destiny:*

MYJLI.COM/GIFTS

TEXT 3b

MAIMONIDES, *MISHNEH TORAH,* LAWS OF KINGS AND THEIR WARS 12:5

וּבְאוֹתוֹ הַזְּמַן לֹא יִהְיֶה שָׁם לֹא רָעָב, וְלֹא מִלְחָמָה, וְלֹא קִנְאָה וְתַחֲרוּת,
שֶׁהַטּוֹבָה תִּהְיֶה מוּשְׁפַּעַת הַרְבֵּה, וְכָל הַמַּעֲדַנִּים מְצוּיִין כֶּעָפָר, וְלֹא יִהְיֶה
עֵסֶק כָּל הָעוֹלָם אֶלָּא לָדַעַת אֶת ה' בִּלְבָד.

In that era, there will be neither famine nor war, neither envy nor rivalry, for there will be abundance, and all delights will be as freely available as dust. The occupation of the entire world will be solely to know G-d.

RABBI MOSHE BEN MAIMON (MAIMONIDES, RAMBAM) 1135–1204

Halachist, philosopher, author, and physician. Maimonides was born in Córdoba, Spain. After the conquest of Córdoba by the Almohads, he fled Spain and eventually settled in Cairo, Egypt. There, he became the leader of the Jewish community and served as court physician to the vizier of Egypt. He is most noted for authoring the *Mishneh Torah,* an encyclopedic arrangement of Jewish law, and for his philosophical work, *Guide for the Perplexed.* His rulings on Jewish law are integral to the formation of halachic consensus.

QUESTION FOR DISCUSSION

Is there a difference between behaving morally due to logic and conscience or due to an absolute, transcendent moral standard? Does the source of our moral convictions matter?

Peaceable Kingdom (Detail), Edward Hicks, oil on canvas, c. 1848. (Albright-Knox Art Gallery, Buffalo)

Figure 6.1

The Path to Absolute Morality

THE SUPERIOR AUTHORITY MUST BE:

The exclusive authority over all of existence and, therefore, "entitled" to dictate right and wrong

An entity that is moral

Interested in the events of the universe and, thus, concerned with how humanity should conduct itself

Exercise 6.1

Read the following verses with a partner. Underline the words or phrases that underscore that G-d Himself is:

1 the sole authority over the universe

2 the epitome of morality

3 concerned about human morality

TEXT 4

GENESIS 18:20–21, 23–25

וַיֹּאמֶר ה' זַעֲקַת סְדֹם וַעֲמֹרָה כִּי רָבָּה, וְחַטָּאתָם כִּי כָבְדָה מְאֹד. אֵרְדָה נָּא וְאֶרְאֶה הַכְּצַעֲקָתָהּ הַבָּאָה אֵלַי עָשׂוּ כָּלָה . . .

וַיִּגַּשׁ אַבְרָהָם וַיֹּאמַר, הַאַף תִּסְפֶּה צַדִּיק עִם רָשָׁע. אוּלַי יֵשׁ חֲמִשִּׁים צַדִּיקִם בְּתוֹךְ הָעִיר, הַאַף תִּסְפֶּה וְלֹא תִשָּׂא לַמָּקוֹם לְמַעַן חֲמִשִּׁים הַצַּדִּיקִם אֲשֶׁר בְּקִרְבָּהּ. חָלִלָה לְּךָ מֵעֲשֹׂת כַּדָּבָר הַזֶּה לְהָמִית צַדִּיק עִם רָשָׁע וְהָיָה כַצַּדִּיק כָּרָשָׁע, חָלִלָה לָּךְ הֲשֹׁפֵט כָּל הָאָרֶץ לֹא יַעֲשֶׂה מִשְׁפָּט.

G-d said to Abraham, "The outcry from Sodom and Gomorah is so great and their sin so grievous that I will go down and see if what they have done is as bad as the outcry that has reached me. If it is, I will destroy them. . . .

Abraham approached and said to G-d, "Will You even destroy the righteous with the wicked? What if there are fifty righteous people in the city; will You destroy it and not spare the place for the sake of the fifty righteous people who are in it?" Far be it from You to do a thing such as this, to kill the righteous along with the wicked and treat the righteous like the wicked. Far be it from You! Will the Judge of the entire earth not perform justice?"

***Rabbi Yitzchak Breitowitz** discusses the novelty of the link between religion and morality:*

MYJLI.COM/GIFTS

TEXT 5

MAIMONIDES, *MISHNEH TORAH*, LAWS OF KINGS 9:1

עַל שִׁשָּׁה דְּבָרִים נִצְטַוָּוה אָדָם הָרִאשׁוֹן: עַל עֲבוֹדָה זָרָה, וְעַל בִּרְכַּת הַשֵּׁם, וְעַל שְׁפִיכוּת דָּמִים, וְעַל גִּילוּי עֲרָיוֹת, וְעַל הַגָּזֵל, וְעַל הַדִּינִים . . . הוֹסִיף לְנֹחַ אֵבֶר מִן הַחַי.

G-d commanded Adam concerning six matters. He forbade (1) idolatry, (2) blasphemy, (3) murder, (4) illicit sexual relations, (5) theft, and He instructed him to (6) establish a judiciary. . . . To Noah, G-d added another prohibition: (7) consuming a limb torn from a living animal.

Visit the post-lesson website for a comprehensive overview of the Seven Noahide Laws, by ***Rabbi Mendel Kaplan****:*

MYJLI.COM/GIFTS

Illustration of Noah after the flood, from the *Harrison Miscellany*. Corfu, first half of 18th century. (The Braginsky Collection)

Figure 6.2

FRAMEWORK FOR MORAL LIVING

Idolatry	Establishes absolute morality and individual purpose.
Blasphemy	
Illicit sexual relations	Establishes the family framework that cultivates our unique identity and establishes a framework for human discipline.
Murder	Don't violate the image of G-d in another.
Theft	Don't abuse others who are created in G-d's image.
Cruelty to animals	Don't be sadistic.
Judiciary	Enforce law and order in society.

TEXT 6a

ISAIAH 60:3

וְהָלְכוּ גוֹיִם לְאוֹרֵךְ, וּמְלָכִים לְנֹגַהּ זַרְחֵךְ.

Nations shall walk by your [Israel's] light and kings by the glow of your radiance.

***Natan Sharansky**, in an exclusive interview with JLI, discusses how modern Israel has been a gift to the entire world:*

MYJLI.COM/GIFTS

TEXT 6b

RABBI OVADIAH SEFORNO, EXODUS 19:6

"וְאַתֶּם תִּהְיוּ לִי מַמְלֶכֶת כֹּהֲנִים" (שְׁמוֹת יט, ו): וּבָזֶה תִּהְיוּ סְגוּלָּה מִכֻּלָּם, כִּי תִהְיוּ מַמְלֶכֶת כֹּהֲנִים לְהָבִין וּלְהוֹרוֹת לְכָל הַמִּין הָאֱנוֹשִׁי, "לִקְרוֹא כֻלָּם בְּשֵׁם ה', לְעָבְדוֹ שְׁכֶם אֶחָד" (צְפַנְיָה ג, ט).

"And you shall be to Me a kingdom of priests" (EXODUS 19:6): You will be a treasure to Me in the sense that you will be a kingdom of priests, to guide and teach the entire human race "to call upon the name of G-d and serve Him with one purpose" (ZEPHANIAH 3:9).

באור על התורה
אשר חבר און וחקר
עובדיה ספורנו

RABBI OVADIAH SEFORNO
1475–1550

Biblical exegete, philosopher, and physician. Seforno was born in Cesena, Italy. After gaining a thorough knowledge of Talmud and the sciences, he moved to Rome, where he studied medicine and taught Hebrew to the German scholar Johannes Reuchlin. Seforno eventually settled in Bologna, where he founded and directed a yeshiva until his death. His magnum opus is a biblical commentary focused on the simple interpretation of the text, with an emphasis on philology and philosophy.

TEXT 7

MAIMONIDES, *MISHNEH TORAH*, LAWS OF KINGS 11:4

אַךְ מַחְשְׁבוֹת בּוֹרֵא עוֹלָם אֵין כֹּחַ בְּאָדָם לְהַשִּׂיגָם כִּי לֹא דְרָכֵינוּ דְרָכָיו וְלֹא מַחְשְׁבוֹתֵינוּ מַחְשְׁבוֹתָיו.

וְכָל הַדְּבָרִים הָאֵלּוּ שֶׁל יֵשׁוּעַ הַנָּצְרִי וְשֶׁל זֶה הַיִּשְׁמְעֵאלִי שֶׁעָמַד אַחֲרָיו אֵינָן אֶלָּא לְיַשֵּׁר דֶּרֶךְ לַמֶּלֶךְ הַמָּשִׁיחַ וּלְתַקֵּן הָעוֹלָם כֻּלּוֹ לַעֲבוֹד אֶת ה' בְּיַחַד. שֶׁנֶּאֱמַר, "כִּי אָז אֶהְפֹּךְ אֶל עַמִּים שָׂפָה בְרוּרָה לִקְרֹא כֻלָּם בְּשֵׁם הַשֵּׁם לְעָבְדוֹ שְׁכֶם אֶחָד".

כֵּיצַד? כְּבַר נִתְמַלֵּא הָעוֹלָם מִדִּבְרֵי הַמָּשִׁיחַ וּמִדִּבְרֵי הַתּוֹרָה וּמִדִּבְרֵי הַמִּצְוֹות, וּפָשְׁטוּ דְבָרִים אֵלּוּ בְּאִיִּים רְחוֹקִים וּבְעַמִּים רַבִּים עַרְלֵי לֵב, וְהֵם נוֹשְׂאִים וְנוֹתְנִים בִּדְבָרִים אֵלּוּ.

The designs of the Creator defy human comprehension, for His ways are not like our ways, nor are His thoughts like our thoughts.

Ultimately, the events of Jesus of Nazareth and those of [Mohammed] the Ishmaelite, who arose after him, only serve to pave the way for the Messiah and to prepare the entire world for the time when all of humanity will serve G-d together. As the verse states, "I will then purify the speech of all people, so that they will all call upon the name of G-d and serve Him with one purpose."

How is this? [By way of these religions,] the world has been filled with talk of the Messiah, the Torah, and the *mitzvot*. As a result, awareness of these concepts has reached the furthermost islands and many spiritually insensitive nations, and these concepts have become regular topics of discussion among them.

TEXT 8

THE REBBE, RABBI MENACHEM MENDEL SCHNEERSON,
LIKUTEI SICHOT 26, PP.141–142

ס'אִיז יָדוּעַ בְּדִבְרֵי יְמֵי יִשְׂרָאֵל אִין דִי זְמַנִים שֶׁעָבְרוּ, אַז אוֹיךְ אִין דִי מְדִינוֹת וואוּ דֶער עִנְיַן הַגִּיוּר אִיז לוֹיטְן גֶעזֶעץ פוּן דֶער מֶמְשָׁלָה דָארְט - נִיט גֶעוֶוען פַארְבָּאטְן מִטַעַם הַמֶמְשָׁלָה, הָאבְּן זִיךְ אִידְן זֵייעֶר גֶעהִיט פוּן יֶעדֶער זַאךְ וָואס קֶען אוֹיסְגֶעטַייטְשְׁט וֶוערְן וִוי אַ פְּעוּלָה צוּ הֶעלְפְן עֶמֶעצְן מְגַיֵיר זַיין (אַפִילוּ אִין אַזֶעלְכֶע פַאלְן וֶוען דֶער גֵר אִיז פוּן זִיךְ אַלֵיין גֶעקוּמֶען זִיךְ מְגַיֵיר זַיין, אוּן אַוַודַאי נִיט צוּ טָאן עֶפֶּעס וָואס קֶען בַּאטְרַאכְט וֶוערְן וִוי אַ הִשְׁתַּדְלוּת אוּן תַּעֲמוּלָה צוּ מְגַיֵיר זַיין גֵרִים). וַוייל אוֹיךְ אִין אַזֶעלְכֶע מְדִינוֹת אִיז דָאס גֶעוֶוען אַ סַכָּנָה צוּלִיבּ דִי בִּלְבּוּלִים אוּן עֲלִילוֹת וָואס דָאס הָאט גֶעקֶענְט אַרוֹיסְרוּפְן. וּבִפְרַט - מִפְּנֵי הַחֲשַׁשׁ גָדוֹל אַז מֶען וֶועט עֶס נוּצְן קֶעגְן דִי אִידְן בִּשְׁאָר הַמְדִינוֹת . . .

וּמוּבָן אַז אוֹיךְ דִי הִשְׁתַּדְלוּת פוּן אִידְן צוּ בַּאוִוירְקְן אַ בֶּן נֹחַ . . . עֶר זָאל מְקַיֵים זַיין דִי שֶׁבַע מִצְוֹת אִיז גֶעוֶוען פַארְבּוּנְדְן מִיט אַ סַכָּנָה כַּיוֹצֵא בָּזֶה. מ'הָאט דָאס גֶעקֶענְט אָנְנֶעמֶען אַלְס אַיין אַרַיינְמִישׁוּנג בֶּאֱמוּנָתָם, וְכוּ' וְכוּ' . . .

אִיז מוּבָן, אַז בְּדֶרֶךְ כְּלַל הָאבְּן זִיךְ אִידְן גֶעמוּזְט אָפְּהַאלְטְן דֶערְפוּן צוּלִיבּ פִּקוּחַ נֶפֶשׁ. אוּן אִין אוֹיסְנַאם פַאלְן, וֶוען מֶען הָאט דָאס גֶעטָאן, אִיז דָאס גֶעוֶוען בִּזְהִירוּת מַתְאִימָה, וּבְלִי פִּרְסוּם. אִיז דֶערִיבֶּער מוּבָן וָואס מ'הָאט אוֹיךְ נִיט מְפַרְסֵם גֶעוֶוען קֵיין שְׁאֵלוֹת וּתְשׁוּבוֹת בָּזֶה. וְיֵשׁ לֹאמַר אַז מִצַד דֶעם זֶעלְבְּן טַעַם אִיז דֶער דִין ("לָכּוּף") אוֹיךְ נִיט דֶערְמָאנְט אִין שׁוּלְחָן עָרוּךְ אוּן נוֹשְׂאֵי כֵּלָיו - אִין יֶענֶע זְמַנִים אִיז עֶס גֶעוֶוען פִּקוּחַ נֶפֶשׁ.

וּמוּבָן אַז אִין אַ פַאל וואוּ דֶער חֲשַׁשׁ אִיז לְגַמְרֵי נִיטָא - וִוי בַּמְדִינוֹת אֵלוּ - אִיז דָא דֶער צִיוּוי לָכּוּף.

RABBI MENACHEM MENDEL SCHNEERSON
1902–1994

The towering Jewish leader of the 20th century, known as "the Lubavitcher Rebbe," or simply as "the Rebbe." Born in southern Ukraine, the Rebbe escaped Nazi-occupied Europe, arriving in the U.S. in June 1941. The Rebbe inspired and guided the revival of traditional Judaism after the European devastation, impacting virtually every Jewish community the world over. The Rebbe often emphasized that the performance of just one additional good deed could usher in the era of Mashiach. The Rebbe's scholarly talks and writings have been printed in more than 200 volumes.

It is well-known that Jews in previous generations were wary of any behavior that could be construed as facilitating conversion to Judaism (even when the prospective convert was the initiator, and certainly if it could be viewed as an attempt to promote conversion).

***Professor Lawrence Schiffman** on the Lubavitcher Rebbe's views concerning the modern-day Jew's universal mission:*

MYJLI.COM/GIFTS

This was the case even in countries where conversion to Judaism was *not* outlawed because even in those countries, such behavior could have resulted in dangerous libels. In addition, there was concern that it could be used against Jews in other lands. . . .

It is self-understood that encouraging non-Jews . . . to observe the Seven Noahide Laws would also have been dangerous because even this could have been construed as an intrusion into their faith. . . .

It is thus understood that Jews generally avoided advocating observance of the Noahide Laws out of concern for their lives. On the rare occasion that something was done in this regard, it was approached with care and discretion. This is likely the reason why this subject is not discussed in Jewish legal responsa and is not mentioned in the Code of Jewish Law.

Obviously, when this concern no longer applies—such as in our current climate—the obligation to promote the Noahide Laws is fully applicable.

TEXT 9

RABBI LORD JONATHAN SACKS, *RADICAL THEN, RADICAL NOW,* PP. 171–172

Matthew Arnold once said, "As long as the world lasts, all who want to make progress in righteousness will come to Israel for inspiration, as to the people who have had the sense for righteousness most glowing and strongest."

Far from having completed its task, it would be fairer to say that a Jewish contribution to civilization has rarely been more urgently needed. For the first time we live in plural societies in which Jews have the opportunity to enter public debate on free and equal terms. And for the first time since the decline and fall of ancient Greece and Rome there is a real battle to be fought between Judaic and neo-pagan ideas of human responsibility, sexuality, the family, the sanctity of human life, the rule of law, the objectivity of moral values and the ethics of the market and the public square.

MATTHEW ARNOLD, 1822–1888

English Victorian poet. In 1851, Arnold was appointed Her Majesty's Inspector of Schools. In this role, he traveled frequently throughout the British provinces, and he was also sent by the government to inquire into the state of education in other European countries. His first volume of verse was *The Strayed Reveller and Other Poems*, first published in 1849.

Rabbi Lord Jonathan Sacks *on why a spiritual and moral basis is a prerequisite to a thriving civilization:*

MYJLI.COM/GIFTS

Yeshiva student on Manhattan street, encouraging passerby to perform *mitzvot*.

Exercise 6.2

Rabbi Sacks points to several examples of when contemporary values—at least in some quarters—conflict with the Torah's vision for humanity. Underline an item on his list that you feel is most crucial and about which you feel that the Torah's voice must be heard.

TEXT 10

WILL HERBERG, *JUDAISM AND MODERN MAN* (NEW YORK: ATHENEUM, 1979), PP. 91–92

The moral principles of Western civilization are, in fact, all derived from the tradition rooted in Scripture and have vital meaning only in the context of that tradition. The attempt made in recent decades by secularist thinkers to disengage these values from their religious context, in the assurance that they could live a life of their own as "humanistic" ethic, has resulted in what one writer has called our "cut flower culture." Cut flowers retain their original beauty and fragrance, but only so long as they retain the vitality that they have drawn from their now-severed roots; after that is exhausted, they wither and die. So with freedom, brotherhood, justice, and personal dignity—the values that form the moral foundation of our civilization. Without the life-giving power of the faith out of which they have sprung, they possess neither meaning nor vitality. Morality ungrounded in G-d is indeed a house built upon sand, unable to stand up against the vagaries of impulse, and the brutal pressures of power and self-interest.

WILL HERBERG
1901–1977

Theologian. Herberg was a graduate professor of Judaic studies and social philosophy at Drew University. He was a leading conservative thinker during the 1950s and a contributing editor to the *National Review* magazine.

TEXT 11

HILLEL HALKIN, "*THE SACRED CHAIN,* BY NORMAN F. CANTOR: DECONSTRUCTING THE JEWS," *COMMENTARY,* FEBRUARY, 1995

Norman Cantor is a well-known medievalist who has written, I am told, some excellent studies in his field. Now he has branched out to write a general history of the Jews. . . .

Cantor makes no bones about the fact that he is out to debunk (or, as he more fashionably puts it, to "deconstruct") his predecessors, and to present what he seems to think are a number of original theses. As it happens, however, nearly all of these have been advanced long before him—and by writers, from Apion in the 1st century to Arnold Toynbee in the 20th, not known for their friendliness toward the Jews.

These theses may be summarized as follows:

. . . Jewish history is now coming to an end and the Jews are fated to vanish through assimilation and intermarriage, not only in the Diaspora but in Israel too, where "a new Judeo-Arab Near Eastern elite will emerge in the next century." This, though, is nothing to get upset about, for "the Jews have fulfilled their role in history" and "pragmatically, they are no longer very much needed as a distinct race."

HILLEL HALKIN
1939–

Literary critic, biographer, and translator. Halkin studied English literature at Columbia University and writes frequently on Israeli culture and politics. He is a member of the editorial board of the *Jewish Review of Books*.

NORMAN F. CANTOR
1929–2004

Historian. Dr. Cantor was emeritus professor of history, sociology, and comparative literature at New York University. His many books include *In the Wake of the Plague; Inventing the Middle Ages;* and *The Civilization of the Middle Ages*, the most widely read narrative of the Middle Ages in the English language.

Exercise 6.3

Will the world suffer a loss if Jews, as an identifiable group in history, were to be assimilated into oblivion? Is there an idea from this course that you would use to answer this question?

TEXT 12

ZEPHANIAH 3:9

כִּי אָז אֶהְפֹּךְ אֶל עַמִּים שָׂפָה בְרוּרָה, לִקְרֹא כֻלָּם בְּשֵׁם ה', לְעָבְדוֹ שְׁכֶם אֶחָד.

I will then purify the speech of all people, so that they will all call upon the name of G-d and serve Him with one purpose.

*Do Jews still have something to offer to the world today? **Rabbi Manis Friedman** addresses this question:*

MYJLI.COM/GIFTS

Morning Prayer on Subway, Lori Grinker, gelatin silver print, 1984. (The Jewish Museum, New York)

KEY POINTS

1 The ancients believed that time is cyclical: what happened in the past will happen again; lasting change is an impossibility. Jews were the first to teach that progress and change are possible. The ultimate state of universal progress will culminate in the messianic era.

2 Moral imperatives can only be absolute if we believe that they are dictated by an absolute moral authority. Thus, along with monotheism, Jews gave the world the concept of absolute morality.

3 G-d provided a universal road map for moral living through the Seven Noahide Laws.

4 Jews have a mandate to be a light unto the nations. The current climate offers us unprecedented opportunity to promote observance of the Noahide Laws.

5 Many of the moral principles of Western civilization are derived from the Torah and thus have meaning and vitality only in the context of that tradition. We need to ensure that these values remain tethered to their original context so that they are able to stand up against the vagaries of impulse and the powers and self-interest.

Appendix

TEXT 13

TOSEFTA, SHEVU'OT 3:6

פַּעַם אַחַת שָׁבַת רַבִּי רְאוּבֵן בִּטְבֶרְיָא וּמְצָאוֹ פּוּלוּסִיפוּת אֶחָד. אָמַר לוֹ: אֵיזֶה הוּא שָׂנְאוּי בָּעוֹלָם? אָמַר לוֹ: זֶה הַכּוֹפֵר בְּמִי שֶׁבְּרָאוֹ. אָמַר לוֹ: הֵיאַךְ? אָמַר לוֹ: "כַּבֵּד אֶת אָבִיךָ וְאֶת אִמֶּךָ", "לֹא תִרְצָח", "לֹא תִנְאָף", "לֹא תִגְנֹב", "לֹא תַעֲנֶה בְרֵעֲךָ עֵד שָׁקֶר", וְ"לֹא תַחְמוֹד" (שְׁמוֹת כ, יב-יד). הָא אֵין אָדָם כּוֹפֵר בְּדָבָר עַד שֶׁכּוֹפֵר בָּעִיקָר.

Rabbi Reuven once spent Shabbat in Tiberius and met a Hellenist philosopher.

The Hellenist asked, “Who is most despised by society?”

Rabbi Reuven replied, “He who denies the Creator.”

“But how is such a person despised by *society*?” [Such a person could only be said to be despised by G-d.]

Rabbi Reuven replied, “The Creator instructed us, ‘Honor your father and mother,’ ‘Do not murder,’ ‘Do not commit adultery,’ ‘Do not steal,’ ‘Do not testify falsely,’ and ‘Do not covet’” (EXODUS 20:12–14). People do not deny the validity of these commandments unless they deny their underlying foundation.

TOSEFTA

A compendium of laws similar in format to that of the Mishnah; it consists of teachings of the sages of the Mishnah. At times, the material in both works is similar; at other times, there are significant differences between the two. The Talmud often compares these texts in its analysis. According to tradition, the *Tosefta* was redacted by Rabbis Chiyah and Oshiyah in the beginning of the 3rd century in the Land of Israel.

TEXT 14

ETHICS OF THE FATHERS 3:1

הִסְתַּכֵּל בִּשְׁלֹשָׁה דְבָרִים וְאֵין אַתָּה בָא לִידֵי עֲבֵרָה:
דַע מַה לְמַעְלָה מִמְּךָ - עַיִן רוֹאָה וְאֹזֶן שׁוֹמַעַת, וְכָל מַעֲשֶׂיךָ בַּסֵּפֶר נִכְתָּבִין.

Contemplate three things, and you will not come to transgress:

Know what is above you—a seeing eye, a listening ear, and all your deeds are recorded in a book.

ETHICS OF THE FATHERS (PIRKEI AVOT)

A 6-chapter work on Jewish ethics that is studied widely by Jewish communities, especially during the summer. The first 5 chapters are from the Mishnah, tractate Avot. Avot differs from the rest of the Mishnah in that it does not focus on legal subjects; it is a collection of the sages' wisdom on topics related to character development, ethics, healthy living, piety, and the study of Torah.

TEXT 15

SEFER HACHINUCH, MITZVAH 416

וְאַל תִּטְעֶה בְּנִי בְּזֶה הַחֶשְׁבּוֹן שֶׁל שֶׁבַע מִצְוֹות בְּנֵי נֹחַ הַיָּדוּעַ וְהַמּוּזְכָּר בַּתַּלְמוּד. כִּי בֶּאֱמֶת שֶׁאוֹתָן שֶׁבַע הֵן כְּעֵין כְּלָלוֹת, אֲבָל יֵשׁ בָּהֶן פְּרָטִים הַרְבֵּה.

כְּמוֹ שֶׁאַתָּה מוֹצֵא שֶׁאִיסּוּר הָעֲרָיוֹת נֶחְשַׁב לָהֶם דֶּרֶךְ כְּלַל לְמִצְוָה אַחַת, וְיֵשׁ בָּהּ פְּרָטִים . . . וְכֵן עִנְיַן עֲבוֹדָה זָרָה כּוּלוֹ נֶחְשַׁב לָהֶם מִצְוָה אַחַת, וְיֵשׁ בָּהּ כַּמָּה וְכַמָּה פְּרָטִים . . . וּכְמוֹ כֵן נֶאֱמַר, אַחַר שֶׁהוּזְהֲרוּ בְּעִנְיַן הַגָּזֵל שֶׁהוּזְהֲרוּ גַּם כֵּן בְּכָל הַרְחָקוֹתָיו . . . וּבִכְלַל הַהַרְחָקָה שֶׁלֹּא לַחְמוֹד.

Although it is well-known that there are Seven Noahide Laws, do not allow this fact to mislead you. The truth is that these seven laws are seven general categories that each contain many detailed laws.

For example, the prohibition against illicit sexual relations is a single Noahide law, but it includes many details. . . . Similarly, the prohibition against idolatry is a single Noahide law, but it includes many details. . . . The same is true for the prohibition against theft, which proscribes all behaviors that lead to theft . . . such as coveting.

SEFER HACHINUCH

A work on the biblical commandments. Four aspects of every mitzvah are discussed in this work: the definition of the mitzvah; ethical lessons that can be deduced from the mitzvah; basic laws pertaining to the observance of the mitzvah; and who is obligated to perform the mitzvah, and when. The work was composed in the 13th century by an anonymous author who refers to himself as "the Levite of Barcelona." It has been widely thought that this referred to Rabbi Aharon Halevi of Barcelona (Re'ah); however, this view has been contested.

Additional Readings

A MODERN WORLD AND ANCIENT PROPHECIES

BY ROCHEL HOLZKENNER

In the 19th century and much of the 20th, war was a game for the players. Territorial invasion and imperialism were considered fair play; the fittest deserved to survive. On European soil, peace was maintained through a delicate balance of power, and when that power shifted, ammunition broke loose. World War I racked up a death toll of 15 million, all in a dispute over power and territory. By the end of World War II, the death toll was at a shocking 78 million.

Yet in 1990, when Saddam Hussein invaded Kuwait to solve Iraq's financial problems, the world was outraged. That kind of move was not considered cool anymore. Something had changed in our moral perceptions.

The United Nations provided a novel means for conflict resolution. Established in 1945, its platform was to provide a space for dialogue between nations and minimize the need for war. Whilst for time immemorial, war had seemed like a natural resolution for disputes, it had become common sense to use war only as a last resort.

The Lubavitcher Rebbe spoke of the formation of the United Nations as a harbinger to the era of Redemption. He pointed out that the wall that stands in front of the UN building is engraved with the words "And they shall beat their swords into plowshares, . . ." quoting Isaiah's description of the era of Redemption. The world has been refined, said the Rebbe, to the extent that a mindset of peace and aid to the less fortunate has become common sense to so many.

ROCHEL HOLZKENNER

Rochel Holzkenner is a mother of four children and the codirector of Chabad of Las Olas, Florida, serving a community of young professionals. She is a high school teacher and a freelance writer, and also lectures on the topics of kabbalah and feminism, and their application to everyday life.

In February of 1992, a conference took place with representatives from many powerful nations. At the end of the conference the leaders resolved to cut back on arms production and redirect these resources to increase food production. Again the Rebbe noted the very tangible manifestation of Isaiah's prophecy, turning swords into plowshares. And the prophecy continues to unfold. Satellites that were developed in order to spy on the enemy from thousands of miles away are now used to detect the resources beneath the earth's surface and develop new areas for agricultural growth. Millions of dollars of defense research budget are being used to take military technology and transfer it for commercial use.

It makes so much sense. An idea that once seemed illogical that is now so sensible.

■■■

The Torah alludes to the shift in ethical sensibility in the opening sentence of the Torah reading of Mishpatim, the portion that discusses many of G-d's logical commandments.

G-d tells Moses:

> *"And these are the ordinances that you shall set before them."*

The Midrash (quoted by Rashi) exposes an insight based on the first two words of the sentence "And these":

> *"Wherever it is said 'and these,' it is adding to what has been previously stated. Thus, just as what has been previously stated [the Ten Commandments] were from Sinai, these too were from Sinai."*

The Torah includes the seemingly superfluous "and" to emphasize that these sensible ordinances were also from Sinai. Meaning, lest you think that these laws are a code of ethics that was generated by the human conscience, G-d clarifies that they were personally designed by G-d just as were the "illogical" laws. The only difference: with regards to the logical mitzvot, G-d gave us the gift to be able to understand their rationale, as opposed to the other mitzvot which we are not privy to understand.

We naturally assume that Jewish rituals are either sensible, like giving charity and respecting our parents, or illogical, like keeping kosher or immersing in the ritual bath. But here, G-d challenges our natural assumptions. "*These too are from Sinai*"—all the mitzvot are generated from a single source, G-d's will and wisdom. He fashioned our minds to comfortably comprehend one part of His will and not the other; the latter He asks us to do because we love Him, not because we understand Him.

But as we travel down the time continuum, moving closer to the era of Redemption, our minds become more in sync with G-d's wisdom. His will becomes more natural. For example, G-d says to respect boundaries, but for as long as history has been recorded, empires have swallowed up weaker nations as they ascended in power. It was the game of politics. If they tried that today, the UN would send in a major peacekeeping mission to keep the bully in check.

G-d says to help others who are in need. Well, for almost all of history this was largely incomprehensible. Why would we invest our hard-earned resources in a country that is of no benefit to us? Let them take care of their own problems. Yet now it's almost instinctive; someone else is hurting and I need to open up my purse. After the devastating earthquake in Haiti in January of 2010, America sent thousands of troops to Haiti and promised $100 million in recovery funds. Globally, more than one billion dollars in aid have been pledged by various governments. Israel's rescue mission to Haiti is costing its government NIS 40 million. US individuals and businesses donated millions of dollars to the Red Cross's philanthropic efforts to help Haiti victims.

Would the response have been comparable two centuries earlier, even a century earlier?

The Rebbe said that we are at the brink of a global transformation, and soon the world will become a wonderful place. We are moving this process along by being good today. It just makes sense.

Based on a talk by the Lubavitcher Rebbe, Parshat Mishpatim 5752 (1992).

Rochel Holzkenner, "A Modern World and Ancient Prophecies," Chabad.org.

SEVEN LAWS FOR A BEAUTIFUL PLANET
THE NOAHIDE TRADITION

BY RABBI TZVI FREEMAN

We are a single organism, a tenuous membrane stretched over a vast but delicate globe, every cell sharing every breath of air, every sip of water, every microbe—even every byte of knowledge. Vast webs of communication and trade have forged us together, much as proteins bond the elements of life.

We are humankind.

But not so fast. We are not cells—we are human beings, each an entire world. We have families and cultures, beliefs and religions. We value these distinctions, for without them each of us is no more than another solitary amoeba floating aimlessly upon the waves of a meaningless universe. Distinctiveness is vital, for in this universe, without diversity there is no life.

So here lies the problem: Can we find a new consciousness that will allow each of us to retain our unique heritage while playing in tune with humanity's grand orchestra?

Sounds like a fairy-tale. If it were not for one thing: The path has been here as long as we have. It is the one thing we all share. Because none of us made it up.

The Un-Religion

There is an ancient teaching that has no houses of worship, no priests, no conversion ceremony. No one needs to abandon his or her heritage to embrace it; only to return, to dig deep, back to the essential truths that are buried within every belief system known to humankind and to discard the outer layers that may have distorted its message.

You may have heard of this teaching, preserved and transmitted over the millennia by the Jewish People —although it is older even than that ancient nation: That all religions sprouted from a single seed and share a single root.

According to this tradition, Noah, the father of us all, planted that seed, a gift he received from the Creator of All Things. It is based on a set of laws he had received from Adam, renewed and expanded for Noah's time. It is a guide from beyond to show humankind how to create a sustainable world that would never again face destruction.

And it is a teaching that brings many voices into harmony, for it is the essence of all of them, yet does not deny to any its own unique beauty. After all, once you have found truth in your own backyard, that doesn't mean no one else is allowed a backyard. Rather, in each backyard is another glowing ember of the truth known to Noah. Each people has cultured and developed a certain wisdom, a certain beauty that others lack.

So that's all we're presenting here: A guide to finding the truths within the traditions we already have. For in those latent truths lie all that we need to breathe together as one harmonious humankind embracing one healthy Planet Earth.

Power from Beyond

The power behind these seven laws is that none of us made them up. You could say they're from "outside the system." That's important. Because, as everyone knows, no system can support itself.

Think about it:

Can you make a perpetual motion machine? No. Because a machine can't run itself.

Can you make a system of logic with no assumptions? No. Because logic can't explain itself.

RABBI TZVI FREEMAN, 1955–

Rabbi, computer scientist, and writer. A published expert, consultant, and lecturer in the field of educational technology, Rabbi Freeman has held posts at the University of British Columbia and the Digipen School of Computer Gaming. Rabbi Freeman's books include *Bringing Heaven Down to Earth* and *Men, Women and Kabbalah.* He is a senior editor at Chabad.org.

Can humankind determine how to live together in peace and harmony for all time? No. Because we didn't put ourselves here. We need to tap into something beyond us, infinitely higher than us, to do that.

We need a set of principles based not on human reason, but on the essential sanctity of life and justice. So here are seven laws that are not relative truths that can change as society changes. They are absolutes; solid ground upon which the world can firmly stand.

The Seven Laws of Noah:
1. Embrace the Relevance of Oneness

> *The first principle of Noah is that the Essence of Being cares about what we are doing and wants something from us.*

Noah looked upon Planet Earth and saw that every life upon it breathes with purpose and meaning. He saw himself and his children as its stewards, charged with a duty and a mission.

To have purpose, the universe must have a singular core—a conscious and deliberate Essence of Being that chooses to care about the reality that extends from it.

Every culture has its names for this essential oneness behind reality. One thing is agreed by all: We are not talking about a being, physical or spiritual, that can be known or defined in any way. After all, this essence is responsible for all being and all form—so it itself transcends all being and form. Even the terms of "existence" or "non-existence" could not apply.

Nevertheless, the Noah tradition insists that this unknowable oneness cares about our reality and is accessible to us through prayer and deeds; that reality is not an accident—every detail of life is deliberate and is filled with purpose and meaning.

The Essence desires to be found in each thing. Why? It is a passion beyond reason. Reason, after all, is just another idea that this Essential Oneness sustains.

That essential consciousness spoke from within the first members of humanity. From its voice, we learned that acts of kindness, caring, prayer, wisdom and enlightenment put us in harmony with the universe. Murder, theft, adultery, incest and wanton cruelty to living creatures—all these and everything associated with them are destructive to that relationship. And we were told to administer justice.

How were these laws forgotten? As time progressed, people came to rely more on their own meek understanding and less on that voice from beyond. They understood that there is only one Supreme Essence, but they decided that the many forces of nature were also worth considering as conscious, semi-autonomous beings. "After all," they said, "how can you talk to the Essence of Being? How could such a being care about us? We need something we can relate to."

That's how the idea of a pantheon of gods first became popular. It wasn't long before temples were raised to those many forces and beings. Soon there were physical representations, so that people could focus their minds and hearts on manipulating the cosmic flow. Later, another generation arose that only knew the outer rituals, completely blind to the inner meaning.

Eventually, humanity deteriorated to the point that the common man and woman knew only the wood and stone and believed these to be the gods who controlled their lives. Those seekers and hermits who knew the truth dared not share it save with their closest disciples.

With idolatry, came the downfall of human dignity. Rulers claimed to be gods and treated their subjects as inferior beings. The only lives that were valued were those that were considered close to the gods.

Until a lofty soul entered the world and turned the tide. His name was Abraham and he too was raised in the idolatry and superstition of the time. But he took these practices seriously, pondered their meaning, and realized they were lies.

With no teacher to guide him, he perceived that all the forces of nature worked in synchronous harmony. He chose to bond his soul not with the fire and not with the sun, not with the sky and not with the wind, not with the heavenly constellations and not with the invisible spirits, but with the singular divinity that breathes within them all. Eventually, he came to understand that this great force of nature, as well, was only a manifestation of the all-transcendent Source of Being from which all existence originates.

Abraham's ideas threatened the authority of the god-kings and their appointed priests. He defied them openly, declaring that every human being could call directly upon the Ultimate Authority for all his needs, for compassion and for justice.

The ancient Greeks and Egyptians mention Abraham as a great sage and astronomer. Three great religions consider him their patriarch. Some Jewish teachings trace that the monotheistic concept of Brahman—which seems closely related to his name—derives from his teachings. Without his conviction that there is harmony in the many opposites of nature, the quest of science would not be possible.

After Abraham's passing, the world slipped back into darkness. His children carried on his path in a hostile world. Eventually they, too, as slaves in Egypt, became steeped in falseness and the seedling Abraham had planted almost withered and died.

It was then that another revolutionary arose. Moses liberated the children of Abraham and brought them to the desolate peninsula of Sinai. There, he arranged a meeting of heaven and earth, so that all the people would not only understand, but also see for themselves that all of reality is sustained by a single Being, one that imbues all life with meaning. They received laws by which to guide their lives and the lives of their children after them. And they were appointed to a mission: to preserve Noah's teaching and Abraham's message, spreading it to all peoples and nations wherever their travels would take them.

Mount Sinai was a watershed event for humankind. Until that point, Abraham's message was the conviction of a single man, arrived at by his own intuition. Abraham was a man reaching upward, to connect with the light beyond. At Sinai, it was that Infinite Light itself that reached inward, touching humankind, asking us to let It in.

The difference is crucial: The foundation was no longer human reason, but the will of that which transcends all reason. Human reason provides a shifting foundation; eventually it must fail—as Abraham's message withered after his passing. The foundation of Sinai came from beyond space and time.

Today, over 50% of the world acknowledges Abraham as the father of their belief systems. Yet Abraham's vision has still yet to ripen. We are standing on the threshold of that dream. The rest is up to us.

2. Do Not Deny That Oneness

> *The second principle of Noah is not to profane that oneness in any way.*

In a simple sense, that means not to damn or curse the one who conducts this universe, or deny that there is one.

This, too, is an essential part of creating a sustainable world for humankind on our planet. If the magnificent plethora of life that surrounds us is nothing more than an accident, why should we bother to make the sacrifices necessary to preserve it? Recognizing that this world has a master who has made us its stewards is a vital step in taking responsibility for our environment in the long term.

It's also an essential part of building a sustainable society. The bedrock of the morality of healthy societies is the human intuition that there is meaning and purpose to life, that this purpose serves as an absolute measure of good and evil, and that the choice is up to us whether or not to work towards fulfilling that purpose.

Purpose requires a higher context. Just as an automobile can have no purpose without a road and a destiny, just as a hammer can have no purpose without a nail and structure to be built, so our world and the life within it cannot have purpose without a higher consciousness that chooses a destiny for the world and gives it meaning.

But without a context greater than itself, life can have no purpose. And when purpose is robbed from human beings, the very fabric of their morality swiftly crumbles.

If there is no meaning, then all courses of life are equally purposeless.

If there is no purpose, then all efforts to defend our values are a joke.

If there is no absolute good or evil, then morality is left to each person to decide, according to his or her whims and benefit.

If we have no free will to choose between good and evil, then all is justified—because no justification is necessary. There is no "me" who did anything wrong. There is only a relentless, blameless, mindless chain of cause and effect. Anything can happen. And it does.

The 20th century provides us with a laboratory demonstration. When human beings abandoned a higher authority to serve the icons of their own making then the most atrocious acts of inhumanity, mass slavery, hatred and genocide ever known to humankind spread across the planet. Nazi Germany, Stalinist Russia, Maoist China and Pol Pot's Cambodia are prime, but not lone, specimens of this truth. These were not the acts of barbarians, but cold and calculated acts perpetrated in the name of G-dless human ideologies.

This is the crucial importance of the second law of Noah: It tells us that to actively and explicitly deny the existence of a single, deliberate and purposeful conductor of this universe is a serious, irresponsible and reckless crime against humanity. Because it undermines the very foundation of responsible human conduct—the knowledge that there is a singular reality beyond our own that gives us purpose and to whom we are held responsible.

3. Guard the Sanctity of Human Life

The third principle of Noah is that the value of human life cannot be measured.

Noah was not simply told, "Do not murder." He was given a reason: Because the human being is made in the divine image.

Just as it is vital to know that there is only one force behind the universe, so it is vital to know that this force breathes within each human being. We are not just functional machines made of meat and standing on two legs; each of us contains the entire universe—each one contains the very soul of the universe. This is what the Book of Genesis calls "the Divine Image."

To destroy a single human life is to destroy the entire universe—because, for that person, this reality has ceased to exist. And so it follows that by sustaining a single human life, you are sustaining an entire universe.

No idea in human history has caused as much upheaval and progress as this basic tenet. Abraham and Moses were its great proponents, but it was not until it finally resurfaced in Europe 500 years ago that the world was transformed beyond recognition. It is the basis of the American Bill of Rights and of the constitution of every progressive nation today.

4. Honor the Sanctity of Measured Consumption

The fourth principle of Noah has to do with how we exploit the life and resources of our world.

This principle is stated clearly in Genesis, "Do not eat meat while its soul is still within it." Quite simply, if we wish to eat meat, we must wait until the entire animal has died before removing one of its limbs. We are not permitted to cause unnecessary suffering to any creature.

But we must look deeper, into the spirit of the words: that we must respect the life and function of whatever we consume. And that is only sustainable when we recognize that all life is purposeful because it is the work of a single, deliberate and purposeful consciousness.

Everywhere on the planet, a grand symphony of life unfolds. Oxygen, carbon and hydrogen are fused by the sun to give life to plants and trees; a multitude of swimming, crawling, running and flying beings each plays its part as simple organisms are consumed by more complex, intelligent and conscious beings.

Which way is up and which is down? There is no way to tell. For it is the simple that gives life to the more complex and each depends on the other—until all together they present a masterful, integrated whole.

The chain of life continues into the non-physical realm, for the human being stands as a bridge between the material and the spiritual. We are meant to live with our feet on the earth and our hearts towards the heavens, tending to the most mundane matters of eating and sleeping in a mindful way, consuming our food with care and respect for the life that brought it to us. In this way, we carry the life we consume one step higher, from the material to the spiritual.

With every bite we eat, every calorie of energy we burn, we can choose to continue dragging our environment into greater disarray—or to bond heaven and earth, connecting the life of this planet with a higher purpose.

Since the Source of all things is an essential oneness, so every detail of the world around us expresses a magnificent unity. As the Kabbalists explain, in every event, every life and every creature an infinite light can be found, because the truth within each thing is divine.

Humankind has the capacity to reveal that divinity within all earthly things and to connect them to the infinite light. But we also have the capacity for the opposite, to cause acrimony and unbalance. This is a challenge for every human being: To choose harmony with the soul of the universe and reveal the harmony of all of the creation.

And this begins with acknowledgment of the world's master and awe for the masterwork we inhabit.

5. Respect the Sanctity of Private Property

The fifth principle of Noah is about respecting the property of others.

In other words, not stealing. But there's much more to stealing than you might have imagined.

Each of our lives has its unique purpose—and those things that enter our lives and become our possessions are key to that purpose. You can't steal purpose from anyone's life, no matter how much you take away from him. But another person's property in your possession becomes a heavy weight that does not allow your own purpose to be fulfilled.

Thinking about it this way, you'll realize that there are many ways of stealing without even taking your hands out of your pockets. How about the person who gets ahead by putting someone else down, for example? Isn't that also a form of taking something that's not really yours? The same with laughing at someone else's expense. Or gossiping about someone else just for entertainment.

Whatever benefits you receive in this world, make sure that none of them are at the unfair expense of someone else.

6. Harness and Sublimate the Human Libido

The sixth principle of Noah is about harnessing and sublimating the human libido. Incest, adultery, rape and other licentious practices are forbidden by this principle.

Sexuality is the fountain of life and so nothing is more divine than the sexual act. So, too, nothing can be more debasing and destructive to the human being.

The union of man and woman is a reflection of the cosmic dance by which all things come to be. It is the union of heaven and earth, spiritual and material, soul and body, energy and matter, oneness and diversity. When man and woman unite in a harmonious, caring way, their union rings throughout the universe like a song resonating in a vast chamber. All of reality plays along as an orchestra plays a grand concerto. They bring healing and blessing to the world, just as they bring new souls, dressed in pure and pristine light.

Yet, as with any art, to achieve such harmony is a struggle. As the artist must master his craft, choosing the beautiful and rejecting the ugly; as a musician disciplines his fingers and a dancer her limbs—so to this primal art of human union has its own rules and discipline.

As art is a supernatural act of the human being, so is marriage. It is not nature, but higher than nature. For some people this requires a superhuman effort. That is what the beauty of human sexuality is all about: The ability to be supernatural. In the long run, nothing could be more satisfying and create more beauty.

7. Create Mechanisms to Ensure Justice

The seventh principle of Noah demands that we ensure justice in our world.

No other creature on the planet but the human being requires a court to enforce law and order. The fish know their place in the sea, the birds their pathways in the skies and the animals know the laws of their kingdoms. Only the human being must have a score set before him so he will not play in grinding discord. Only the human being has the ability to disrupt the order of the entire planet, to step out of synch with his own purpose and the divine plan.

If the Creator has a purpose for humankind, why doesn't He Himself rein humankind in? Let Him mete out justice Himself—why should we meddle into His business?

But this itself is the reason—both for our freedom and for our responsibilities: We are meant to be partners in the Creation. And that, most of all, is through determining and delivering justice.

We are not meant to passively observe oppression, inequality and injustice and accept this as fate. We are meant to be outraged, to cry out to the Creator of all things, "How could this be?" And then to do something about it.

Even a small act of justice for a single human being impacts every other human being on the planet. We are restoring harmony to our reality, placing it in synch with a higher reality, a supernal order. In that order, every life is an entire world, no one is insignificant. And so, in establishing justice for one person, all the world is healed.

The Goal

Why have these seven principles become so crucial today? Because today we stand at the doorstep of a whole new world. All our technology, all our advances in science and social justice, all drive us up a steady track towards an age promised by the prophets and described by the sages—an age of wisdom and of peace.

The know-how is in place. We can feed everyone. We can teach everyone. We can all join together in dialog and creativity. We only need a common ground. Not one that any human being can establish for us, not one that can arise from our consensus. That's just more dusty topsoil, easily blown away by the first wind. The common ground we need must be the ground from which we were formed, at the essence of humanity's purpose and the meaning of reality.

And that lies only in the hand of the Infinite Light that formed us. The voice that Noah heard.

Rabbi Tzvi Freeman, "Seven Laws for a Beautiful Planet," Chabad.org

WHAT IS MORALITY?

BY DR. YITZCHOK BLOCK

How is one to know whether any moral judgment is true or false? What, indeed, is the basis of morality?

The answer that many theists give at this point is that moral actions are actions that G-d has commanded. The fact that G-d has commanded an act is sufficient to transform it into a moral one. I suppose these theists would argue that if G-d commanded us to play the piano, then playing the piano would also become for us a moral act.

Would it? There are numerous commands in the Bible that one would be hard pressed to understand as a moral act. What is moral about the biblical prohibitions on mixing linen with wool or eating non-kosher food? Furthermore, G-d was not beyond commanding Abraham to sacrifice his son Isaac. Was that a moral command? G-d Himself said on another occasion that one should not offer human sacrifice to idols. Did human sacrifice suddenly become a morally good act when G-d commanded it?

When G-d told Abraham that He was going to destroy the wicked people of Sodom and Gomorra, Abraham argued with G-d that this would not be just if there were good people living in these cities. "G-d forbid, that the Judge of the whole world should not do what is just!" (Genesis 18:25). G-d agreed with Abraham that to destroy the good people together with the bad, would not be just, but the truth is that there were no good people in those cities. If what G-d commands is *eo ipso* good, however, then Abraham should never have argued with G-d in the first place. He should have said something like, "G-d, I always thought that it was immoral to punish the righteous together with the wicked, but now that you have commanded your angels to do so, I see that I was mistaken and that it is indeed the morally right thing to do." Had Abraham said this, G-d would no doubt have called Abraham an idiot and have had nothing more to do with him. After all, how could an idiot be the father of our faith?

It is true that what G-d demands of us is obedience whether we understand Him or not. What G-d commands is a categorical command, but that does not make it "moral." Being categorical may be a necessary property of a command by G-d, but it does not follow that G-d's command is a sufficient condition for it being moral. G-d has commanded us not to wear clothes made of wool and linen, but no one can claim to understand that this is a moral imperative simply because G-d commanded it. Rashi says that the true test of faith is obedience to G-d whether one understands the command or not. If it were true, however, that G-d's commanding something is a sufficient condition for our understanding it as morally good, it would be impossible for *chukkim* (commands of G-d which appear to have no compelling reason behind them other than the fact that G-d commanded them) to exist.

When G-d commands us not to steal, no one puts up an argument except the thief, who might complain that G-d has taken away his livelihood. When, however, G-d commands us not to wear woolen and linen garments, we all wonder what could possibly be the reason for this command. If we are devoted to G-d we will obey Him anyway, for who can understand G-d?

The conclusion of all this is that it is false to suppose that G-d's commanding something is a sufficient condition for our understanding it as morally good. In other words, one cannot argue for the moral goodness of anything by simply appealing to the fact that G-d has commanded it. To what, then, can one appeal? What, indeed, is the ground of morality? I believe the ground of morality rests upon something I

DR. YITZCHOK BLOCK, 1931–2017

Dr. Block earned a PhD in philosophy from Harvard University. He published many scholarly papers and served as professor of philosophy at the University of Western Ontario in London, Ontario. His main areas of expertise were Aristotle and Wittgenstein. As a Chabad representative to London, he also addressed many of the needs of the local Jewish community.

call "the moral sense." In the remainder of this paper, I will try to explain what I mean by this.

The Moral Sense

What I mean by the moral sense is well-illustrated in one of Plato's earlier Dialogues.[1] Plato recounts how the gods gave to each species of animal the precise kind of abilities and instincts to survive. To the weak they gave speed, to those with strength they gave slowness of movement so the weaker could escape. To the smallest of all animals, the birds, they gave flight. To the animals living in cold countries they provided thick hair for warmth, and to each species they gave those kinds of bodily mechanisms and instincts to survive in its respective environment. After they had taken care of all the animals, they finally came to man and to their consternation discovered that all the natural protections and instincts had already been apportioned out and there was nothing left for man. Man was about to come naked into the world without any means of survival. The situation was saved by Zeus. He imparted to humans ". . . respect for one another and a sense of justice." This enabled man to form societies and live together in friendship and unity and thus survive.

I know of no other ground of morality or the moral sense than this. I do not mean that it was Zeus who implanted this sense of justice in human beings, but however it got there, the point I want to argue here is that it needs no ground or justification any more than *modus ponens* needs a proof of its validity. (We remind our readers that *modus ponens* is the Latin term for the following valid logical inference: from the two premises, i) if p then q, and ii) p; it follows that iii) q.) No proof could be more persuasive than *modus ponens* itself, and no argument supporting justice could be more compelling than justice itself. It is to the credit of John Rawls to have pointed out that justice as fairness cannot be reduced to some utilitarian value.[2] It is an a priori good in itself apart from the social and utilitarian values it so eminently serves. Even in those cases when it may not serve a utilitarian value, one still feels the compelling call of the biblical command, "Justice, justice shall you pursue!" (Deuteronomy 16:20).

Another integral element that composes this sense of morality is the compassion we feel for the suffering of another human being. These two—the sense of justice and the sense of compassion—comprise what I mean by the sense of morality. There may be other elements that enter into morality, but these are the primary ones. It is no accident that these two senses—the sense of compassion and the sense of justice—are intimately connected with love (*chessed*) and sternness (*gevurah*) which Chasidism and Kabbalah propound as the basic emotions in man and as the primary *middot* (moral qualities) with which G-d created the world.

The first thing I want to call attention to are the emotions one instinctively feels when one witnesses acts of injustice or suffering. They are called, respectively, "righteous indignation" and "compassion." Why do we have these emotions? Injustice is really an act or a fact about human relations, and suffering is a state of human existence. Why is it that these facts call forth these emotions? There is no necessity in our feeling these emotions, and indeed we may know individuals or have read about certain people for whom the appropriate situations do not call forth such emotions. We call such people insensitive or lacking in moral feelings. Though they may not yet be said to be evil or cruel, it is nonetheless the sine qua non of being a morally good person that one *feels* indignation and compassion on the appropriate occasions.

I believe there is something innate about these feelings, such that we find it quite natural to have them and think it unnatural when we do not. This is particularly true of cruelty, which is so unnatural that we call perpetrators of cruel acts "inhuman." A human being feels compassion for the suffering of another human being, and a decent person feels indignant when he sees injustice.

These feelings are as natural as laughing at a joke. It is silly to ask why one laughs at a joke if it is truly funny, and it is just as odd to ask why one feels indignation and compassion on the appropriate occasions. How else should one react to injustice and suffering? It is difficult to imagine reacting in any other way, just as we would find it difficult to react to a funny joke other than by laughing.

If one feels no indignation or compassion, this is a sign of something seriously amiss with one's humanity or goodness. The association of moral character with these feelings is so intimate that we are inclined to say that a decent person would never knowingly consent to injustice and a compassionate person could never inflict unnecessary pain or suffering on anyone. The "would never" and "could never" here is "logical" in that what one *means* by a moral person is someone who would never act unjustly and could never bring oneself to cause unnecessary pain or misery to anyone. To say that someone is morally good but acts unjustly or is cruel is a "logical" contradiction in the same sense in which it is a "logical" contradiction to say that a bachelor is married.

The reason the term "logical" is flagged here is that it is being used a bit differently from the way it is ordinarily used by logicians. Logical contradiction is usually applied to statements that negate logically valid inferences. Thus if *modus ponens* is a valid inference, then to say i) if p then q, and ii) p, but iii) not q, is a logical contradiction. However, the contradiction in saying that someone is a bachelor and is married contradicts no valid inference. What it contradicts is how we use words in English. It has to do with our understanding of concepts or ideas. What ordinarily is meant in English by the term "bachelor" excludes the possibility that a bachelor could be married. To ask of someone to whom you have been introduced as a bachelor, "By the way, are you married?" shows that either you do not understand English very well, or that you are trying to be funny, or that you are an imbecile. One might imagine other ways of explaining how or why someone might ask such a nonsensical question, but the point is that it is nonsensical, given the common meaning of the term "bachelor" in English.

In a similar way, I think it is nonsensical to say of someone, that he is morally good or decent, but nonetheless unjust or cruel. I want to say that what one *means* by a good person is at least a person about whom one would say that it is unthinkable that this person could act unjustly or cruelly. (It goes without saying that no one is morally perfect. We are all prone to weakness and temptations. Occasionally, we are unjust or lose our tempers and are mean. If we are morally decent, we will recognize these backslidings and regret them.)

There might be other traits that define our concept of moral goodness, but certainly justice and compassion are necessary aspects of this concept and perhaps even sufficient aspects. In any event, they are crucial, such that anyone who lacked these qualities would not be said to be a morally good person.

If it is true, as we claim here, that these feelings are innate or that all human beings are born with them, how is it that some people feel them more strongly than others and some seem to lack them altogether? I do not think these are counter examples to our point. People get side-tracked through bad nurturing or training from parents or teachers. It is a matter of education, as is any kind of character or emotional development.

This is Plato's point that the evil that men fall into is inadvertent and unintentional. No one willingly sets out to become evil. Some people are raised in an environment that is hostile to their basic moral feelings. The moral growth of such people becomes stunted, much as musical talent is stunted by an environment that fails to nurture and develop that talent. The difference between a talent for music and the sense of justice and compassion is that lack of the latter is a more serious character fault than the lack of the former. One who lacks a talent for music or a sense of humor is missing out on something important that adds to the value of human life, but someone who is unjust or cruel should be ostracized from human society.

Such people are cancerous. They destroy the trust and friendship that is the glue holding society together. Sometimes these moral sentiments shine through the thick skin of the most hardened criminals or those whom one would ordinarily consider cruel or inhumane. A close friend of mine who survived the infamous death march from Auschwitz was saved by a Nazi guard who, along with shooting straggling prisoners on the way, would come over to my friend every day and share his canteen of coffee with him. When they reached the railroad junction after days of marching and they boarded the cattle cars that transported them to Bergen-Belsen, the guard disappeared and my friend never saw him again. Why the guard showed my friend this kindness, and who this person was has remained a mystery to this very day.

In Kabbalah, the term for evil is *klipah* ('shell' or 'covering'). The idea here is that the world and man are essentially good, but an external layer of evil covers and conceals this good. One simply has to peel back this layer to reveal a basic underlying goodness. Sometimes a glimmer of humanity peeks through the outer shell of evil.

A similar idea was expressed in a lecture I once heard by Robert Frost who described what a poem is using the following metaphor: The ancients thought that the black sky at night was a curtain that was stretched over the heavens when the sun set. Beyond that curtain was a supernal light which we could not see. Powerful archers would shoot arrows at the curtain and sometimes they would pierce it and pinpoints of the supernal light would shine through. The ancients thought that was a star. Robert Frost said it is a poem. Kabbala proclaims it a ray of that elemental goodness which is the essence of man and the world. The mysterious kindness shown by the Nazi guard mentioned in the previous footnote was a fleeting glimpse of that goodness in the midst of evil.

No one is all good or all evil. Each of us is a mixture of both, varying in the degree that goodness is able to shine through the shell of egoism that encrusts us all.

Egoism is the dark curtain that conceals the supernal goodness concealed in the soul of every human being and the bad and evil among us are simply those unfortunate ones who, for whatever reason, have been unable to unearth this goodness. From time to time on rare occasions, it manages to poke a hole through the mire of our entanglements.

However we come by this sense of morality, we do not come by it as a result of G-d's commands, though the commentators on the Bible tell us that in pursuing morality we are emulating G-d. Man naturally feels compassion with or without G-d. Furthermore, as we said earlier, Abraham actually challenged G-d for not displaying a sense of justice in dealing with the wicked people of Sodom and Gomorra.

The interesting thing about this story is that it is taken for granted by both G-d and Abraham that it would not be fair to treat righteous men and wicked men in the same way, and that it is unthinkable that G-d could act unjustly. Suppose G-d had challenged Abraham to produce an argument that it is morally wrong or evil to treat people unfairly. What could Abraham have said? I myself do not know of any argument that Abraham could have produced. I doubt if G-d would have been impressed by either a Kantian or a Nietzschean argument, and certainly not a utilitarian one.

Abraham, as a matter of fact, had preempted the question. He challenged G-d: "G-d forbid, that the Judge of the world should not do what is fair!" If G-d indeed had answered by saying something like, "What is so terrible in treating the righteous and the wicked in the same way? Prove to Me that this is wrong," we would then have to throw up our hands in despair, for all would be lost. If the Judge of the whole world is not just, G-d have mercy on us! If a fellow human being of flesh and blood would have asked this question, we would question his sanity. How can any decent person ask why it is good to be fair?

Something similar can be said about the sense of compassion. Why should one feel compassion for the suffering of another human being? The only possible answer is that if you don't, you are morally insensitive and probably capable of cruelty yourself. If someone were to ask, what is evil about cruelty? There is no answer. One simply throws up one's hands in horror and stays as far away as one can from such people. This is the only proper response. Such people do not deserve an argument! If G-d Himself were cruel (and there is no contradiction to His being an omniscient, omnipotent Creator of the world and also cruel), could one go on living? If the ultimate end of the righteous as well as the wicked is eternal damnation, what is the point of it all?

Søren Kierkegaard wrote a book, *Fear and Trembling*, in which he imagines how the biblical story of the binding of Isaac might have been written a bit differently had Abraham not been the true hero of faith that he was. He might have pleaded with G-d, complained against G-d, held in repressed anger or disappointment, and so forth. It never occurred to Kierkegaard to rewrite the story as if G-d were not G-d but an evil demon. The evil demon would not have saved Isaac at the last moment and moreover would have gloated over his sacrifice and laughed at Abraham's suffering in gleeful joy. If he had said to Abraham, "You fool—the only reason I created you and tested your faith is that I should have the enjoyment of watching you suffer!" The only proper response to this is that Abraham plunge the knife into himself, for there would be no point in going on living. If G-d is cruel, that is the end—the world gets turned upside down. This shows how fundamental is the idea that the world and G-d are good.

The Necessity of Goodness

This fundamental role that moral goodness plays in human life, however, is derived from man, not from G-d. It is not that we consider moral goodness crucial because G-d has commanded it—rather we consider it crucial because we cannot imagine living without it. In some ways, it is even more fundamental in our thinking than is G-d. Many people claim they can live without G-d, but no one can say honestly they can get along without goodness. This attests to the efficacy with which G-d implanted it within us, and it is important that one should not forget that it was G-d Who implanted it. That is, it did not come about by chance or through some evolutionary process.

This certainly adds to our responsibility. If one has a talent, one should try to develop it if it enhances one's life. However, one has no *responsibility* to develop it unless it is "G-d-given." If the Creator of Heaven and Earth has given someone a talent that enhances the value and the goodness of human life, then one has a categorical responsibility to nourish this talent. That is, it is not up to one's individual choice to decide whether one should develop it.

How much more does this apply if we are talking about one's "talent" for goodness, i.e., one's sense of compassion. This is nothing else than the emulation of G-d. "As I am merciful," says G-d, "so shall you be merciful." The sense of compassion in man is a reflection of G-d's image in us. As G-d is good, so are we, or rather our dependency on goodness is due to the fact that this is how G-d made us, and the development of our talent for goodness is an emulation of G-d.

The only difference is that this is a talent that every human being has, by right of being human. This talent was not reserved for a select few. The exhortation by G-d that we should be merciful is not a command as such. It is more of an encouragement. "I know it is difficult," He says, "but you can do it. You have it in you. I know—I put it there!" It is similar to G-d's exhortation to be holy. "You shall be holy because I am holy" (Leviticus 19:2). At first, this does not sound like much of an argument. If G-d had said, "You shall be omnipotent because I am omnipotent," we would think it a joke. The difference is that G-d has given us the ability to attain a degree of holiness or goodness, but not His omnipotence. Don't let it go to your head. Just because G-d shares with man some of His attributes, man does not, therefore, become G-d.

That goodness is a G-d-given talent is significant. It implies that man has a categorical responsibility to develop that talent, which otherwise he would not have.[3] If one's feeling for justice and compassion for suffering are evolutionary traits that evolved in the course of man's cultural development, there is no moral duty or obligation to nurture them except for prudential reasons, i.e., to help stabilize society or lead to pleasure and happiness, but then we are no longer talking about morality but about prudence. In order for righteous indignation and compassion to be a genuine barometer for morality, one needs G-d. Human compassion is a moral feeling because G-d is compassionate. Justice is a moral trait because G-d is just. Without G-d, the feeling we all have that righteous indignation and compassion are the sine qua non of morality could be "explained" as some kind of evolutionary development that has survival value. The only way one can say that these feelings constitute morality as we know it, is not because that's the way we have been taught or nurtured, but because the moral life is some form of emulation of G-d. To be what it is, morality must be "G-d-like."

Thus the Bible says one must ". . . walk in His ways" (Deuteronomy 28.9). Various rabbinic commentators interpret this to mean that one must emulate the characteristics that G-d Himself displays. To quote Maimonides, "Just as He (G-d) is called kind, so you should be kind. As He is called merciful, so you should be merciful. As He is called holy, so you should be holy" (*Mishneh Torah, Hilchot Deot*, chap. 1, paragraph 6). One of the interpretations of the biblical statement that man was made in the image of G-d is that the feelings we call moral feelings are such as they are and have the categorical demands that they do, because they are the feelings that G-d has also, insofar as it makes sense to talk of G-d as having feelings similar to those of human beings.

When Plato asked his famous question in the *Euthyphro*, "Is something holy because G-d desires it or does G-d desire it because it is holy?" (for our purpose, we can substitute "good" for "holy"; the logic of the question is the same) the answer is a bit of both. When we say that the feelings of moral indignation and compassion are moral feelings, we mean that this is so because that's how G-d Himself feels on certain occasions, and man has these feelings because G-d implanted them in him. Without G-d, man might still have them but there is no way one can justify its categorical demands. G-d and morality are essentially one and the same thing. This dimension of human life that distinguishes mankind from animals disappears with the view that there is no G-d and man has no peculiar virtue other than that of being at the top of the evolutionary process. What we call morality would be nothing more than the end point of evolution; that does not make it moral but simply successful.

Should some evolutionary process replace our present moral feelings with others, then man would simply have outgrown what we all call morality, and the evolutionary value of survival will have replaced these moral feelings and values with others which we might then call the "new morality." One can well imagine that if Hitler had won the Second World War and established his dream of the thousand year *Reich*, he might indeed have created a new "morality" altogether.

In a word, the categorical element in moral judgment has no basis without G-d.

Endnotes

1 See Plato's *Protagoras*, 320d–322e.

2 See his "Justice as Fairness" in *The Philosophical Review*, vol. LXVII (1958) and his book, *A Theory of Justice* (Cambridge, MA: Harvard University Press, 1971) chap. 1.

3 Kant assumed that one has a categorical responsibility to develop whatever talents one might have, but he never argues for this in any convincing fashion. He simply says that ". . . as a rational being, he necessarily wills that his faculties be developed since they serve him, and have been given to him for all sorts of possible purposes." (*Fundamental Principles of the Metaphysics of Morals*, pp. 450–490 in original German edition, ed. Rosencranz and Schubert, 1938). I do not see how reason can dictate the necessity of developing our talents unless it is on the basis of prudential or utilitarian considerations, which Kant actually suggests here. However, the duty then becomes hypothetical and not categorical, as Kant would like. If one has no desire to develop his talent for music, why should he feel obliged to do so just because he has it?

Adapted with permission from Dr. Yitzchok Block, "G-d and Morality," *B'Or Ha'Torah: Science, Art and Modern Life in the Light of the Torah,* vol. 12 (2001) (Jerusalem College of Technology Publications)

Order it online: www.TorahandScienceBooks.com
Published and copyright by F.R.E.E. Publishing House and Shamir; www.RussianJewry.org

Acknowledgments

We are grateful to the following individuals for helping shape this course:

Rabbis Mordechai Dinerman and **Naftali Silberberg**, who codirect the JLI Curriculum Department and the Flagship editorial team; **Rabbi Dr. Shmuel Klatzkin**, JLI's senior editor; and **Rabbi Zalman Abraham**, who skillfully provides the vision and strategic planning of JLI course offerings.

Rabbis Baruch Shalom Davidson, Mordechai Dinerman, Lazer Gurkow, and **Shmuel Super** designed and authored this course. **Rabbi Yakov Gershon**—of JLI's Machon Shmuel: The Sami Rohr Research Institute—provided extensive research for this course, with assistance from **Rabbi Shmuel Gomes.**

We thank **Avi Webb** for leading the vision for the marketing of this course, and **Mushka Kanner** and **Shifra Tauber** for creating and designing the marketing materials.

Rabbis Levi Dubinsky, Shmuel Gancz, Mendy Kasowitz, and **Mendy Lewis,** the Instructor Advisory Board for this course, spent many hours reviewing the course materials with the JLI team and provided numerous useful suggestions that have enhanced the course and ensured its suitability for a wide range of students.

Rivki Mockin streamlined and ensured the smoothness and timeliness of the content production, and **Chana Dechter**, JLI Flagship's administrator, capably oversaw the entire project. **Mushka Backman** provided editorial assistance, and **Rakefet Orobona, Mimi Palace, Rabbi Shmuel Super, Shmuel Telsner,** and **Ya'akovah Weber** enhanced the quality and accuracy of the writing with their proofreading. **Rivky Fieldsteel, Shayna Grosh, Rabbi Zalman Korf,** and **Shternie Zaltzman** designed the textbooks with taste and expertise, and the textbook images were researched and selected by **Chany Block. Rabbi Mendel Sirota** directed the book's publication and distribution.

Chany Block, Mushka Druk, Baila Goldstein and **Rivka Rapoport** designed the aesthetically pleasing PowerPoint presentations, and **Moshe Raskin** and **Getzy Raskin** produced the videos. The video scripts were masterfully written by **Rabbi Yaakov Paley.**

We are immensely grateful for the encouragement of JLI's visionary chairman, and vice-chairman of *Merkos L'Inyonei Chinuch*—Lubavitch World Headquarters, **Rabbi Moshe Kotlarsky**. Rabbi Kotlarsky has been highly instrumental in building the infrastructure for the expansion of Chabad's international network and is also the architect of scores of initiatives and services to help Chabad representatives across the globe succeed in their mission. We are blessed to have the unwavering support of JLI's principal benefactor, **Mr. George Rohr**, who is fully invested in our work, continues to be instrumental in JLI's monumental growth and expansion, and is largely responsible for the Jewish renaissance that is being spearheaded by JLI and its affiliates across the globe.

The commitment and sage direction of JLI's dedicated Executive Board—**Rabbis Chaim Block, Hesh Epstein, Ronnie Fine, Yosef Gansburg, Shmuel Kaplan, Yisrael Rice**, and **Avrohom Sternberg**—and the countless hours they devote to the development of JLI are what drive the vision, growth, and tremendous success of the organization.

Finally, JLI represents an incredible partnership of more than 1,600 *shluchim* and *shluchot* in more than 1,000 locations across the globe, who contribute their time and talent to further Jewish adult education. We thank them for generously sharing feedback and making suggestions that steer JLI's development and growth. They are our most valuable critics and our most cherished contributors.

Inspired by the call of the **Lubavitcher Rebbe**, of righteous memory, it is the mandate of the Rohr JLI to **provide a community of learning** for all Jews throughout the world where they can participate in their precious heritage of Torah learning and experience its rewards. May this course succeed in fulfilling this sacred charge!

On behalf of the Rohr Jewish Learning Institute,

RABBI EFRAIM MINTZ
Executive Director

RABBI YISRAEL RICE
Chairman, Editorial Board

20 Av, 5779

The Rohr Jewish Learning Institute

AN AFFILIATE OF MERKOS L'INYONEI CHINUCH,
THE EDUCATIONAL ARM OF THE CHABAD-LUBAVITCH MOVEMENT
822 EASTERN PARKWAY, BROOKLYN, NY 11213

CURRICULUM DEVELOPMENT

Rabbi Mordechai Dinerman
Rabbi Naftali Silberberg
EDITORS IN CHIEF

Rabbi Shmuel Klatzkin, PhD
Rabbi Yanki Tauber
SENIOR EDITORS

Rabbi Binyomin Bitton
Rabbi Baruch Shalom Davidson
Rabbi Chaim Fieldsteel
Rabbi Mendel Glazman
Rabbi Shmuel Gomes
Rabbi Eliezer Gurkow
Rabbi Michoel Lipskier
Rabbi Ahrele Loschak
Rabbi Yaakov Paley
Rabbi Berry Piekarski
Rabbi Mendel Rubin
Rabbi Shmuel Super
Rabbi Boruch Werdiger
Rabbi Yosi Wolf
CURRICULUM TEAM

Mrs. Rivki Mockin
CONTENT COORDINATOR

MARKETING AND BRANDING

Rabbi Zalman Abraham
DIRECTOR

Ms. Mashie Vogel
ADMINISTRATOR

Rabbi Avi Webb
BRAND COPYWRITER

Mrs. Chaya Mushka Kanner
Ms. Shira Levine
Mrs. Shifra Tauber
Mrs. Rikkie Wolf
GRAPHIC DESIGN

Mrs. Chany Block
Mrs. Rivky Fieldsteel
Mrs. Shayna Grosh
Rabbi Zalman Korf
Mrs. Aliza Mayteles
Rabbi Moshe Wolff
Mrs. Shternie Zaltzman
PUBLICATION DESIGN

Lazer Cohen
SOCIAL MEDIA

Rabbi Yaakov Paley
WRITER

Rabbi Yossi Grossbaum
Rabbi Mendel Lifshitz
Rabbi Shraga Sherman
Rabbi Ari Sollish
Rabbi Mendel Teldon
MARKETING COMMITTEE

MARKETING CONSULTANTS

JJ Gross
Israel

Joseph Jaffe
EVOL8TION
New York, NY

Warren Modlin
MEDNETPRO, INC.
Orange County, CA

Alan Rosenspan
ALAN ROSENSPAN & ASSOCIATES
Sharon, MA

Gary Wexler
PASSION MARKETING
Los Angeles, CA

JLI CENTRAL

Rabbi Isaac Abelsky
Rabbi Mendel Abelsky
Mrs. Mussi Abelsky
Ms. Rochel Karp
Rabbi Mendel Klein
Ms. Zehavah Krafchik
Mrs. Aliza Mayteles
Ms. Adina Posner
ADMINISTRATION

Rabbi Mendel Sirota
AFFILIATE SUPPORT

Rabbi Shlomie Tenenbaum
PROJECT MANAGER

Mrs. Mindy Wallach
AFFILIATE ORIENTATION

Ms. Mushka Backman
Mrs. Chany Block
Mrs. Bunia Chazan
Mrs. Mushka Druk
Mrs. Baila Goldstein
Ms. Mimi Rabinowitz
Getzy Raskin
Moshe Raskin
MULTIMEDIA DEVELOPMENT

Rabbi Mendy Elishevitz
Mendel Grossbaum
Rabbi Aron Liberow
Yoni Ben-Oni
Mrs. Rochie Rivkin
Mrs. Chana Weinbaum
ONLINE DIVISION

Mrs. Ya'akovah Weber
LEAD PROOFREADER

Dr. Rakefet Orobona
Ms. Mimi Palace
PROOFREADERS

Rabbi Mendel Sirota
Yosef Feigelstock
PRINTING AND DISTRIBUTION

Mrs. Musie Liberow
Mrs. Shaina B. Mintz
Mrs. Shulamis Nadler
ACCOUNTING

Rabbi Zalman Abraham
Ms. Mushka Backman
Mrs. Shulamis Nadler
Mrs. Mindy Wallach
Mr. Yehuda Wengrofsky
DEVELOPMENT

Mrs. Musie Liberow
Mrs. Mindy Wallach
CONTINUING EDUCATION

JLI FLAGSHIP

Rabbi Yisrael Rice
CHAIRMAN

Mrs. Chana Dechter
PROJECT MANAGER

Rabbi Yisroel Altein
Rabbi Hesh Epstein
Rabbi Sholom Raichik
Mrs. Michla Schanowitz
Rabbi Shraga Sherman
Mrs. Rivkah Slonim
Rabbi Ari Sollish
Rabbi Avraham Steinmetz
Rabbi Avrohom Sternberg
EDITORIAL BOARD

PAST FLAGSHIP AUTHORS

Rabbi Yitschak M. Kagan
of blessed memory

Rabbi Zalman Abraham
Brooklyn, NY

Rabbi Berel Bell
Montreal, QC

Rabbi Nissan D. Dubov
London, UK

Rabbi Tzvi Freeman
Toronto, ON

Rabbi Eliezer Gurkow
London, ON

Rabbi Aaron Herman
Pittsburgh, PA

Rabbi Simon Jacobson
New York, NY

Rabbi Chaim D. Kagan, PhD
Monsey, NY

Rabbi Shmuel Klatzkin, PhD
Dayton, OH

Rabbi Nochum Mangel
Dayton, OH

Rabbi Moshe Miller
Chicago, IL

Rabbi Yosef Paltiel
Brooklyn, NY

Rabbi Yehuda Pink
Solihull, UK

Rabbi Yisrael Rice
S. Rafael, CA

Rabbi Eli Silberstein
Ithaca, NY

Mrs. Rivkah Slonim
Binghamton, NY

Rabbi Avrohom Sternberg
New London, CT

Rabbi Shais Taub
Cedarhurst, NY

Rabbi Shlomo Yaffe
Longmeadow, MA

ROSH CHODESH SOCIETY

Rabbi Shmuel Kaplan
CHAIRMAN

Mrs. Shaindy Jacobson
DIRECTOR

Mrs. Baila Goldstein
ADMINISTRATOR

Mrs. Malky Bitton
Mrs. Shula Bryski
Mrs. Chanie Wilhelm
EDITORIAL BOARD

Mrs. Devorah Kornfeld
Mrs. Chana Lipskar
Mrs. Chana Alte Mangel
Mrs. Ahuva New
Mrs. Dinie Rapoport
Mrs. Sorah Shemtov
Mrs. Binie Tenenbaum
Mrs. Yehudis Wolvovsky
STEERING COMMITTEE

JLI TEENS
IN PARTNERSHIP WITH
CTEEN: CHABAD TEEN NETWORK

Rabbi Chaim Block
CHAIRMAN

Rabbi Shlomie Tenenbaum
DIRECTOR

Mrs. Aliza Mayteles
ADMINISTRATOR

TORAH STUDIES

Rabbi Yosef Gansburg
CHAIRMAN

Mrs. Naomi Heber
PROJECT MANAGER

Rabbi Ahrele Loschak
EDITOR

Rabbi Levi Fogelman
Rabbi Yaacov Halperin
Rabbi Nechemia Schusterman
Rabbi Ari Sollish
STEERING COMMITTEE

SINAI SCHOLARS SOCIETY
IN PARTNERSHIP WITH
CHABAD ON CAMPUS

Rabbi Menachem Schmidt
CHAIRMAN

Rabbi Dubi Rabinowitz
DIRECTOR

Mrs. Manya Sperlin
COORDINATORS

Mrs. Devorah Zlatopolsky
ADMINISTRATOR

Rabbi Moshe Chaim Dubrowski
Rabbi Yossy Gordon
Rabbi Efraim Mintz
Rabbi Menachem Schmidt
Rabbi Avi Weinstein
EXECUTIVE COMMITTEE

Rabbi Chaim Shaul Brook
Rabbi Shlomie Chein
Rabbi Moshe Leib Gray
Rabbi Zev Johnson
Rabbi Yossi Lazaroff
Rabbi Shmuel Tiechtel
Rabbi Zalman Tiechtel
Rabbi Shmuli Weiss
Rabbi Yisroel Wilhelm
STEERING COMMITTEE

JLI INTERNATIONAL

Rabbi Avrohom Sternberg
CHAIRMAN

Rabbi Dubi Rabinowitz
DIRECTOR

Rabbi Berry Piekarski
ADMINISTRATOR

Rabbi Eli Wolf
ADMINISTRATOR, JLI IN THE CIS IN PARTNERSHIP WITH THE FEDERATION OF JEWISH COMMUNITIES OF THE CIS

Rabbi Shevach Zlatopolsky
EDITOR, JLI IN THE CIS

Rabbi Nochum Schapiro
REGIONAL REPRESENTATIVE, AUSTRALIA

Rabbi Avraham Golovacheov
REGIONAL REPRESENTATIVE, GERMANY

Rabbi Shmuel Katzman
REGIONAL REPRESENTATIVE, NETHERLANDS

Rabbi Avrohom Steinmetz
REGIONAL REPRESENTATIVE, BRAZIL

Rabbi Bentzi Sudak
REGIONAL REPRESENTATIVE, UNITED KINGDOM

Rabbi Shlomo Cohen
FRENCH COORDINATOR, REGIONAL REPRESENTITIVE

NATIONAL JEWISH RETREAT

Rabbi Hesh Epstein
CHAIRMAN

Mrs. Shaina B. Mintz
DIRECTOR

Bruce Backman
HOTEL LIAISON

Rabbi Menachem Klein
PROGRAM COORDINATOR

Rabbi Shmuly Karp
SHLUCHIM LIAISON

Rabbi Mendel Rosenfeld
LOGISTICS COORDINATOR

Mrs. Mussi Abelsky
Ms. Rochel Karp
Ms. Zehavah Krafchik
Mrs. Aliza Mayteles
SERVICE AND SUPPORT

JLI LAND & SPIRIT

ISRAEL EXPERIENCE

Rabbi Shmuly Karp
DIRECTOR

Mrs. Shaina B. Mintz
ADMINISTRATOR

Rabbi Yechiel Baitelman
Rabbi Dovid Flinkenstein
Rabbi Chanoch Kaplan
Rabbi Levi Klein
Rabbi Mendel Lifshitz
Rabbi Mendy Mangel
Rabbi Sholom Raichik
Rabbi Ephraim Silverman
STEERING COMMITTEE

SHABBAT IN THE HEIGHTS

Rabbi Shmuly Karp
DIRECTOR

Mrs. Shulamis Nadler
SERVICE AND SUPPORT

Rabbi Chaim Hanoka
CHAIRMAN

Rabbi Mordechai Dinerman
Rabbi Zalman Marcus
STEERING COMMITTEE

MYSHIUR

ADVANCED LEARNING INITIATIVE

Rabbi Shmuel Kaplan
CHAIRMAN

Rabbi Shlomie Tenenbaum
ADMINISTRATOR

TORAHCAFE.COM

ONLINE LEARNING

Rabbi Mendy Elishevitz
WEBSITE DEVELOPMENT

Moshe Levin
CONTENT MANAGER

Avrohom Shimon Ezagui
FILMING

MACHON SHMUEL

THE SAMI ROHR RESEARCH INSTITUTE

Rabbi Zalman Korf
ADMINISTRATOR

Rabbi Gedalya Oberlander
Rabbi Chaim Rapoport
Rabbi Levi Yitzchak Raskin
Rabbi Chaim Schapiro
Rabbi Moshe Miller
RABBINIC ADVISORY BOARD

Rabbi Yakov Gershon
RESEARCH FELLOW

FOUNDING DEPARTMENT HEADS

Rabbi Mendel Bell
Rabbi Zalman Charytan
Rabbi Mendel Druk
Rabbi Menachem Gansburg
Rabbi Meir Hecht
Rabbi Levi Kaplan
Rabbi Yoni Katz
Rabbi Chaim Zalman Levy
Rabbi Benny Rapoport
Dr. Chana Silberstein
Rabbi Elchonon Tenenbaum
Rabbi Mendy Weg

Faculty Directory

ALABAMA

BIRMINGHAM
Rabbi Yossi Friedman 205.970.0100

MOBILE
Rabbi Yosef Goldwasser 251.265.1213

ALASKA

ANCHORAGE
Rabbi Yosef Greenberg
Rabbi Mendy Greenberg 907.357.8770

ARIZONA

CHANDLER
Rabbi Mendy Deitsch 480.855.4333

FLAGSTAFF
Rabbi Dovie Shapiro 928.255.5756

FOUNTAIN HILLS
Rabbi Mendy Lipskier 480.776.4763

ORO VALLEY
Rabbi Ephraim Zimmerman 520.477.8672

PHOENIX
Rabbi Zalman Levertov
Rabbi Yossi Friedman 602.944.2753

SCOTTSDALE
Rabbi Yossi Levertov 480.998.1410

TUCSON
Rabbi Yehuda Ceitlin 520.881.7956

ARKANSAS

LITTLE ROCK
Rabbi Pinchus Ciment 501.217.0053

CALIFORNIA

AGOURA HILLS
Rabbi Moshe Bryski
Rabbi Yisroel Levine 818.991.0991

BAKERSFIELD
Rabbi Shmuli Schlanger
Mrs. Esther Schlanger 661.331.1695

BEL AIR
Rabbi Chaim Mentz 310.475.5311

BURBANK
Rabbi Shmuly Kornfeld 818.954.0070

CARLSBAD
Rabbi Yeruchem Eilfort
Mrs. Nechama Eilfort 760.943.8891

CHATSWORTH
Rabbi Yossi Spritzer 818.718.0777

CONTRA COSTA
Rabbi Dovber Berkowitz 925.937.4101

CORONADO
Rabbi Eli Fradkin 619.365.4728

DANVILLE
Rabbi Shmuli Raitman 213.447.6694

ENCINO
Rabbi Aryeh Herzog 818.784.9986
Chapter founded by Rabbi Joshua Gordon, OBM

FOLSOM
Rabbi Yossi Grossbaum 916.608.9811

FREMONT
Rabbi Moshe Fuss 510.300.4090

GLENDALE
Rabbi Simcha Backman 818.240.2750

HUNTINGTON BEACH
Rabbi Aron David Berkowitz 714.846.2285

LA JOLLA
Rabbi Baruch Shalom Ezagui 858.455.5433

LAGUNA BEACH
Rabbi Elimelech Gurevitch 949.499.0770

LAGUNA NIGUEL
Rabbi Mendy Paltiel 949.831.8475

LOMITA
Rabbi Eli Hecht
Rabbi Sholom Pinson 310.326.8234

LONG BEACH
Rabbi Abba Perelmuter 562.621.9828

LOS ANGELES
Rabbi Leibel Korf 323.660.5177
Rabbi Dovid Liberow 424.261.8770

MALIBU
Rabbi Levi Cunin 310.456.6588

MARINA DEL REY
Rabbi Danny Yiftach-Hashem
Rabbi Dovid Yiftach 310.859.0770

NORTH HOLLYWOOD
Rabbi Nachman Abend 818.989.9539

NORTHRIDGE
Rabbi Eli Rivkin 818.368.3937

OJAI
Rabbi Mordechai Nemtzov 805.613.7181

PACIFIC PALISADES
Rabbi Zushe Cunin 310.454.7783

PALO ALTO
Rabbi Menachem Landa 415.418.4768
Rabbi Yosef Levin
Rabbi Ber Rosenblatt 650.424.9800

PASADENA
Rabbi Chaim Hanoka
Rabbi Sholom Stiefel 626.539.4578

PLEASANTON
Rabbi Josh Zebberman 925.846.0700

POWAY
Rabbi Mendel Goldstein 858.208.6613

RANCHO CUCAMONGA
Rabbi Sholom B. Harlig 909.949.4553

RANCHO MIRAGE
Rabbi Shimon H. Posner 760.770.7785

RANCHO PALOS VERDES
Rabbi Yitzchok Magalnic 310.544.5544

RANCHO S. FE
Rabbi Levi Raskin 858.756.7571

REDONDO BEACH
Rabbi Yossi Mintz
Rabbi Zalman Gordon 310.214.4999

RIVERSIDE
Rabbi Shmuel Fuss 951.329.2747

S. CLEMENTE
Rabbi Menachem M. Slavin 949.489.0723

S. CRUZ
Rabbi Yochanan Friedman 831.454.0101

S. DIEGO
Rabbi Rafi Andrusier 619.387.8770
Rabbi Motte Fradkin 858.547.0076

S. FRANCISCO
Rabbi Gedalia Potash 415.648.8000
Rabbi Shlomo Zarchi 415.752.2866

S. MATEO
Rabbi Yossi Marcus 650.341.4510

S. MONICA
Rabbi Boruch Rabinowitz 310.394.5699

S. RAFAEL
Rabbi Yisrael Rice 415.492.1666

SOUTH LAKE TAHOE
Rabbi Mordechai Richler 530.314.7677

SUNNYVALE
Rabbi Yisroel Hecht 408.720.0553

TEMECULA
Rabbi Yonason Abrams 951.234.4196

THOUSAND OAKS
Rabbi Chaim Bryski 805.370.5770

TUSTIN
Rabbi Yehoshua Eliezrie 714.508.2150

UNIVERSITY CITY
Rabbi Yechiel Cagen 832.691.1825

VENTURA
Rabbi Yakov Latowicz 805.658.7441

WEST HILLS
Rabbi Avi Rabin 818.337.4544

WEST HOLLYWOOD
Rabbi Mordechai Kirschenbaum 310.275.1215

WEST LOS ANGELES
Rabbi Mordechai Zaetz 424.652.8742

YORBA LINDA
Rabbi Dovid Eliezrie 714.693.0770

COLORADO

ASPEN
Rabbi Mendel Mintz 970.544.3770

AURORA
Rabbi David Araiev 720.388.2704

DENVER
Rabbi Mendel Popack 720.515.4337
Rabbi Yossi Serebryanski 303.744.9699

FORT COLLINS
Rabbi Yerachmiel Gorelik 970.407.1613

HIGHLANDS RANCH
Rabbi Avraham Mintz 303.694.9119

LONGMONT
Rabbi Yakov Borenstein 303.678.7595

VAIL
Rabbi Dovid Mintz 970.476.7887

WESTMINSTER
Rabbi Benjy Brackman 303.429.5177

CONNECTICUT

FAIRFIELD
Rabbi Shlame Landa 203.373.7551

GLASTONBURY
Rabbi Yosef Wolvovsky 860.659.2422

GREENWICH
Rabbi Yossi Deren
Rabbi Menachem Feldman 203.629.9059

MILFORD
Rabbi Schneur Wilhelm 203.887.7603

NEW HAVEN
Rabbi Mendy Hecht 203.589.5375

NEW LONDON
Rabbi Avrohom Sternberg 860.437.8000

STAMFORD
Rabbi Yisrael Deren
Rabbi Levi Mendelow 203.3.CHABAD

WEST HARTFORD
Rabbi Shaya Gopin 860.232.1116

WESTPORT
Rabbi Yehuda L. Kantor 203.226.8584

DELAWARE

WILMINGTON
Rabbi Chuni Vogel 302.529.9900

DISTRICT OF COLUMBIA

WASHINGTON
Rabbi Levi Shemtov
Rabbi Yitzy Ceitlin 202.332.5600

FLORIDA

ALTAMONTE SPRINGS
Rabbi Mendy Bronstein 407.280.0535

BAL HARBOUR
Rabbi Dov Schochet 305.868.1411

BOCA RATON
Rabbi Zalman Bukiet
Rabbi Arele Gopin 561.994.6257
Rabbi Moishe Denburg 561.526.5760
Rabbi Ruvi New 561.394.9770

BONITA SPRINGS
Rabbi Mendy Greenberg 239.949.6900

BOYNTON BEACH
Rabbi Yosef Yitzchok Raichik 561.732.4633

BRADENTON
Rabbi Menachem Bukiet 941.388.9656

CAPE CORAL
Rabbi Yossi Labkowski 239.963.4770

CORAL GABLES
Rabbi Avrohom Stolik 305.490.7572

CORAL SPRINGS
Rabbi Yankie Denburg 954.471.8646

CUTLER BAY
Rabbi Yossi Wolff 305.975.6680

DAVIE
Rabbi Aryeh Schwartz 954.376.9973

DELRAY BEACH
Rabbi Sholom Ber Korf 561.496.6228

FISHER ISLAND
Rabbi Efraim Brody 347.325.1913

FLEMING ISLAND
Rabbi Shmuly Feldman 904.290.1017

FORT LAUDERDALE
Rabbi Yitzchok Naparstek 954.568.1190

FORT MYERS
Rabbi Yitzchok Minkowicz
Mrs. Nechama Minkowicz 239.433.7708

HALLANDALE BEACH
Rabbi Mordy Feiner 954.458.1877

HOLLYWOOD
Rabbi Leizer Barash 954.965.9933
Rabbi Leibel Kudan 954.801.3367

KENDALL
Rabbi Yossi Harlig 305.234.5654

KEY WEST
Rabbi Yaakov Zucker 305.304.7713

LAKELAND
Rabbi Moshe Lazaros 863.510.5968

LONGWOOD
Rabbi Yanky Majesky 407.636.5994

MAITLAND
Rabbi Sholom Dubov
Rabbi Levik Dubov 470.644.2500

MIAMI
Rabbi Mendy Cheruty 305.219.3353
Rabbi Yakov Fellig 305.445.5444

MIAMI BEACH
Rabbi Yisroel Frankforter 305.534.3895

N. MIAMI BEACH
Rabbi Eli Laufer 305.770.4412

OCALA
Rabbi Yossi Hecht 352.330.4466

ORLANDO
Rabbi Yosef Konikov 407.354.3660

ORMOND BEACH
Rabbi Asher Farkash 386.672.9300

PALM BEACH
Rabbi Zalman Levitin 561.659.3884

PALM BEACH GARDENS
Rabbi Dovid Vigler 561.624.2223

PALM CITY
Rabbi Shlomo Uminer 772.288.0606

PALM HARBOR
Rabbi Pinchas Adler 727.789.0408

PALMETTO BAY
Rabbi Zalman Gansburg 786.282.0413

PARKLAND
Rabbi Mendy Gutnick 954.796.7330

PEMBROKE PINES
Rabbi Mordechai Andrusier 954.874.2280

PLANTATION
Rabbi Pinchas Taylor 954.644.9177

PONTE VEDRA BEACH
Rabbi Nochum Kurinsky 904.543.9301

S. AUGUSTINE
Rabbi Levi Vogel 904.521.8664

S. PETERSBURG
Rabbi Alter Korf 727.344.4900

SARASOTA
Rabbi Chaim Shaul Steinmetz 941.925.0770

SATELLITE BEACH
Rabbi Zvi Konikov 321.777.2770

SOUTH PALM BEACH
Rabbi Leibel Stolik 561.889.3499

SOUTH TAMPA
Rabbi Mendy Dubrowski 813.922.1723

SOUTHWEST BROWARD COUNTY
Rabbi Aryeh Schwartz 954.252.1770

SUNNY ISLES BEACH
Rabbi Alexander Kaller 305.803.5315

VENICE
Rabbi Sholom Ber Schmerling 941.493.2770

WELLINGTON
Rabbi Mendy Muskal 561.386.3090

WESLEY CHAPEL
Rabbi Mendy Yarmush
Rabbi Mendel Friedman 813.731.2977

WEST PALM BEACH
Rabbi Yoel Gancz 561.659.7770

WESTON
Rabbi Yisroel Spalter 954.349.6565

GEORGIA

ALPHARETTA
Rabbi Hirshy Minkowicz 770.410.9000

ATLANTA
Rabbi Yossi New
Rabbi Isser New 404.843.2464
Rabbi Alexander Piekarski 678.267.6418

ATLANTA: INTOWN
Rabbi Eliyahu Schusterman
Rabbi Ari Sollish 404.898.0434

CUMMING
Rabbi Levi Mentz 310.666.2218

GWINNETT
Rabbi Yossi Lerman 678.595.0196

MARIETTA
Rabbi Ephraim Silverman 770.565.4412

HAWAII

KAPA'A
Rabbi Michoel Goldman 808.647.4293

IDAHO

BOISE
Rabbi Mendel Lifshitz 208.853.9200

ILLINOIS

CHAMPAIGN
Rabbi Dovid Tiechtel 217.355.8672

CHICAGO
Rabbi Mendy Benhiyoun 312.498.7704
Rabbi Meir Hecht 312.714.4655
Rabbi Dovid Kotlarsky 773.495.7127
Rabbi Yosef Moscowitz 773.772.3770
Rabbi Levi Notik 773.274.5123

DES PLAINES
Rabbi Lazer Hershkovich 224.392.4442

ELGIN
Rabbi Mendel Shemtov 847.440.4486

GLENVIEW
Rabbi Yishaya Benjaminson 847.910.1738

GRAYSLAKE
Rabbi Sholom Tenenbaum 847.782.1800

HIGHLAND PARK
Mrs. Michla Schanowitz 847.266.0770

NAPERVILLE
Rabbi Mendy Goldstein 630.778.9770

NORTHBROOK
Rabbi Meir Moscowitz 847.564.8770

OAK PARK
Rabbi Yitzchok Bergstein 708.524.1530

PEORIA
Rabbi Eli Langsam 309.692.2250

SKOKIE
Rabbi Yochanan Posner 847.677.1770

VERNON HILLS
Rabbi Shimmy Susskind 847.984.2919

WILMETTE
Rabbi Dovid Flinkenstein 847.251.7707

INDIANA

INDIANAPOLIS
Rabbi Avraham Grossbaum
Rabbi Dr. Shmuel Klatzkin 317.251.5573

IOWA

BETTENDORF
Rabbi Shneur Cadaner 563.355.1065

KANSAS

OVERLAND PARK
Rabbi Mendy Wineberg 913.649.4852

KENTUCKY

LOUISVILLE
Rabbi Avrohom Litvin 502.459.1770

LOUISIANA

BATON ROUGE
Rabbi Peretz Kazen 225.267.7047

METAIRIE
Rabbi Yossie Nemes
Rabbi Mendel Ceitlin 504.454.2910

NEW ORLEANS
Rabbi Mendel Rivkin 504.302.1830

MAINE

PORTLAND
Rabbi Levi Wilansky 207.650.1783

MARYLAND

BALTIMORE
Rabbi Velvel Belinsky 410.764.5000
Classes in Russian

BEL AIR
Rabbi Kushi Schusterman 443.353.9718

BETHESDA
Rabbi Sender Geisinsky 301.913.9777

CHEVY CHASE
Rabbi Zalman Minkowitz 301.260.5000

COLUMBIA
Rabbi Hillel Baron
Rabbi Yosef Chaim Sufrin 410.740.2424

FREDERICK
Rabbi Boruch Labkowski 301.996.3659

GAITHERSBURG
Rabbi Sholom Raichik 301.926.3632

OLNEY
Rabbi Bentzy Stolik 301.660.6770

OWINGS MILLS
Rabbi Nochum H. Katsenelenbogen 410.356.5156

POTOMAC
Rabbi Mendel Bluming 301.983.4200
Rabbi Mendel Kaplan 301.983.1485

ROCKVILLE
Rabbi Shlomo Beitsh 646.773.2675
Rabbi Moishe Kavka 301.836.1242
Rabbi Levi Raskin 240.444.3345

MASSACHUSETTS

ANDOVER
Rabbi Asher Bronstein 978.470.2288

BOSTON
Rabbi Yosef Zaklos 617.297.7282

BRIGHTON
Rabbi Dan Rodkin 617.787.2200

CAPE COD
Rabbi Yekusiel Alperowitz 508.775.2324

HINGHAM
Rabbi Levi Lezell 617.862.2770

LONGMEADOW
Rabbi Yakov Wolff 413.567.8665

NEWTON
Rabbi Shalom Ber Prus 617.244.1200

SUDBURY
Rabbi Yisroel Freeman 978.443.0110

SWAMPSCOTT
Rabbi Yossi Lipsker 781.581.3833

MICHIGAN

ANN ARBOR
Rabbi Aharon Goldstein 734.995.3276

BLOOMFIELD HILLS
Rabbi Levi Dubov 248.949.6210

GRAND RAPIDS
Rabbi Mordechai Haller 616.957.0770

WEST BLOOMFIELD
Rabbi Elimelech Silberberg 248.855.6170

MINNESOTA

MINNETONKA
Rabbi Mordechai Grossbaum
Rabbi Shmuel Silberstein 952.929.9922

S. PAUL
Rabbi Shneur Zalman Bendet 651.998.9298

MISSOURI

S. LOUIS
Rabbi Yosef Landa 314.725.0400

NEVADA

LAS VEGAS
Rabbi Yosef Rivkin 702.217.2170

SUMMERLIN
Rabbi Yisroel Schanowitz
Rabbi Tzvi Bronchtain 702.855.0770

NEW JERSEY

BASKING RIDGE
Rabbi Mendy Herson
Rabbi Mendel Shemtov 908.604.8844

CHERRY HILL
Rabbi Mendel Mangel 856.874.1500

CLINTON
Rabbi Eli Kornfeld 908.623.7000

FAIR LAWN
Rabbi Avrohom Bergstein 201.362.2712

FORT LEE
Rabbi Meir Konikov 201.886.1238

FRANKLIN LAKES
Rabbi Chanoch Kaplan 201.848.0449

GREATER MERCER COUNTY
Rabbi Dovid Dubov
Rabbi Yaakov Chaiton 609.213.4136

HASKELL
Rabbi Mendy Gurkov 201.696.7609

HOLMDEL
Rabbi Shmaya Galperin 732.772.1998

MADISON
Rabbi Shalom Lubin 973.377.0707

MANALAPAN
Rabbi Boruch Chazanow
Rabbi Levi Wolosow 732.972.3687

MEDFORD
Rabbi Yitzchok Kahan 609.451.3522

MOUNTAIN LAKES
Rabbi Levi Dubinsky 973.551.1898

MULLICA HILL
Rabbi Avrohom Richler 856.733.0770

OLD TAPPAN
Rabbi Mendy Lewis 201.767.4008

RED BANK
Rabbi Dovid Harrison 718.915.8748

ROCKAWAY
Rabbi Asher Herson
Rabbi Mordechai Baumgarten 973.625.1525

RUTHERFORD
Rabbi Yitzchok Lerman 347.834.7500

SCOTCH PLAINS
Rabbi Avrohom Blesofsky 908.790.0008

SHORT HILLS
Rabbi Mendel Solomon
Rabbi Avrohom Levin 973.725.7008

SOUTH BRUNSWICK
Rabbi Levi Azimov 732.398.9492

TEANECK
Rabbi Ephraim Simon 201.907.0686

TENAFLY
Rabbi Mordechai Shain 201.871.1152

TOMS RIVER
Rabbi Moshe Gourarie 732.349.4199

VENTNOR
Rabbi Avrohom Rapoport 609.822.8500

WAYNE
Rabbi Michel Gurkov 973.694.6274

WEST ORANGE
Rabbi Mendy Kasowitz 973.325.6311

WOODCLIFF LAKE
Rabbi Dov Drizin 201.476.0157

NEW MEXICO

LAS CRUCES
Rabbi Bery Schmukler 575.524.1330

S. FE
Rabbi Berel Levertov 505.983.2000

NEW YORK

BAY SHORE
Rabbi Shimon Stillerman 631.913.8770

BEDFORD
Rabbi Arik Wolf 914.666.6065

BINGHAMTON
Mrs. Rivkah Slonim 607.797.0015

BRIGHTON BEACH
Rabbi Moshe Winner 718.946.9833

BRONXVILLE
Rabbi Sruli Deitsch 917.755.0078

BROOKLYN
Rabbi Nissi Eber 347.677.2276

BROOKVILLE
Rabbi Mendy Heber 516.626.0600

CEDARHURST
Rabbi Zalman Wolowik 516.295.2478

COMMACK
Rabbi Mendel Teldon 631.543.3343

DIX HILLS
Rabbi Yaakov Saacks 631.351.8672

DOBBS FERRY
Rabbi Benjy Silverman 914.693.6100

EAST HAMPTON
Rabbi Leibel Baumgarten
Rabbi Mendy Goldberg 631.329.5800

ELLENVILLE
Rabbi Shlomie Deren 845.647.4450

FOREST HILLS
Rabbi Yossi Mendelson 917.861.9726

GREAT NECK
Rabbi Yoseph Geisinsky 516.487.4554

KINGSTON
Rabbi Yitzchok Hecht 845.334.9044

LARCHMONT
Rabbi Mendel Silberstein 914.834.4321

LITTLE NECK
Rabbi Eli Shifrin 718.423.1235

LONG BEACH
Rabbi Eli Goodman 516.897.2473

MONTEBELLO
Rabbi Shmuel Gancz 845.746.1927

NYACK
Rabbi Chaim Zvi Ehrenreich 845.356.6686

NYC KEHILATH JESHURUN
Rabbi Elie Weinstock 212.774.5636

NYC UPPER EAST SIDE
Rabbi Uriel Vigler 212.369.7310

NYC UPPER WEST SIDE
Rabbi Shlomo Kugel 212.864.5010

OCEANSIDE
Rabbi Levi Gurkow 516.764.7385

OSSINING
Rabbi Dovid Labkowski 914.923.2522

OYSTER BAY
Rabbi Shmuel Lipszyc
Rabbi Shalom Lipszyc 347.853.9992

PARK SLOPE
Rabbi Menashe Wolf 347.957.1291

PORT WASHINGTON
Rabbi Shalom Paltiel 516.767.8672

PROSPECT HEIGHTS
Rabbi Mendy Hecht 347.622.3599

ROCHESTER
Rabbi Nechemia Vogel 585.271.0330

ROSLYN
Rabbi Yaakov Reiter 516.484.8185

SEA GATE
Rabbi Chaim Brikman 917.975.2792

SOUTHAMPTON
Rabbi Chaim Pape 917.627.4865

STATEN ISLAND
Rabbi Mendy Katzman 718.370.8953

STONY BROOK
Rabbi Shalom Ber Cohen 631.585.0521

SUFFERN
Rabbi Shmuel Gancz 845.368.1889

YORKTOWN HEIGHTS
Rabbi Yehuda Heber 914.962.1111

NORTH CAROLINA

ASHEVILLE
Rabbi Shaya Susskind 828.505.0746

CARY
Rabbi Yisroel Cotlar 919.651.9710

CHARLOTTE
Rabbi Yossi Groner
Rabbi Shlomo Cohen 704.366.3984

GREENSBORO
Rabbi Yosef Plotkin 336.617.8120

RALEIGH
Rabbi Pinchas Herman
Rabbi Lev Cotlar 919.637.6950

OHIO

BEACHWOOD
Rabbi Shmuli Friedman 216.282.0112

CINCINNATI
Rabbi Yisroel Mangel 513.793.5200

COLUMBUS
Rabbi Yitzi Kaltmann 614.294.3296

DAYTON
Rabbi Nochum Mangel
Rabbi Shmuel Klatzkin 937.643.0770

OKLAHOMA

OKLAHOMA CITY
Rabbi Ovadia Goldman 405.524.4800

TULSA
Rabbi Yehuda Weg 918.492.4499

OREGON

PORTLAND
Rabbi Chaim Wilhelm 503.309.4490
Rabbi Mordechai Wilhelm 503.977.9947

SALEM
Rabbi Avrohom Yitzchok Perlstein 503.383.9569

PENNSYLVANIA

AMBLER
Rabbi Shaya Deitsch 215.591.9310

BALA CYNWYD
Rabbi Shraga Sherman 610.660.9192

DOYLESTOWN
Rabbi Mendel Prus 215.340.1303

LAFAYETTE HILL
Rabbi Yisroel Kotlarsky 484.533.7009

LANCASTER
Rabbi Elazar Green 717.368.6565

MONROEVILLE
Rabbi Mendy Schapiro 412.372.1000

NEWTOWN
Rabbi Aryeh Weinstein 215.497.9925

PHILADELPHIA: CENTER CITY
Rabbi Yochonon Goldman 215.238.2100

PITTSBURGH
Rabbi Yisroel Altein .... 412.422.7300 EXT. 269

PITTSBURGH: SOUTH HILLS
Rabbi Mendy Rosenblum 412.278.3693

READING
Rabbi Yosef Lipsker 610.921.1522

RYDAL
Rabbi Zushe Gurevitz 267.536.5757

WYNNEWOOD
Rabbi Moishe Brennan 610.529.9011

PUERTO RICO

CAROLINA
Rabbi Mendel Zarchi 787.253.0894

RHODE ISLAND

LINCOLN
Rabbi Aryeh Laufer 401.499.2574

WARWICK
Rabbi Yossi Laufer 401.884.7888

SOUTH CAROLINA

COLUMBIA
Rabbi Hesh Epstein
Rabbi Levi Marrus 803.782.1831

GREENVILLE
Rabbi Leibel Kesselman 864.256.1770

MYRTLE BEACH
Rabbi Doron Aizenman 843.385.2240

TENNESSEE

CHATTANOOGA
Rabbi Shaul Perlstein 423.490.1106

KNOXVILLE
Rabbi Yossi Wilhelm 865.588.8584

MEMPHIS
Rabbi Levi Klein 901.754.0404

TEXAS

AUSTIN
Rabbi Mendy Levertov 512.905.2778

BELLAIRE
Rabbi Yossi Zaklikofsky 713.839.8887

DALLAS
Rabbi Mendel Dubrawsky
Rabbi Moshe Naparstek 972.818.0770

FORT WORTH
Rabbi Dov Mandel 817.263.7701

FRISCO
Rabbi Mendy Kesselman 214.460.7773

HOUSTON
Rabbi Dovid Goldstein
Rabbi Zally Lazarus 281.589.7188
Rabbi Moishe Traxler 713.774.0300

HOUSTON: RICE UNIVERSITY AREA
Rabbi Eliezer Lazaroff 713.522.2004

LEAGUE CITY
Rabbi Yitzchok Schmukler 281.724.1554

MISSOURI CITY
Rabbi Mendel Feigenson 832.758.0685

PLANO
Rabbi Mendel Block
Rabbi Yehudah Horowitz 972.596.8270

S. ANTONIO
Rabbi Chaim Block
Rabbi Levi Teldon 210.492.1085
Rabbi Tal Shaul 210.877.4218

SOUTHLAKE
Rabbi Levi Gurevitch 817.451.1171

THE WOODLANDS
Rabbi Mendel Blecher 281.719.5213

UTAH

SALT LAKE CITY
Rabbi Benny Zippel 801.467.7777

VERMONT

BURLINGTON
Rabbi Yitzchok Raskin 802.658.5770

VIRGINIA

ALEXANDRIA/ARLINGTON
Rabbi Mordechai Newman 703.370.2774

FAIRFAX
Rabbi Leibel Fajnland 703.426.1980

GAINESVILLE
Rabbi Shmuel Perlstein 571.445.0342

LOUDOUN COUNTY
Rabbi Chaim Cohen 248.298.9279

NORFOLK
Rabbi Aaron Margolin
Rabbi Levi Brashevitzky 757.616.0770

RICHMOND
Rabbi Shlomo Pereira 804.740.2000

TYSONS CORNER
Rabbi Chezzy Deitsch 703.829.5770
Chapter founded by Rabbi Levi Deitsch, OBM

WASHINGTON

BELLINGHAM
Rabbi Yosef Truxton 360.224.9919

MERCER ISLAND
Rabbi Elazar Bogomilsky 206.527.1411
Rabbi Nissan Kornfeld 206.851.2324

OLYMPIA
Rabbi Yosef Schtroks 360.867.8804

SPOKANE COUNTY
Rabbi Yisroel Hahn 509.443.0770

WISCONSIN

BAYSIDE
Rabbi Cheski Edelman 414.439.5041

KENOSHA
Rabbi Tzali Wilschanski 262.359.0770

MADISON
Rabbi Avremel Matusof 608.231.3450

MEQUON
Rabbi Menachem Rapoport 262.242.2235

MILWAUKEE
Rabbi Mendel Shmotkin 414.961.6100

WAUKESHA
Rabbi Levi Brook 925.708.4203

ARGENTINA

BUENOS AIRES
Mrs. Chani Gorowitz 54.11.4865.0445
Rabbi Menachem M. Grunblatt 54.911.3574.0037
Rabbi Mendi Mizrahi 54.11.4963.1221
Rabbi Mendy Gurevitch 55.11.4545.7771
Rabbi Pinhas Sudry 54.1.4822.2285
Rabbi Shloimi Setton 54.11.4982.8637
Rabbi Shiele Plotka 54.11.4634.3111
Rabbi Yosef Levy 54.11.4504.1908

SALTA
Rabbi Rafael Tawil 54.387.421.4947

S. MIGUEL DE TUCUMÁN
Rabbi Ariel Levy 54.381.473.6944

AUSTRALIA

NEW SOUTH WALES

DOUBLE BAY
Rabbi Yanky Berger 612.9327.1644

DOVER HEIGHTS
Rabbi Motti Feldman 614.0400.8572

NORTH SHORE
Rabbi Nochum Schapiro
Rebbetzin Fruma Schapiro 612.9488.9548

QUEENSLAND

BRISBANE
Rabbi Levi Jaffe 617.3843.6770

VICTORIA

CAULFIELD
Rabbi Mendel Groner 613.9532.7299

MOORABBIN
Rabbi Elisha Greenbaum 614.0349.0434

WESTERN AUSTRALIA

PERTH
Rabbi Shalom White 618.9275.2106

AZERBAIJAN

BAKU
Mrs. Chavi Segal 994.12.597.91.90

BELARUS

BOBRUISK
Mrs. Mina Hababo 375.29.104.3230

MINSK
Rabbi Shneur Deitsch
Mrs. Bassie Deitsch 375.29.330.6675

BELGIUM

BRUSSELS
Rabbi Shmuel Pinson 375.29.330.6675

BRAZIL

CURITIBA
Rabbi Mendy Labkowski 55.41.3079.1338

S. PAULO
Rabbi Avraham Steinmetz 55.11.3081.3081

CANADA

ALBERTA

CALGARY
Rabbi Mordechai Groner 403.281.3770

EDMONTON
Rabbi Ari Drelich
Rabbi Mendy Blachman 780.200.5770

BRITISH COLUMBIA

KELOWNA
Rabbi Shmuly Hecht 250.575.5384

RICHMOND
Rabbi Yechiel Baitelman 604.277.6427

VANCOUVER
Rabbi Dovid Rosenfeld 604.266.1313

VICTORIA
Rabbi Meir Kaplan 250.595.7656

MANITOBA

WINNIPEG
Rabbi Shmuel Altein 204.339.8737

ONTARIO

LAWRENCE/EGLINTON
Rabbi Menachem Gansburg 416.546.8770

MAPLE
Rabbi Yechezkel Deren 647.883.6372

MISSISSAUGA
Rabbi Yitzchok Slavin 905.820.4432

NIAGARA FALLS
Rabbi Zalman Zaltzman 905.356.7200

OTTAWA
Rabbi Menachem M. Blum 613.843.7770

RICHMOND HILL
Rabbi Mendel Bernstein 905.770.7700

THORNHILL
Rabbi Yisroel Landa 416.897.3338
Rabbi Moishe Schurder 647.770.9351

THORNHILL WOODS
Rabbi Chaim Hildeshaim 905.881.1919

TORONTO AREA
Rabbi Sholom Lezell 416.809.1365

GREATER TORONTO REGIONAL OFFICE & THORNHILL
Rabbi Yossi Gansburg 905.731.7000

WATERLOO
Rabbi Moshe Goldman 226.338.7770

YORK MILLS
Rabbi Levi Gansburg 416.551.9391

QUEBEC

CÔTE S.-LUC
Rabbi Levi Naparstek 438.409.6770

HAMPSTEAD
Rabbi Moshe New
Rabbi Berel Bell 514.739.0770

MONTREAL
Rabbi Ronnie Fine
Pesach Nussbaum 514.738.3434

OLD MONTREAL/GRIFFINTOWN
Rabbi Nissan Gansbourg
Rabbi Berel Bell 514.800.6966

S. LAZARE
Rabbi Nochum Labkowski 514.436.7426

TOWN OF MOUNT ROYAL
Rabbi Moshe Krasnanski
Rabbi Shneur Zalman Rader 514.342.1770

WESTMOUNT
Rabbi Yossi Shanowitz
Mrs. Devorah Leah Shanowitz 514.937.4772

SASKATCHEWAN

SASKATOON
Rabbi Raphael Kats 306.384.4370

CAYMAN ISLANDS

GRAND CAYMAN
Rabbi Berel Pewzner 717.798.1040

COLOMBIA

BOGOTA
Rabbi Chanoch Piekarski 57.1.635.8251

COSTA RICA

S. JOSÉ
Rabbi Hershel Spalter
Rabbi Moshe Bitton 506.4010.1515

CROATIA

ZAGREB
Rabbi Pinchas Zaklas 385.1.4812227

DENMARK

COPENHAGEN
Rabbi Yitzchok Loewenthal 45.3316.1850

DOMINICAN REPUBLIC

S. DOMINGO
Rabbi Shimon Pelman 829.341.2770

ESTONIA

TALLINN
Rabbi Shmuel Kot 372.662.30.50

FRANCE

BOULOGNE
Rabbi Michael Sojcher 33.1.46.99.87.85

DIJON
Rabbi Chaim Slonim 33.6.52.05.26.65

LA VARENNE-S.-HILAIRE
Rabbi Mena'hem Mendel Benelbaz 33.6.17.81.57.47

MARSEILLE
Rabbi Eliahou Altabe 33.6.11.60.03.05
Rabbi Mena'hem Mendel Assouline 33.6.64.88.25.04
Rabbi Emmanuel Taubenblatt 33.4.88.00.94.85

PARIS
Rabbi Yona Hasky 33.1.53.75.36.01
Rabbi Acher Marciano 33.6.15.15.01.02
Rabbi Avraham Barou'h Pevzner 33.6.99.64.07.70

PONTAULT-COMBAULT
Rabbi Yossi Amar 33.6.61.36.07.70

SEINE-ET-MARNE
Rabbi Yossi Amar 33.1.60.29.50.17

VILLIERS-SUR-MARNE
Rabbi Mena'hem Mendel Mergui 33.1.49.30.89.66

GEORGIA

TBILISI
Rabbi Meir Kozlovsky 995.32.2429770

GERMANY

BERLIN
Rabbi Yehuda Tiechtel 49.30.2128.0830

DUSSELDORF
Rabbi Chaim Barkahn 49.173.2871.770

HAMBURG
Rabbi Shlomo Bistritzky 49.40.4142.4190

HANNOVER
Rabbi Binyamin Wolff 49.511.811.2822

GREECE

ATHENS
Rabbi Mendel Hendel 30.210.323.3825

GUATEMALA

GUATEMALA CITY
Rabbi Shalom Pelman 502.2485.0770

ISRAEL

ASHKELON
Rabbi Shneor Lieberman 054.977.0512

BALFURYA
Rabbi Noam Bar-Tov 054.580.4770

CAESAREA
Rabbi Chaim Meir Lieberman 054.621.2586

EVEN YEHUDA
Rabbi Menachem Noyman 054.777.0707

GANEI TIKVA
Rabbi Gershon Shnur 054.524.2358

GIV'ATAYIM
Rabbi Pinchus Bitton 052.643.8770

JERUSALEM
Rabbi Levi Diamond 055.665.7702
Rabbi Avraham Hendel 054.830.5799

KARMIEL
Rabbi Mendy Elishevitz 054.521.3073

KFAR SABA
Rabbi Yossi Baitch 054.445.5020

KIRYAT BIALIK
Rabbi Pinny Marton 050.661.1768

KIRYAT MOTZKIN
Rabbi Shimon Eizenbach 050.902.0770

KOCHAV YAIR
Rabbi Dovi Greenberg 054.332.6244

MACCABIM-RE'UT
Rabbi Yosef Yitzchak Noiman 054.977.0549

NES ZIYONA
Rabbi Menachem Feldman 054.497.7092

NETANYA
Rabbi Schneur Brod 054.579.7572

RAMAT GAN-KRINITZI
Rabbi Yisroel Gurevitz 052.743.2814

RAMAT GAN-MAROM NAVE
Rabbi Binyamin Meir Kali 050.476.0770

RAMAT YISHAI
Rabbi Shneor Zalman Wolosow 052.324.5475

RISHON LEZION
Rabbi Uri Keshet 050.722.4593

ROSH PINA
Rabbi Sholom Ber Hertzel 052.458.7600

TEL AVIV
Rabbi Shneur Piekarski 054.971.5568

JAPAN

TOKYO
Rabbi Mendi Sudakevich 81.3.5789.2846

KAZAKHSTAN

ALMATY
Rabbi Shevach Zlatopolsky 7.7272.77.59.49

KYRGYZSTAN

BISHKEK
Rabbi Arye Raichman 996.312.68.19.66

LATVIA

RIGA
Rabbi Shneur Zalman Kot
Mrs. Rivka Glazman 371.6720.40.22

LITHUANIA

VILNIUS
Rabb Sholom Ber Krinsky 370.6817.1367

LUXEMBOURG

LUXEMBOURG
Rabbi Mendel Edelman 352.2877.7079

MEXICO

S. MIGUEL DE ALLENDE
Rabbi Daniel Huebner 347.559.1304

NETHERLANDS

ALMERE
Rabbi Moshe Stiefel 31.36.744.0509

AMSTERDAM
Rabbi Yanki Jacobs 31.644.988.627
Rabbi Jaacov Zwi Spiero 31.652.328.065

EINDHOVEN
Rabbi Simcha Steinberg 31.63.635.7593

HAGUE
Rabbi Shmuel Katzman 31.70.347.0222

HEEMSTEDE-HAARLEM
Rabbi Shmuel Spiero 31.23.532.0707

MAASTRICHT
Rabbi Avrohom Cohen 32.48.549.6766

NIJMEGEN
Rabbi Menachem Mendel Levine 31.621.586.575

ROTTERDAM
Rabbi Yehuda Vorst 31.10.265.5530

PANAMA

PANAMA CITY
Rabbi Ari Laine
Rabbi Gabriel Benayon 507.223.3383

RUSSIA

ASTRAKHAN
Rabbi Yisroel Melamed 7.851.239.28.24

BRYANSK
Rabbi Menachem Mendel Zaklas 7.483.264.55.15

CHELYABINSK
Rabbi Meir Kirsh 7.351.263.24.68

MOSCOW
Rabbi Aizik Rosenfeld 7.906.762.88.81
Rabbi Mordechai Weisberg 7.495.645.50.00

NIZHNY NOVGOROD
Rabbi Shimon Bergman 7.920.253.47.70

NOVOSIBIRSK
Rabbi Shneur Zalmen Zaklos 7.903.900.43.22

OMSK
Rabbi Osher Krichevsky 7.381.231.33.07

PERM
Rabbi Zalman Deutch 7.342.212.47.32

ROSTOV
Rabbi Chaim Danzinger 7.8632.99.02.68

S. PETERSBURG
Rabbi Shalom Pewzner 7.911.726.21.19
Rabbi Zvi Pinsky 7.812.713.62.09

SAMARA
Rabbi Shlomo Deutch 7.846.333.40.64

SARATOV
Rabbi Yaakov Kubitshek 7.8452.21.58.00

TOGLIATTI
Rabbi Meier Fischer 7.848.273.02.84

UFA
Rabbi Dan Krichevsky 7.347.244.55.33

VORONEZH
Rabbi Levi Stiefel 7.473.252.96.99

SINGAPORE

SINGAPORE
Rabbi Mordechai Abergel 656.337.2189
Rabbi Netanel Rivni 656.336.2127
Classes in Hebrew

SOUTH AFRICA

CAPE TOWN
Rabbi Levi Popack 27.21.434.3740

JOHANNESBURG
Rabbi Dovid Masinter
Rabbi Ari Kievman 27.11.440.6600

SWITZERLAND

BASEL
Rabbi Zalmen Wishedski 41.77.958.8418

LUZERN
Rabbi Chaim Drukman 41.41.361.1770

THAILAND

BANGKOK
Rabbi Yosef C. Kantor 6681.837.7618

UKRAINE

BERDITCHEV
Mrs. Chana Thaler 380.637.70.37.70

DNEPROPETROVSK
Rabbi Dan Makagon 380.504.51.13.18

NIKOLAYEV
Rabbi Sholom Gotlieb 380.512.37.37.71

ODESSA
Rabbi Avraham Wolf
Rabbi Yaakov Neiman .... 38.048.728.0770 EXT. 280

ZAPOROZHYE
Mrs. Nechama Dina Ehrentreu 380.957.19.96.08

ZHITOMIR
Rabbi Shlomo Wilhelm 380.504.63.01.32

UNITED KINGDOM

BOURNEMOUTH
Rabbi Bentzion Alperowitz 44.749.456.7177

CHEADLE
Rabbi Peretz Chein 44.161.428.1818

LEEDS
Rabbi Eli Pink 44.113.266.3311

LONDON

Rabbi Mendel Cohen 44.777.261.2661
Rabbi Shneor Glitzenstein 44.792.585.7050
Rabbi Chaim Hoch 44.753.879.9524
Rabbi Dovid Katz 44.207.624.2770
Rabbi Yisroel Lew 44.207.060.9770
Rabbi Gershon Overlander 44.208.202.1600
Rabbi Hillel Gruber 44.208.202.1600
Rabbi Shlomo Odze 44.791.757.3558
Rabbi Yossi Simon 44.208.458.0416
Rabbi Bentzi Sudak 44.207.078.7469

MANCHESTER

Rabbi Levi Cohen 44.161.792.6335
Rabbi Shmuli Jaffe 44.161.766.1812

URUGUAY

MONTEVIDEO

Rabbi Mendy Shemtov 598.2628.6770

The Jewish Learning Multiplex

Brought to you by the Rohr Jewish Learning Institute

In fulfillment of the Mandate of the Lubavitcher Rebbe, of blessed memory, whose leadership guides every step of our work, the mission of the Rohr Jewish Learning Institute is to transform Jewish life and the greater community through the study of Torah, connecting each Jew to our shared heritage of Jewish learning.

While our flagship program remains the cornerstone of our organization, JLI is proud to feature additional divisions catering to specific populations, in order to meet a wide array of educational needs.

The Rohr **JEWISH LEARNING INSTITUTE**

A subsidiary of Merkos L'Inyonei Chinuch,
the adult educational arm of the Chabad-Lubavitch movement.

Torah Studies provides a rich and nuanced encounter with the weekly Torah reading.

MyShiur courses are designed to assist students in developing the skills needed to study Talmud independently.

This rigorous fellowship program invites select college students to explore the fundamentals of Judaism.

Jewish teens forge their identity as they engage in Torah study, social interaction, and serious fun.

The Rosh Chodesh Society gathers Jewish women together once a month for intensive textual study.

TorahCafe.com provides an exclusive selection of top-rated Jewish educational videos.

This yearly event rejuvenates mind, body, and spirit with a powerful synthesis of Jewish learning and community.

Participants delve into our nation's past while exploring the Holy Land's relevance and meaning today.

Select affiliates are invited to partner with peers and noted professionals, as leaders of innovation and excellence.

Machon Shmuel is an institute providing Torah research in the service of educators worldwide.